Praise for

Leading Every Day, Third Edition

"Daily inspirations and guidance for putting them into action.

With *Leading Every Day*, I am able to make a difference every day.

The reason this book is in its third edition is because its messages continues to resonate, encourage, and motivate action. Congratulations.

The memory of the inspirational leadership of Susan Loucks Horsley is retained in volume 3 and provides me with the daily motivation to be the best I can be.

A powerful combination of inspirational, critical, and practical guidance delivered in daily doses."

> Stephanie Hirsh
> *Executive Director*
> *Learning Forward*

"An excellent resource for developing your own leadership action plan."

> Cynthia Willingham
> *Project Instructor*
> *Alabama Science in Motion*
> *University of Alabama at Birmingham*
> *Birmingham, AL*

"This book joins the ranks of Covey and Carnegie in helping readers to enhance and improve their leadership skills. *Leading Every Day* falls right in line with our school's implementation of PLC's and RTI. It gives me knowledge to be an effective change agent in my school."

> Paul Hurt
> *Assistant Principal*
> *Snow Canyon High School*
> *St. George, UT*

"*Leading Every Day* is a practical reinforcement of the idea that leadership is taking responsibility for something you care about. The daily entries, which can be used separately or together, encourage leaders to be reflective practitioners."

> Kathy DiRanna
> *Education Director*
> *K-12 Alliance/WestEd*
> *Santa Ana, CA*

"The premise of *Leading Every Day* is that all of us who work in education need to be effective leaders. Leadership is not the purview of a chosen few, but the responsibility of all of us. This idea has never been more important than it is today. But where and how do we begin? This book puts the power to improve leadership skills in the hands of every working educator who wants the best for his/her students, teachers, schools, and communities.

The authors have culled and condensed the broad research literature on leadership and presented it in a very accessible way for all of us to apply. It's easy to find yourself and your own situation among the book's contemplations and then to determine your own learning path. The book's organization around change, learning communities, effective groups and results is at the same time practical and stimulating. This is a book to keep on your desk for easy reference and to share with colleagues and friends.

Each new edition of this book gets better and better as the authors refine their own understanding, listen to their readers, and tackle timely and important topics for educators. The addition of Book Five, Leadership for Results, is especially significant now as we see numerous educational improvement efforts flounder in the absence of a commitment to feasible, reasonable and valued outcomes."

>Patricia Bourexis
>*President*
>*The Study Group, Inc.*
>*Kill Devil Hills, NC*

"Skillful leadership requires pattern recognition and answering the question: Is this pattern productive for our group, organization or project? If not, how do I most effectively break that pattern and help those involved develop new and more productive ways of interacting? This practical and engaging book offers practical tools for leaders who want to be better creators of patterns that take hold and become the new habits in powerful groups."

>Bruce Wellman
>*Co-Director*
>*MiraVia LLC*
>*Guilford, VT*

"In my career, I have worked with a few actual leaders in education and many aspiring leaders. This book affirms the characteristics of educational leaders and provides a roadmap for those aspiring to effective educational leadership. The third edition of *Leading Every Day* is required reading for educators."

>Rodger W. Bybee
>*Executive Director (Retired)*
>*Biological Sciences Curriculum Study (BSCS)*

"*Leading Every Day* is an excellent resource for aspiring, new and seasoned STEM leaders. This book includes a wealth of information that is organized to provide leaders the flexibility to reflect on small nuggets of knowledge and the application of that information to his/her specific work on a day-to-day basis. As such, it effectively promotes a culture of continuous and improved learning in the school community.

This book is unique in considering every leader's demanding schedules and acknowledging the many challenges, they face. The daily quotes provide inspiring messages and motivation, coupled with a related discussion topic that helps leaders increase their effectiveness from day to day.

As we strive to ensure that we are preparing STEM-literate students, it is especially important that we equip leaders with the necessary tools to make this a reality. This book is a "must-have" for all STEM Leaders."

Zipporah Miller
Associate Executive Director for Professional Programs and Conferences National Science Teachers Association
Arlington, VA

"*Leading Every Day* is a staple of our principal leadership program. Each chapter elevates our students' thinking about what it takes to become a leader in order to transform themselves and others toward a common outcome.

Leading Every Day is the clockworks of leadership: It compels us to see leadership as a delicate system of balance, precision and perpetual movement toward a common end."

John Somers
Professor of Teacher Education, Director of Graduate Programs
University of Indianapolis
Indianapolis, IN

"Leading schools and districts today has never been more challenging. The courageous people who choose this work need thoughtful, practical strategies that are easily accessible to reflect upon and refer to throughout the year. *Leading Every Day: Actions for Effective Leadership, Third Edition* delivers this resource. The new addition to the book on *Leadership for Results* is timely and addresses an actual leadership need apparent across the country. This book is a must-have for all education leaders, both new and experienced."

Linda M. Paul, EdD
Executive Director
New Mexico School Leadership Institute
Albuquerque, NM

Leading Every Day

Third Edition

Leading Every Day

Actions for Effective Leadership

Third Edition

Joyce Kaser
Susan Mundry
Katherine E. Stiles
Susan Loucks-Horsley
WestEd

FOR INFORMATION:

Corwin

A SAGE Company

2455 Teller Road

Thousand Oaks, California 91320

(800) 233-9936

www.corwin.com

SAGE Publications Ltd.

1 Oliver's Yard

55 City Road

London EC1Y 1SP

United Kingdom

SAGE Publications India Pvt. Ltd.

B 1/I 1 Mohan Cooperative Industrial Area

Mathura Road, New Delhi 110 044

India

SAGE Publications Asia-Pacific Pte. Ltd.

3 Church Street

#10-04 Samsung Hub

Singapore 049483

Acquisitions Editor: Arnis Burvikovs
Associate Editor: Desiree Bartlett
Editorial Assistant: Ariel Price
Production Editor: Brittany Bauhaus
Copy Editor: Laurie Pitman
Typesetter: C&M Digitals (P) Ltd.
Proofreader: Jeff Bryant
Indexer: Diggs Publication Services, Inc.
Graphic Designer: Anupama Krishnan
Marketing Manager: Katie Stoddard

Copyright © 2013 by Corwin

All rights reserved. When forms and sample documents are included, their use is authorized only by educators, local school sites, and/or noncommercial or nonprofit entities that have purchased the book. Except for that usage, no part of this book may be reproduced or utilized in any form or by any means, electronic or mechanical, including photocopying, recording, or by any information storage and retrieval system, without permission in writing from the publisher.

All trade names and trademarks recited, referenced, or reflected herein are the property of their respective owners who retain all rights thereto.

Printed in the United States of America

Library of Congress Cataloging-in-Publication Data

A catalog record of this book is available from the Library of Congress.

9781452260938

This book is printed on acid-free paper.

13 14 15 16 17 10 9 8 7 6 5 4 3 2 1

Brief Contents

Acknowledgments	xvi
About the Authors	xviii
About the National Academy for Science and Mathematics Education Leadership	xxi
Introduction	xxiii
Dedication	xxvi
Book 1: Leadership Every Day	1
Book 2: Leading Change	46
Book 3: Leading Learning Communities	92
Book 4: Leading Effective Groups	144
Book 5: Leadership for Results	196
Index	254

Detailed Contents

Acknowledgments — xvi
About the Authors — xviii
About the National Academy for Science and Mathematics Education Leadership — xxi
Introduction — xxiii
Dedication — xxvi

Book 1: Leadership Every Day — 1
    Day 1: We Are All Leaders — 2
    Day 2: Effective Leadership Practices — 3
    Day 3: Making Conscious Choices — 5
    Day 4: Committing to a Moral Imperative — 7
    Day 5: Using Power Appropriately — 8
    Day 6: Building Shared Vision — 10
    Day 7: Promoting Diversity — 11
    Day 8: Leading for Results — 12
    Day 9: Using Habits to Our Advantage — 14
    Day 10: Generating and Sharing Knowledge — 15
    Day 11: Keeping a Client-Centered Focus — 17
    Day 12: Recognizing and Celebrating Success — 18
    Day 13: Networking — 19
    Day 14: Embracing Innovative Thinking — 20
    Day 15: Aligning Actions and Beliefs — 22
    Day 16: Examining Your Culture — 23
    Day 17: Building a Trusting Climate — 24
    Day 18: Collaborative Leadership — 26

Day 19: Building Relationships	27
Day 20: Trying Something New	28
Day 21: Coping with Ambiguity, Change, and Confusion	29
Day 22: Leading through Crisis	30
Day 23: Balancing Leadership and Management	32
Day 24: Living with Paradox	33
Day 25: Paying Attention to Leadership Actions and Traits	34
Day 26: Getting Support	35
Day 27: Asking Good Questions	37
Day 28: Finding Win/Win Solutions	38
Day 29: Modeling Leadership	40
Day 30: Ethical Leadership	41
Day 31: Doing the Right Thing	42
References	43
Book 2: Leading Change	**46**
Day 1: Change as a Process	47
Day 2: Change Happens in People First	48
Day 3: The Impact of Change	49
Day 4: Moving through the Stages of Change-Concerns	50
Day 5: Moving through the Stages of Change-Behavior	52
Day 6: Change as Continuous Improvement	53
Day 7: Speed of Change	54
Day 8: The Missing Piece in Change	56
Day 9: Balancing Constants and Change	57
Day 10: Recognizing Assumptions	59
Day 11: Crafting a Shared Vision	60
Day 12: Mission and Goals	61
Day 13: Motivating Others	62
Day 14: Planning for Change	63
Day 15: Origins of Change	65
Day 16: Accepting Loss	66
Day 17: Dealing with Disappointment	68
Day 18: Change and Resilience	69
Day 19: Facing Problems	70

Day 20: Neutralizing Resistance	71
Day 21: Capitalizing on Resistance	73
Day 22: Knowing Your Constituents	75
Day 23: Managing Multiple Change Efforts	76
Day 24: Systems Thinking	78
Day 25: Examining Change History	80
Day 26: The Downside of Change	81
Day 27: Building Ownership for Change	82
Day 28: Individuals as Agents of Change	83
Day 29: Self-Assessment as a Change Leader	85
Day 30: Sustaining Individual Leadership	86
Day 31: Initiating, Implementing, and Institutionalizing Change	88
References	89
Book 3: Leading Learning Communities	**92**
Day 1: Leading Communities of Learning	93
Day 2: Leading Learning in Organizations	95
Day 3: Building Cultural Proficiency	96
Day 4: Powerful Learning Experiences	98
Day 5: How People Learn	99
Day 6: Transformative Learning	100
Day 7: Transforming Situational Learning	102
Day 8: Defining Expertise	103
Day 9: Characteristics of Effective Professional Learning	105
Day 10: Aligning Beliefs and Behaviors	107
Day 11: Designing Professional Development	108
Day 12: Committing to Vision and Standards	110
Day 13: Using Data to Guide Professional Development Designs	111
Day 14: Inputs into Professional Development Design	112
Day 15: Knowledge and Beliefs in Science and Mathematics	114
Day 16: Professional Development in Context	115
Day 17: Critical Issues to Consider	117
Day 18: Ensuring Equity	119

Day 19: Strategies for Professional Learning	120
Day 20: Selecting and Combining Strategies	123
Day 21: Professional Development for Student Impact	125
Day 22: Balancing Philosophy and Pragmatism	126
Day 23: Incorporating Reflexive Practice	128
Day 24: Reaching Everyone or Scaling Up	129
Day 25: Team Learning	131
Day 26: Sharing Knowledge and Capturing Lessons Learned	132
Day 27: Using Program Logic Models	134
Day 28: Achieving Realistic Outcomes	135
Day 29: Gathering Evaluation Data	137
Day 30: Leading Learning by Example	138
Day 31: Taking Responsibility for Learning	139
References	141
Book 4: Leading Effective Groups	**144**
Day 1: Leading Groups	145
Day 2: Four Roles of Group Leaders	146
Day 3: Group Norms of Collaboration	147
Day 4: Group Norm #1—Pausing	149
Day 5: Group Norm #2—Paraphrasing	151
Day 6: Group Norm #3—Posing Questions	153
Day 7: Group Norm #4—Putting Ideas on the Table	155
Day 8: Group Norm #5—Providing Data	157
Day 9: Group Norm #6—Paying Attention to Self and Others, Verbal Communication	157
Day 10: Group Norm #6—Paying Attention to Self and Others, Nonverbal Communication	159
Day 11: Group Norm #7—Presuming Positive Intentions	160
Day 12: Dialogue Versus Discussion	162
Day 13: Dialogue as Reflective Learning Process	164
Day 14: Eliciting Participation from Everyone	165
Day 15: Cultural Proficiency	167
Day 16: Establishing Clear Roles and Functions	170
Day 17: Structuring an Effective Meeting	172

Day 18: Providing Logistical Supports	174
Day 19: Setting Up the Meeting Room	175
Day 20: Group Decision Making	177
Day 21: Reaching Consensus	178
Day 22: Giving Feedback	179
Day 23: Receiving Feedback	181
Day 24: Handling Problems	182
Day 25: Options for Resolving Conflict	183
Day 26: Conflict as Opportunity	185
Day 27: Facilitating Conflict	186
Day 28: Resolving Value Conflicts	187
Day 29: Dealing with Disruptive People	188
Day 30: Beginnings and Endings	190
Day 31: Six Domains of Group Development	192
References	195
Book 5: Leadership for Results	**196**
Day 1: Results-Based Leadership	197
Day 2: Role of Leader to Achieve Results	199
Day 3: Using Rigorous Evidence	201
Day 4: Being an Accountable Leader	202
Day 5: Role of Policy in Achieving Results	204
Day 6: Building a Culture of Continuous Improvement	205
Day 7: Equitable Access to Data	206
Day 8: Purposeful Use of Data	208
Day 9: The Power of Data	209
Day 10: Collaborative Inquiry	211
Day 11: Engaging Everyone with Data	213
Day 12: Data-Driven Dialogue	215
Day 13: Root Cause Analysis	217
Day 14: Cause and Effect	219
Day 15: Cause and Effect Analysis: The Fishbone	221
Day 16: Identifying Problems	223
Day 17: Communicating about Problems	224
Day 18: Criteria for Selecting Outcomes	226

Day 19: Selecting the Right Intervention	228
Day 20: Rapid Prototyping	230
Day 21: Assessing Evaluation	232
Day 22: Reflecting on Results	233
Day 23: Planning for Success	235
Day 24: Components of Trust	237
Day 25: Keeping the Trust	238
Day 26: Time Required for Results	240
Day 27: Getting Better Results	242
Day 28: Seeking Collective Impact	243
Day 29: Sustaining a Focus on Continuous Improvement	245
Day 30: Results over Time	247
Day 31: Continuing to Learn	249
References	251

Index   **254**

Acknowledgments

Translating the curriculum of the National Academy for Science and Mathematics Education Leadership, along with current research and best practice, into three editions of this book has not been a solitary task. For more than a decade Leadership Academy fellows, mentors, colleagues, advisors, reviewers, and friends have generously provided us with their ideas, resources, and time, contributions that are now reflected throughout the contemplations of *Leading Every Day*. We thank the following individuals, each of whom has made a significant contribution to one or more of the three editions.

Stan Altrock	Nancy Love
Richard Audet	Marilyn Lutz
Susan Brady	Norm Mitchell
Terry Brell	Judith Noel
Shannon CdeBaca	Ronald Richmond
Kathy DiRanna	Stacey Roddy
Karen Falkenberg	Cheryl Rose
Kelly Jacobs	Marlene Ross
Karen Kearney	Robert Terry
Page Keeley	Emma Walton
Nancy Kellogg	Sybil Yastrow
Paul Kuerbis	Kendall Zoller
Nelson Letts	

Our special thanks goes to Diane Enright, Deanna Maier, and Julie Colton who made many helpful suggestions as they prepared the final manuscripts. We appreciate their hard work and dedication.

Our colleagues at Corwin Press provided the motivation and guidance in producing all three editions. For this edition we thank Arnis Burvikovs for having a niche for our ideas, Mayan White for keeping us on target with the submission process, and Laurie Pitman for helping us refine our words.

We also gratefully acknowledge the National Science Foundation. Their confidence in Susan Loucks-Horsley's vision and support for the Leadership Academy enabled us to reach hundreds of science and mathematics education leaders. We appreciate our parent organization, WestEd, for hosting the academy and supporting us to do great mission-driven work.

We also thank our families, who—yet again—have allowed us the space and time to write while providing unconditional support throughout the process of preparing the manuscripts.

Finally, we gratefully acknowledge the contributions of the following reviewers:

Kathy DiRanna, *WestEd*

Paul Hurt, *Snow Canyon High School*

Karen Kearney, *WestEd*

Michelle LaPointe, *Lesley University*

Carl Nagin, *WestEd*

Cynthia Willingham, *University of Alabama at Birmingham*

About the Authors

Joyce Kaser is a Senior Program Associate in the Science, Technology, Engineering, and Mathematics (STEM) Program at WestEd. She has extensive experience in program evaluation, primarily the evaluation of STEM programs. She has served as a team member for the development of two frameworks for the National Assessment of Educational Progress: Science, 2009 and Technology and Engineering Literacy, 2014. Joyce also led the development of the background variables for students, teachers, and administrators participating in NAEP and was co-lead of the standard setting for the NAEP 2009 science project. Joyce has had numerous experiences in evaluating STEM professional development, including co-developing an external validation system for professional development and student enrichment programs. She is first author of *Enhancing Program Quality in Science and Mathematics*, also published by Corwin. Joyce has been the facilitator for the New Mexico Secretary of Education's Math and Science Advisory Council and has evaluated National Science Foundation educational outreach projects. Prior to joining WestEd, Joyce directed the Washington, D.C. office of The NETWORK, a research and development organization, headed up an equity assistance center, and served as a district administrator and high school teacher. Currently she is involved in research of mathematics and science programs, looking specifically at learning progressions in science, computer-based tutoring systems, and program implementation. She holds an EdD from The American University.

Susan Mundry is Deputy Director of Learning Innovations and Science, Technology, Engineering, and Mathematics (STEM) at WestEd. For the past 20 years, she has engaged in technical assistance and research focused on effective professional development and developing leaders for educational change. She currently serves as a Senior Researcher for the Regional Education

Laboratory-Northeast & Islands (REL-NEI) where she has co-authored studies on teacher quality and is the lead facilitator for the REL-NEI's Research Alliance on Educator Effectiveness. Susan also serves as the project director for the evaluation of a National Science Foundation funded Math-Science Partnership program at The Pennsylvania State University. She is the project director for the technical assistance project supporting the Nellie Mae Education Foundation's school redesign project to implement innovative student-centered approaches in secondary education and a Senior Researcher for the National Center for Cognition and Mathematics Instruction. Prior to this, Susan was a Principal Investigator for two National Science Foundation projects on teacher development: *Curriculum Topic Study*, which developed and field tested professional development materials for mathematics and science teachers; and *Building Systems for Quality Professional Development* where she co-designed a simulation game and professional development materials on building professional learning communities. She has also served as an advisor to National Science Foundation projects, to the National Research Council, and to the National Science Teachers Association. Susan is an author of several books, book chapters, articles, and the co-developer of two simulation games on educational change. She co-authored: *Designing Effective Professional Development for Teachers of Science and Mathematics (2nd and 3rd editions)*; *The Data Coach's Guide to Improving Learning for all Students: Unleashing the Power of Collaborative Inquiry*; *Professional Learning Communities for Science Teaching*; *The Leader's Guide to Science Curriculum Topic Study*; *The Leader's Guide to Mathematics Curriculum Topic Study*; and *Leading Every Day: 124 Actions for Effective Leadership*, which received a Book of the Year Award from Learning Forward.

Katherine E. Stiles is a Senior Program Associate in the STEM Program at WestEd. Katherine is Co-Director of WestEd's National Academy for Science and Mathematics Education Leadership, providing professional development and support for education leaders nationwide. The foci of the Leadership Academy–effective leadership, educational change, professional development and communities of learners, facilitation, and using data and evidence to achieve results–are reflected in the book, *Leading Every Day: Actions for Effective Leadership, Third Edition* (2013). She designs and leads science and mathematics education program evaluation projects at the school, district, state, and national level, focusing on assessing the quality of professional development, and the relationship between teachers' conceptual learning, changes in practice, and student learning. Katherine works with schools and districts to enhance student learning through the development of collaborative inquiry into data among staff as part of her work on the Using Data Project and as co-author of *The Data Coach's Guide to Improving Learning for All Students: Unleashing the Power of Collaborative Inquiry,* (2008). She was co-director of an NSF-funded project, Building Systems for Quality Teaching and Learning in Science, that resulted in the publication of professional development materials and a simulation board game on science education. The project extended the work of the seminal book on professional development that she co-authored, *Designing Professional Development for Teachers of Science and Mathematics, Third Edition* (2010). Prior to joining WestEd in 1995, Katherine worked at the National Science Resources Center in Washington, D.C., as a science curriculum developer and authored four curriculum units for the *Science and Technology for Children* program.

Susan Loucks-Horsley was Associate Executive Director at Biological Sciences Curriculum Study (BSCS) and Senior Research Associate for Science and Mathematics at WestEd. She directed the Professional Development Project at the National Institute for Science Education and was senior author of the project's *Designing Professional Development for Teachers of Science and Mathematics,* published in 1998. Previously, she was the Director of Professional Development and Outreach at the National Research Council (NRC) Center for Science, Mathematics, and Engineering Education. Her work at the NRC included promoting, supporting, and monitoring the progress of standards-based education, especially the *National Science Education Standards.* Her work as Associate Director of the Northeast/Islands Regional Lab and the National Center for Improving Science Education focused on developing approaches, products, and training activities to help educators build their knowledge and skills in collaborative approaches to staff development, program change, and program evaluation. She led the development team of *Facilitating Systemic Change in Science and Mathematics Education: A Toolkit for Professional Developers,* a product of the 10 regional education laboratories. She was senior author of *Continuing to Learn: A Guidebook for Teacher Development, An Action Guide for School Improvement, Elementary School Science for the '90s,* reports from the National Center for Improving Science Education on teacher development and support, and numerous chapters and articles on related topics. While at the University of Texas (Austin) Research and Development Center for Teacher Education, she worked on the development team of the Concerns-Based Adoption Model (CBAM), which describes how individuals experience change.

About the National Academy for Science and Mathematics Education Leadership

Since 1997, the Leadership Academy has supported leaders throughout the United States—from Puerto Rico to Alaska—to implement wide-scale science and mathematics education reform through in-depth professional development experiences. The Leadership Academy's curriculum focuses on leadership styles, practice, and models; organizational and individual change; strategic planning and organizational development; facilitation and development of collaborative groups; data-driven decision making and using data to guide teaching and improve student learning; and professional development design, implementation, and evaluation.

The first three cohorts of leaders were supported with funding from the National Science Foundation; and cohorts four, five, six, and seven have been supported with funding from the Susan Loucks-Horsley Educational Fund and individual tuition. During the past 16 years, participating leaders have achieved many impressive outcomes. They have put some of the best resources for learning in place, returned to their own settings to lead learning for others, contributed to the knowledge base by writing and publishing books, developed new approaches to teacher professional development, advanced their careers, and most important, improved outcomes for teachers and students.

The Leadership Academy is a project of WestEd—a research, development, and service agency working with education and other communities to promote excellence, achieve equity, and improve learning for children, youth, and adults. The Leadership Academy was started in collaboration with several national organizations:

- Association for the Education of Teachers in Science (AETS)
- Association for State Supervisors of Mathematics (ASSM)
- Council of State Science Supervisors (CSSS)
- National Council of Supervisors of Mathematics (NCSM)
- Learning Forward (formerly the National Staff Development Council)
- National Science Education Leadership Association (NSELA)
- National Science Teachers Association (NSTA)
- National Research Council's Center for Science, Mathematics, and Engineering Education (CSMEE)

For additional information about the Leadership Academy, contact Julie Colton, Learning Innovations at WestEd, 300 Unicorn Park Drive, 5th Floor, Woburn, MA, 01801-3324, Telephone: (781) 481–1135. Fax: (781) 481–1120.

Introduction

Welcome to the third edition of *Leading Every Day: Actions for Effective Leadership.* If you have read the first and second editions, a special "Welcome back" to you. We were delighted with the impact of those two editions and with the many people who shared their stories of how the book influenced their practice. The book was recognized by the National Staff Development Council (now Learning Forward) with the 2003 Outstanding Book of the Year Award. This new edition has been substantially updated. Our underlying purpose—helping you to be an effective leader during a time of rapid change—remains the same. However, informed by new research and thinking in the field, our suggestions for getting you there have been reshaped and sharpened.

Most of the content in this book is part of the curriculum of the National Academy for Science and Mathematics Education Leadership at WestEd, which provides participants with the knowledge and perspectives to carry out their roles as leaders. The primary audience for this book is leaders—leaders at all levels of the system. We consider leaders to be anyone who facilitates the learning and work of and with others, including teacher leaders, instructional coaches, principals, district administrators, state-level coordinators, and those from higher education, technical assistance agencies, and informal learning institutions.

Leading Every Day is divided into five books: Leadership Every Day, Leading Change, Leading Learning Communities, Leading Effective Groups, and Leadership for Results. These five topics are, in the authors' experience, the key areas for developing and sustaining leaders. For each book, the material is presented in 31 contemplations, one for each day of the month. Each contemplation begins with an inspiring quote, discusses important aspects of the topic, and ends with a reflection, usually a series of questions or a scenario for the reader to consider.

So, what's different about the third edition? Book One, Leadership Every Day, Book Two, Leading Change, and Book Four, Leading Effective Groups, have been sharpened and updated. Over the past 7 years we have continued to work closely with leaders who have shaped our experiences and learning; thus, our own learning has led us to make some shifts in the topics addressed in those books. Book Four focuses on the updated and revised work of Bob Garmston and Bruce Wellman (2012, 2009), and we gratefully thank the authors for allowing us to include so much of their work in *Leading Every Day.*

Book Three, Leading Learning Communities, has been completely revised to reflect the new content in the third edition of our book, *Designing Professional Development for Teachers of Science and Mathematics* (Corwin Press, 2010).

Book Five, Leadership for Results, is completely new. We believe that with the growing emphasis on accountability, leaders need guidance on creating cultures of success and commitment to results. As we have worked with educational organizations over the years, we have seen how often a focus on results is missing from the education improvement equation. We've come to believe that an essential role of leaders is to engage and involve everyone in setting worthwhile goals, defining what success will look like, and taking actions that will lead to desired results. Therefore, the new Book Five provides 31 contemplations that support leaders to engage in results-based leadership as a way of working and thinking that focuses on achieving the most important outcomes.

During the past 7 years—since the publication of the second edition—there has been a wealth of new research and literature about how people learn, the relationship of leadership practices to improved student learning, the role of data to guide improvement efforts, and the value of developing schools as professional learning communities. This new research has guided our overall revisions in this edition of the book.

For example, there's more discussion in this edition about instructional leadership, collaborative leadership, and what it takes to support a community of learners *and* leaders. There's greater emphasis on building trusting climates, innovative thinking, and new forms of networking, as well as the use of data for decision making, leading change, and designing adult learning experiences based on student needs. The importance of reflecting on and monitoring progress toward achievement of goals is a theme included throughout each of the five books. In response to readers' requests, we have included more scenarios to guide the readers' engagement with topics. The five books are more closely integrated, with several themes interwoven throughout the entire volume. The references and examples have been updated in each book.

The contemplations of *Leading Every Day* can be read in order, or a reader may select a specific theme to pursue throughout the five books. However you choose to engage with this volume, the contemplations are best read in an environment that is conducive to reflection, when you have time and energy to consider the questions and compose thoughtful and meaningful responses. Readers of the prior editions of this book will notice that we removed the "Notes" section after each Reflection. We encourage you to keep a journal or notes as you reflect on and respond to the questions provided in each contemplation so that you can document your own learning and growth as a leader.

In the spirit of continuous learning, we hope that the contemplations in the third edition of *Leading Every Day* help readers reflect on their leadership roles, styles, and practices and gain insights that improve their effectiveness and sustain them through challenging transitions.

Dedication

Susan Loucks-Horsley
1947–2000

This book is dedicated to our co-author and dear friend, Susan Loucks-Horsley, whose visionary leadership and tireless dedication to education improvement inspired so many. The National Academy for Science and Mathematics Education Leadership (on which this book is based) was a dream realized for Susan. For many years, she had talked with colleagues about the need to build the next generation of leaders for education. She had a vision of a leadership academy that would be a national network, in which leaders learned from and supported each other. The academy she developed and directed, like Susan's many other endeavors, was a tremendous success. Through this and other achievements, she carried out the work she cared so passionately about—the continual improvement of education for children and professional development opportunities for educators.

Susan will live on in the work and hearts of the many people with whom she shared herself so generously during her remarkable career. We give tribute to her and promise to carry on her vision and passion for leadership development. Susan's middle name was Hope, and she had it in abundance. Our hope is that her work lives on in you as you take up and use the ideas and reflections on leadership, change, learning, group facilitation, and achieving results in this book.

Joyce S. Kaser, Susan Mundry, and
Katherine E. Stiles

Book 1

Leadership Every Day

At no other time in education have we needed quality leadership more than we do today. Schools are striving to support all students to learn and meet challenging standards. This requires rethinking how schools operate, developing new roles for teachers and administrators, and changing expectations as well as behaviors.

Without supportive and proactive leadership, the increased pressure for high performance can be exhausting and demoralizing. It can encourage blaming and lead people to lose hope. With visionary and collaborative leadership, schools and the people in them feel supported as they focus on improving processes and practices and work together to achieve high performance. They can set a course for success, monitoring and celebrating milestones, and supporting one another along the way.

Quality leadership requires collaboration among many to make it work well and practice, practice, practice to get it right. With today's challenges and opportunities in education, we need many, rather than a few, people leading collaboratively and creatively every day.

The contemplations in Book One introduce leadership as a way of thinking and acting every day. They are organized by major themes, including:

- What do effective leaders do? How do they build a shared commitment to the work? What specific practices increase student achievement?
- What are the environments that support excellent leadership, such as shared leadership and professional learning communities?
- What are some of the challenges leaders face, and how can they address them?
- What are the traits of leaders, and how do they keep doing the right things?

These topics are interwoven through the contemplations for Days 1 through 31.

DAY 1: WE ARE ALL LEADERS

A community is like a ship; everyone ought to be prepared to take the helm.

Henrik Ibsen

Are you a leader?

Have you wrestled with this question maybe once or twice in your life, or maybe more frequently? Do you eagerly take responsibility for leading others, or is it harder for you to take the helm? What does it mean to you to be a leader?

One common definition of leadership is an individual's ability to work with others to accomplish an agreed-upon result. What isn't in this definition is as important as what is. It says absolutely nothing about position, title, or status.

Everyone can demonstrate extraordinary leadership when he or she learns and uses effective practices such as those described in this book. You do not need to be an administrator to be a leader. Sometimes having an impressive job title helps to get things done, but not always. In fact, when leaders rely only on their positional power to make things happen, their coworkers or followers may be compelled to do what the leader wants, but they may not be committed to their work. Rather, it is the ability to cultivate leadership in others and build commitment to the goals of the organization that is a hallmark of a good leader. For example, the Wallace Foundation (2013) has found that school leaders "have to be (or become) leaders of learning who can develop a team delivering effective instruction" (p. 6), a process that entails five key responsibilities:

1. Shaping a vision of academic success for all students, one based on high standards

2. Creating a climate hospitable to education in order that safety, a cooperative spirit, and other foundations of fruitful interaction prevail

3. Cultivating leadership in others so that teachers and other adults assume their part in realizing the school vision

4. Improving instruction to enable teachers to teach at their best and students to learn at their utmost
5. Managing people, data, and processes to foster school improvement

Reflection

Consider how prepared you are to be an effective leader and to develop a team of co-workers who share leadership roles and responsibilities with you. Do you:

- Have a clear vision of academic success based on standards? Support others to share this vision?
- Create an environment based on trust and cooperation?
- Empower others to take on leadership responsibilities and roles?
- Provide opportunities for teachers and students to teach and learn?
- Have systems in place to manage people, data, and processes aligned with your vision?
- What are your strengths? What would you like to enhance?

DAY 2: EFFECTIVE LEADERSHIP PRACTICES

If your actions inspire others to dream more, learn more, do more and become more, you are a leader.

John Quincy Adams

According to researchers Kouzes and Posner (2012), leaders who accomplish extraordinary results with others use five leadership practices. Their actions contribute to their effectiveness and the success of those with whom they work. Effective leaders intentionally and deliberately use these five leadership practices every day:

1. *Model the way.* It is no surprise that effective leaders are credible. People usually know what to expect from them. They are clear about their own personal values and views and build a consensus among others about the values that will guide all of them. Leaders "model the way" by checking to make sure their actions are consistent with their values, sending a strong message about what is important to them and their work.

2. *Inspire a shared vision.* Effective leaders care deeply about what they want to accomplish and work with their colleagues to identify common, shared goals and aspirations for the future.

3. *Challenge the process.* Effective leaders question and work to change the status quo. They take on challenging projects that help them learn something new. They learn from their failures as well as their successes and see every day as a chance to do their job smarter and better than the day before.

4. *Enable others to act.* Leaders foster collaboration and teamwork. They share power and responsibility. They actively remove hierarchy and other roadblocks to increase interactions among people who need to work together. They coach and support others so that they have the confidence they need to succeed. They continually ask themselves, "What can I do to help this person continue to grow and be highly competent?"

5. *Encourage the heart.* Effective leaders build a strong, caring community in which people praise and recognize success. They know success breeds success and celebrate each small milestone. They support and encourage everyone when the going gets tough. (Kouzes & Posner, 2012)

Reflection

How often do you demonstrate the leadership practices described? Review the short descriptions of each, and rank order them from those you do most frequently to those you do least frequently. Reflect on the ones you practice frequently. How well are you performing these practices? What would you like to do better?

Reflect on the ones you practice infrequently. How might you use these more often? What support do you need to do that? Who can help you?

Here are some examples of behaviors related to the leadership practices. How might you incorporate these into your daily practice?

- For a week, make a list of every task you perform. About each ask yourself, "Why am I doing this? Why am I doing it this way? Can this task be eliminated or done better?"
- Establish a norm of asking everyone to share things they have done recently to enhance performance and outcomes.
- Ask staff to identify areas in the organization that need improvement. Commit to changing three of the most frequently mentioned items.
- Write down what you aspire to accomplish in your current position and why. Talk with others about their hopes and goals. Find

areas of common goals and shared aspirations that you can work on together.
- Publicize the work of your colleagues. Let others know about their accomplishments.

Think about what you say and do each day for a week. Are your actions consistent with your values? If you say you believe in creating a place where all students will succeed, are your behaviors supporting that vision? Are you setting the example you want? If there are inconsistencies, identify what you need to change (Kouzes, Posner, & Morrow, 2010).

DAY 3: MAKING CONSCIOUS CHOICES

One's philosophy is not best expressed in words; it is expressed in the choices one makes.

Eleanor Roosevelt

Choose. Choose often—hundreds of times a day, in fact.

Choose. Choose based on what you desire—what you truly want for yourself and others.

Choose. Choose deliberately and consciously. Choose, if you want to move forward. Don't choose, and you stay stationary or fall back.

One of the key characteristics of leaders is that they consciously make all kinds of choices—not just the big ones, such as instituting new policies or programs. They make medium-sized choices, such as choosing not to blame themselves for failure or not being deterred from their mission by adversaries. They also make many small choices: choosing to check in on a colleague who has a serious illness in the family or picking up the coffee cups at the end of a meeting. Each of the choices leaders make says something about what they stand for and what they want for themselves and their organizations.

As a leader in your organization, there are two choices that are essential for you to make:

1. *Choose to know what you want.* Oftentimes, people cannot move ahead because they don't know what they want. They are stagnant, often waiting for some external force to push them in a direction. Although it is not easy, you can develop a conscious habit of knowing what you want and pursing it. Maybe you need to set up a meeting with an influential person in your community to help

get the budget passed; perhaps you want to get small groups of staff working together to better track your results; or maybe you would rather not serve on a group or committee that you have been assigned to for years. Be clear about and consciously choose what you want. Think of yourself as always having an answer to the question, if it were posed, "What is it that you want right now? Five days from now? Five years from now?"

2. *Choose to act to achieve what you want.* How much of your time do you spend doing what you want to do to achieve your goals? How often do you feel as if you are compelled to spend time doing things that are not connected to your goals but imposed on you? Listen to your language as you talk with others. How often do you say you "have to" or "should" do something?

According to Dave Ellis (2002), this language communicates that you are living in a world of obligation—your actions are controlled by external influence, not by your own goals and desires. Ellis points out that people communicate more powerfully when they clarify what they want and speak less in terms of what they "have to" do and more in terms of what they "plan" or "promise" to do. People often don't get what they want because they never make their wishes known to themselves and others and act on them. The sheer act of stating what you want will accomplish a great deal. Perhaps to achieve what you want, you must take a next step: set a meeting date, write a memo, or recommend a new program. Each day, try to take at least one step that moves you toward your goals.

Reflection

During the day, stop periodically to ask yourself what choices you are making and why. If you want something at that moment, what is it? Take an extra minute or two for yourself if you don't readily have an answer to that question. Chances are that you do want something—maybe even just 5 minutes to call home or to sign a contract for a new professional development program. Once you find what it is, choose it for yourself. At the end of the day, tally what you gained for yourself and your organization by making conscious, deliberate choices.

Look over your list. How many of the items relate directly to what you are trying to accomplish? How can you do more of these things and less of the things that may not affect your goals?

DAY 4: COMMITTING TO A MORAL IMPERATIVE

Most educators inherently believe that racism is morally wrong. The challenge is to advance that moral position into real, comprehensive, cognitive, and intellectual foundations of understanding that will allow us to challenge racism in our everyday personal interactions and professional practices.

Glenn Singleton & Curtis Linton

One of the conscious choices that leaders must make is to commit to a "moral imperative." According to Lindsey, Robins, and Terrell (2003), educators must make a "moral commitment to confronting entitlement and eliminating oppression" (p. 294). Without such a commitment, racial inequalities and achievement gaps will continue to persist within our educational system. It is imperative for leaders to confront racial inequalities, and the beliefs that underlie them, in order for the vision of all students learning and thriving to become a reality.

Glenn Singleton and Curtis Linton (2006) advocate that leaders need to have the courageous conversations about race in order to confront the actions and the beliefs that "play a primary role in students' struggle to achieve at high levels" (p. 2). They note that three critical factors are necessary for educators to close the racial achievement gap: having the passion to directly confront the problem, enacting the educational practices that research shows are effective for students of color, and maintaining the persistence that is needed to relentlessly address inequality (pp. 6–7).

In order to enact the second factor, Singleton and Linton propose that leaders engage in courageous conversation following their "six conditions" that can guide leaders' through racial dialogue. The six conditions include:

1. *Getting Personal*—"establishing a racial context that is personal, local, and immediate," which entails an examination of one's own racial attitudes, beliefs, and expectations (p. 73)

2. *Keeping the Spotlight on Race*—"isolating race while acknowledging the broader scope of diversity and the variety of factors that contribute to a racialized problem," which means that conversations focus exclusively and intentionally on race and not, for example, on poverty, language, or gender; which are also important issues to discuss but leaders need to promote dialogue that focuses on one issue at a time (p. 88)

3. *Engaging Multiple Racial Perspectives*—"normalizing social construction of knowledge, thus engaging multiple racial points of view in order to surface critical perspectives," which means acknowledging that individuals bring experienced-based and unique perspectives on race to the conversation, forming a "broad continuum of willingness and ability to examine and understand racial matters" (pp. 105–106)

4. *Keeping Us All at the Table*—"monitoring the parameters of the conversation by being explicit and intentional about the number of participants, prompts for discussion, and time allotted for listening, speaking and reflecting," which means that leaders pay attention to the elements of the conversation that promote safety and trust (pp. 117–119)

5. *What Do You Mean by "Race"?*—"establishing agreement around a contemporary working definition of race that clearly differentiates it from ethnicity and nationality," which means consulting the literature so that everyone at the table is clear about the distinctions and definitions (p. 158)

6. *Let's Talk About Whiteness*—"examining the presence and role of Whiteness, its impact on the conversation, and the problem being addressed," which means acknowledging that this dominant racial group has historically shaped the definition of race (p. 181) and "subordinates other cultures" (p. 204)

Reflection

Do you have a strong commitment to confronting and addressing racial inequality and racial achievement gaps? In what ways do you act upon this moral commitment?

Do you engage your colleagues in "courageous conversations"? To what extent do you engage and encourage those in your organization to examine the racial beliefs and assumptions operating within the system?

What more might you do to ensure that your organizational culture values and routinely acts upon a moral imperative to address inequalities and discuss race?

DAY 5: USING POWER APPROPRIATELY

The key to successful leadership today is influence, not authority.

Kenneth Blanchard

What do you think of when you hear the word *power* being used in relation to people, as in "She's a powerful woman" or "He's got a lot of power in this organization"?

Power can be defined as having great influence and control over others. Leaders gain it through positional authority and/or by earning respect and developing a following. Regardless of how leaders gain power, they must use it appropriately and morally. If they fall in love with the idea of power, they may end up taking actions that are in the interest of retaining their power, not in meeting their mission.

Stephen Covey (1990) identified three different types of power used by leaders. When a leader uses *coercive power*, followers follow because they are afraid. They will either be punished in some way or lose something if they fail to do what the leader wants. For example, too often we see education leaders use accountability for student learning as a threat instead of as an opportunity to work together to solve problems. When a leader relies on *utility power*, followers follow because of the benefits they will receive if they comply. This model sees the leader-follower relationship as transactional—the follower will do something for some reward (for example, paycheck, bonus, or recognition). This type of power is the most commonly used in organizations. The third type—*legitimate power*—is focused on building commitment and trust. Followers follow because they believe in the leaders, trust them, and want to achieve the same purpose. This is the type of power that is the strongest and most effective.

Each type of power has different consequences. Coercive power relies on fear and works only as long as there is something to be feared. Although it is based on equity, utility power often encourages individualism rather than group efforts. Legitimate power relies on mutual respect and honor and produces a sustained, proactive response from followers.

Reflection

Pay attention to your own language. Do you often cite the consequences of noncompliance, as in "Those who fail to do this will . . . "? If so, you may be drawing too heavily on coercive power. Do you make promises, as in "Those who do this will get extra credit, a raise, a bonus . . . "? If so, you may be over relying on utility power. Pay attention to the times you may use these words and think about whether it would be more effective to build trust and commitment so that people are more personally motivated to make desired changes.

After considering these questions, ask yourself what type of power base you see yourself relying on most frequently. How do followers respond? What type of power base would you prefer to use more often? How do you think followers would respond?

DAY 6: BUILDING SHARED VISION

Few, if any, forces in human affairs are as powerful as shared vision.

Peter Senge

Vision! What is your reaction to this word?

Is it negative? Perhaps you have been involved in vision-building activities that never really made a difference in how your organization functioned or in your results. Perhaps your organization, like many others, failed to live by its vision once it was created.

Effective leaders engage people throughout the organization in building commitment toward the shared vision that becomes the guiding force for all action. A great example of this is schools that have established a vision of an unyielding commitment to ensuring that all students gain important and relevant content knowledge. The vision drives all behaviors and informs all of the school's operations, structures, and allocation of resources. Another example is schools that envision themselves as providing the best quality instruction, without exception. Again, the vision shapes what the staff does, including making sure every teacher is supported to learn and carry out best practice and use ongoing analysis of data and results to find out what is working and what needs to be changed.

Many organizations have vision and mission statements. Most visions, however, are not shared visions. They are imposed on others by the head of the organization or a group of people at the top. These visions are not effective long term because they "command compliance—not commitment" (Senge, 1990, p. 206). A shared vision is different. A shared vision incorporates individual visions, engenders commitment, and focuses energy. As Senge (1990) says, "When people truly share a vision, they are connected, bound together by a common aspiration. Shared visions derive their power from a common caring" (p. 206).

Kouzes and Posner (2012) suggest that leaders inspire people to come to a shared vision that is appropriate for them based on carefully considering how future trends will affect them and what reputable people are predicting about their business in the next 10 years. As leaders you must look at this information and identify patterns to predict how you will be affected in the future and help to build a shared vision based on that. Schools that have visions based on old trends and data from prior decades are going to be locked in the past.

Don't confuse vision and mission. Vision is knowing where you want to be or what you want to become. It includes tangibles, as well as intangibles, such as virtues and the culture that you want to surround you.

Mission is your reason for being and the work you pursue to realize your vision. Your mission guides your actions to achieve what you envision for yourself and your organization. Both are necessary, especially for leaders of organizations.

> **Reflection**
>
> Do the people in your organization have a common, clear, and shared vision of what you are working toward? How well does the vision drive decisions and actions? Does it permeate your organization's culture and decision making on a daily basis? Do you have a personal vision for yourself? Are you clear about your mission in life?

DAY 7: PROMOTING DIVERSITY

Recognizing the inevitable diversity within cultures is just as important as acknowledging the differences that exist between diverse cultures.

Lindsey, Roberts, & CampbellJones

Consider the following scenario: You meet a new staff member at the fall orientation. You quickly discover that this person graduated from your alma mater, has relatives in your hometown, lives two blocks away from you, and has children the same age as yours. Such similarities often facilitate a quick and immediate bond. The two of you agree to have lunch soon to get better acquainted.

Here is a different take: You meet a new staff member who was born in Peru. This person speaks fluent Spanish, is single with no children, has traveled extensively around the world, is a technology expert, and keeps two exotic birds as pets. You don't speak Spanish, are married with several children, haven't traveled outside the United States, are technology anxious, and are philosophically opposed to keeping exotic animals or birds as pets. You think that you have little in common with this person. Are you more likely to set up a lunch or walk away and meet someone else? If you are like most other human beings, you will move on to someone else. However, think for a moment how much you might learn from this person.

While it is much less challenging to be with others of one's own culture, ethnicity, socioeconomic group, or religion, interactions among people with varied backgrounds can offer the greatest learning opportunities. Leaders have a responsibility to model the value of diversity and create opportunities for everyone to associate with a variety of people, share perspectives, and promote deeper understanding.

Leaders can promote diversity through formal team-building activities as well as informal groupings and assignments. Mix people up in learning situations and in team assignments. Set up opportunities for everyone to share their backgrounds, cultures, and what they consider as the strengths they bring to creating a diverse perspective in the organization. During staff or team meetings, ask people to speak from a particular diverse perspective. For example, have wide representation of different groups provide input to a decision you are making. Ask staff to point out when an action or a decision may not be in the best interest of all groups. Find alternatives that better serve everyone.

> **Reflection**
>
> How do you ensure diversity in your organization? Whom do you involve to ensure a broad perspective? How are work groups of various kinds structured? When people are free to choose, with whom do they choose to work?
>
> What is the turnover rate in your organization? Does it differ based on race, ethnicity, or gender?
>
> What is the racial, ethnic, and gender composition of your administrators and organizational leaders? How do they model the importance of seeking diverse involvement and building unity among all?
>
> What more can you do to demonstrate the value of diversity?

DAY 8: LEADING FOR RESULTS

> *If I have seen farther than others, it is because I was standing on the shoulders of giants.*
>
> Isaac Newton

Current leaders can learn so much from the leaders that have come before them. We all benefit from knowing what has worked for other leaders and getting insight into the question, "If you can only use a few leadership practices, which ones are likely to have the greatest results?" For example, what leaders do in schools can have a significant impact (positive or negative) on student learning. In a meta-analysis of 35 years of research on school leadership, Marzano, Waters, and McNulty (2005) identified 21 principal leadership practices that enhance student achievement. They are many of the actions we discuss throughout this book for leaders to use in general. Savvy school leaders actively seek to use these 21 approaches.

1. *Affirmation*—recognizing and celebrating school accomplishments
2. *Change Agent*—consciously challenging the status quo and considering new and better ways of doing things
3. *Contingent Rewards*—recognizing and rewarding individual accomplishments
4. *Communication*—establishing effective means for communication with and between administrators, teachers, and students
5. *Culture*—fostering shared beliefs and sense of community and cooperation
6. *Discipline*—protecting instructional time and teachers from interruptions and external distractions
7. *Flexibility*—adapting behavior to fit with specific situations
8. *Focus*—establishing clear goals and keeping attention focused on the goals
9. *Ideals/Beliefs*—possessing, sharing, and modeling well-defined beliefs about teaching and learning
10. *Input*—involving teachers in the design and implementation of decisions and policies
11. *Intellectual Stimulation*—ensuring that school staff are aware of and discussing current research and best practices
12. *Involvement in Curriculum, Instruction, and Assessment*—being actively involved in helping teachers with instructional issues
13. *Knowledge of Curriculum, Instruction, and Assessment*—possessing extensive knowledge about instructional practices
14. *Monitoring/Evaluating*—continually monitoring the effectiveness of the school's practices and being aware of their impact
15. *Optimizer*—inspiring others to accomplish and implement challenging innovations
16. *Order*—establishing routines, structures, rules, and procedures for teachers and students
17. *Outreach*—ensuring compliance with district and state mandates and being an advocate with the larger community

18. *Relationships*—being informed about personal needs of teachers and events in their lives

19. *Resources*—ensuring that teachers have the necessary materials, equipment, and professional learning opportunities

20. *Situational Awareness*—paying attention to the current and potential issues that can interfere with teaching and learning

21. *Visibility*—engaging in frequent contact with teachers and students and the larger community (Marzano, Waters, & McNulty, 2005, pp. 41–61)

Reflection

These are the effective principal leadership actions shown to best influence student learning. To what extent have you developed the capacity to use them? For those of you who are or who work with principals and school leaders, what are some ways you can increase the use of these practices that are tied to student achievement?

What gets in the way of using these research-based practices in schools?

Review the list and select three you think could have a significant impact on your own leadership. What are they? What will you need to do to learn to use them? What is your plan for making them a part of your leadership repertoire?

DAY 9: USING HABITS TO OUR ADVANTAGE

Your brain can't tell the difference between bad and good habits, and so if you have a bad one, it's always lurking there, waiting for the right cues and rewards.

Charles Duhigg

How much of our behavior is habitual? Do you think it's 10 percent, 30 percent, 40 percent, or 60 percent?

According to one study, more than 40 percent of our behavior stems from habits rather than from decisions that we make (Duhigg, 2012). And how many habits are helpful, and how many are a hindrance? Ah, that's a study to be done. But for right now, let's look at the anatomy of a habit.

According to Duhigg, from a neurological perspective a habit has three parts (1) a cue, something that triggers a craving, (2) a routine, something that is an automatic act, and (3) a reward, something that is pleasurable. Here's an example: Driving past an ice cream store triggers a craving for an ice cream cone (cue). So you stop and order two scoops of vanilla on a sugar cone and promptly eat every bite (routine). Your craving has been satisfied, and you feel a sense of pleasure instead of the craving (reward).

So is it possible to develop new habits? According to Duhigg, one can do so "by putting together a cue, a routine and a reward, and then cultivating a craving that drives the loop" (p. 49).

What's all this got to do with leadership? Our tendency to form habits goes right into the workplace with us and influences the ways in which we behave as leaders. As you read the different contemplations in this book, you will probably find that some of the suggestions for actions are new to you and may conflict with an existing "habit." For example, one of the effective leadership practices associated with student achievement (Day 8) is Affirmation, recognizing and celebrating school accomplishments. Perhaps you have gotten into the habit of neglecting to acknowledge others' accomplishments, in effect, developing a "bad habit." Enhancing your leadership practices will sometimes involve consciously finding new cues, routines, and rewards to help you learn new and more effective "habits."

Reflection

Write down five habits that you believe serve you well as a leader and five that are truly not reflective of effective leadership. What does each group have in common? How do the positive habits serve you and others well? What impact do the negative habits have on you as a leader and those with whom you work and lead? Are there any that you want to change? How will you go about identifying new cues, routines, and rewards to support the development of new habits?

DAY 10: GENERATING AND SHARING KNOWLEDGE

Knowledge can't be separated from the communities that create it, use it, and transform it. In all types of knowledge work, people require conversation, experimentation, and shared experiences...

Etienne Wenger

One of the critical skills for leaders is the generating and sharing of knowledge. Nowhere is that organizational value emerging more clearly than in education. Information about best practices and research on teaching and learning abound in today's publications. Part of a leader's job is to help staff get access to and apply information so that it becomes actively used in practice.

As a leader, this means that you need to establish an environment for bringing new knowledge to your staff and encourage them to share information and knowledge with each other. By doing so, you are building on what Hargreaves and Fullan (2012) refer to as professional capital, which has three components: human, social, and decisional. *Human capital* refers to the quality of the individuals, which is complemented by *social capital*—teachers working collaboratively to make substantial improvements and problem-solve issues together. Hargreaves and Fullan have found that social capital can greatly contribute to individual human capital, since working in teams enhances the people, processes, and outcomes that result. *Decisional capital* is at the core of what the profession of teaching is all about—assessing complex situations and making decisions.

As a leader, how can you support the development of knowledge sharing and professional capital? Here are a few suggestions:

Generating knowledge from practice: Teams of teachers try out new teaching and learning strategies, and share artifacts and examples of how they worked. They document what they learned. One of our Leadership Academy participants worked with a colleague on a commercially published book that documents the use of science journals. She spread her knowledge from her own colleagues to teachers nationwide. In another project we are involved with, teachers are generating knowledge of students' misconceptions by using common assessments and comparing their student responses to the research on misconceptions. Educators also produce knowledge by conducting discrete action research projects, discovering what works, and sharing that knowledge with colleagues. The Internet and social networking sites provide a wealth of avenues for teachers to share their learning with each other.

Reading and applying research results: Teams of teachers read and discuss journal articles related to issues or problems they face. They discuss, "To what extent are the findings or issues illuminated in the research generalizable to our situation? How might we apply the research findings?"

Learning strategies and approaches from others: Educators are organizing study groups in which staff read and discuss cases, books, and other information to inform their own thinking and practice.

These organizational arrangements that bring staff together to share and create knowledge are "de-privatizing" education and contributing to increased collegial cultures and professional capital.

Reflection

Think of a meeting that you will be attending in the next couple of weeks. Is it an opportunity to share and/or generate knowledge that will inform practice in your organization? How might you design the meeting to be knowledge sharing and/or producing? Sometimes all it takes is setting aside time in the meeting for one person to bring work they are doing, share it with others, and allot time for thinking about how others might use or adapt it. Often it involves group members identifying and trying outside resources and learning how they work. Sharing this information and getting in the practice of managing your knowledge is a hallmark of effective organizations.

In what ways are you establishing a culture and structures that promote the development of professional capital? Do you tend to focus more on opportunities for human, social, or decisional capital? How could you refine your efforts to provide opportunities that merge the three components of professional capital?

DAY 11: KEEPING A CLIENT-CENTERED FOCUS

Consumers know more about what they want—and are more determined to get what they want—than ever before.

Jim Taylor

Think about a time you felt that you didn't get the service you wanted, needed, and deserved. Perhaps you had taken time off to have someone come fix an appliance, and that person didn't show up and didn't call. Maybe you had paid a bill, but the accounting department kept sending you statements. Possibly you had made arrangements with your supervisor to take a personal leave day, but he or she had forgotten and scheduled you into a meeting.

Try to remember what you were feeling. Frustration? Anger? Resentment? Now, think of just the opposite situation.

Think about a time you were treated as a valued customer. Perhaps the accounting department notified you of an overpayment. Maybe someone from your clinic called to tell you that the doctor was running late. Possibly your supervisor stopped by to make sure that you had everything you needed to get the proposal in on time.

More and more leaders in schools are finding it essential to adopt a client-centered focus and to be accountable to their students, teachers, and the larger community. In the old paradigm, if students did not have basic skills in reading and mathematics, it was their fault. After all, they had the opportunity to learn, didn't they? If that situation occurs now, schools are more inclined to look at their own systems to determine what else can be done to ensure that the students reach the learning goals. Changing something in the system—instruction, curriculum, opportunities to learn—reflects the more positive side of accountability and model a school's core mission to teach students, not just to "deliver" lessons.

> **Reflection**
>
> Here are a few key questions to ask yourself to gauge your "client centeredness."
>
> - Who are your primary clients or customers—both internal and external?
> - What do your customers value? How do you know?
> - Are you providing them with what they value?
> - In what ways are you accountable to and for your clients?
> - What improvements are needed?
> - How do you continuously assess your clients' satisfaction?

DAY 12: RECOGNIZING AND CELEBRATING SUCCESS

In the end people will forget what you said, forget what you did, but people will never forget how you make them feel.

Maya Angelou

In the Day 2 contemplation of this book we introduce five practices used by ordinary leaders to accomplish extraordinary results (Kouzes & Posner, 2012). One of the practices—"Encourage the heart"—often surprises people when we teach these practices in our Leadership Academy. Too often as leaders we focus on the "hard" practices of planning, visioning, and the provision of resources and forget the power and energy that comes from making people feel valued and recognized for their accomplishments.

About 20 years ago one of the authors received a note of congratulations from her then-boss. She had just led a team through a very challenging proposal submission that resulted in winning a large contract. In the note, her boss said, "Today we celebrate your work and the great team that came together to produce this project—with you, I would attempt anything." His note conveyed such a deep sense of trust and confidence in what the team had accomplished that it fueled them to take on challenging work and achieve more success. Saying "Thank you" and "Job well done" may be the easiest thing leaders can add to their repertoire. In staff meetings, give the entire team an opportunity to share recent successes.

Post letters or notes of praise from clients or coworkers. Kouzes and Posner suggest that leaders should write three thank-you notes a day!

In one organization we worked in, we instituted a peer award that was named after a staff member who exemplified the practice of recognizing and celebrating staff contributions. Each staff member was entitled to give two of these awards per year to their colleagues (individuals or teams) for contributions and successes. The organization funded gift certificates that accompanied the awards. Staff proudly displayed these awards, and they were announced in the organization's weekly newsletter. Using these everyday leadership practices communicates that people are valued and helps to maintain the high morale needed to get challenging work done.

In education, practices such as setting data-driven goals for improvement are helping everyone see what the desired outcomes are, and by publicly sharing data and results, everyone can be clearer about when it's time for celebration! Reward hard work and results, and it will reward you—success breeds success.

Reflection

How often do you recognize, reward, thank people, and/or celebrate success in your organization? Are you careful to make sure that everyone who contributes is recognized? Do you have regular systems for peers to recognize each other? Are the goals clear so that everyone knows when you have achieved success? What one or two things can you do to increase recognition and celebration of success?

DAY 13: NETWORKING

I have seen that in any great undertaking it is not enough for a man to depend simply upon himself.

Lone Man (Isna-la-wica), Teton Sioux

What networks are you part of, and what types of relationships do you have within these networks? How can you bring these relationships to bear on issues you care about?

There is a natural human desire to work in groups and to work well together. Information of all kinds is both generated and shared through networks of all types: organizational, professional, community, religious, and family. "Working the networks" is one way that leaders exert influence, communicate vision, share information, provide support, enhance continuity, and bring about change.

One of the consistent findings from our Leadership Academy is the value educational leaders derive from in-person networking and learning from each other. They share common problems and strategies they have used. They listen to each other and share perspectives that enrich their abilities to lead in their own contexts. Change in organizations is so complex that it cannot occur without strong relationships among people making up a variety of networks, some that exist within the boundaries of an organization and some that go outside.

In recent years, social networking has exploded as a means of collaboration, communication, sharing, and developing new relationships outside the boundaries of one's organization. Professional learning networks are also a means of linking leaders and other educators, providing opportunities for online learning, and sharing with a specific focus on areas of interest to a collection of individuals.

Reflection

Which relationships provide you with diverse information and help you in your role as a leader of reform? Do you have relationships from different worlds that keep your mind open to new ideas and approaches and keep you from becoming too insular? What new relationships do you need to forge, and what networks do you need to become part of to broaden your influence? How often do you participate in an online community of learners versus in-person networking? What might be the benefits for you of exploring a wider array of options for networking?

DAY 14: EMBRACING INNOVATIVE THINKING

We have entered the Transformation Decade of 2010 to 2020, a decade of greater change than in any other decade in human history. Legacy thinking can no longer serve our purposes—and it will certainly not lead to the education system we need.

David Houle

What is innovation?

The U.S. Department of Education (2011) states that, "In education, innovations are the strategies, products, or approaches that improve significantly upon the status quo and can be taken to scale to address persistent educational challenges." Scott Anthony (2012) writes that innovation is "something different that has impact." Inherent in both definitions is a focus on thinking about problems in new ways to identify solutions that achieve results. In the Day 2 contemplation of this book, we introduce five practices used by ordinary leaders to accomplish extraordinary results (Kouzes & Posner, 2012). One of the practices—"Challenge the status quo"—requires that leaders "challenge their own and others' assumptions and encourage divergent points of view" (Schoemaker, Krupp, & Howland, 2013). Often, it is these divergent points of view that can result in the most innovative and effective solutions to problems.

Many corporations and businesses have created environments that are conducive to innovative thinking by deliberately structuring opportunities for employees and designers to think outside the box to generate novel solutions and products. Educational leaders can take many of these lessons learned from business to transform the ways in which they create similar environments and contexts within schools. For example, Susan Wojciki, an employee at Google, identifies "eight pillars of innovation" that guide Google's investment in innovation:

1. *Have a mission that matters.* "Our mission is one that has the potential to touch many lives, and we make sure that all our employees feel connected to it and empowered to help achieve it."

2. *Think big but start small.* "No matter how ambitious the plan, you have to roll up your sleeves and start somewhere."

3. *Strive for continual innovation, not instant perfection.* "Our iterative process often teaches us invaluable lessons. Watching users 'in the wild' as they use our products is the best way to find out what works, then we can act on that feedback."

4. *Look for ideas everywhere.* "Some of the best ideas at Google are sparked . . . when small groups of Googlers take a break on a random afternoon and start talking about things that excite them."

5. *Share everything.* "By sharing everything, you encourage the discussion, exchange, and re-interpretation of ideas, which can lead to unexpected and innovative outcomes. We try to facilitate this by working in small, crowded teams in open cube arrangements, rather than individual offices."

6. *Spark with imagination, fuel with data.* "What begins with intuition is fueled by insights. If you're lucky, these reinforce one another. . . . That's the beautiful thing about data—it can either back up your instincts or prove them totally wrong."

7. *Be a platform.* "There is so much awe-inspiring innovation being driven by people all over the globe. That's why we believe so strongly in the power of open technologies. They enable anyone, anywhere, to apply their unique skills, perspectives, and passions to the creation of new products and features on top of our platforms."

8. *Never fail to fail.* "The thing is, people remember your hits more than your misses. It's okay to fail as long as you learn from your mistakes and correct them fast. . . . Knowing that it's okay to fail can free you up to take risks" (Wojciki, n.d.).

> **Reflection**
>
> Consider the list of eight pillars of innovation and ask yourself:
>
> - In what ways do you communicate to others the value of innovative thinking?
> - What structures and opportunities are currently in place to support innovation? What more might you do?
> - To what extent do you pay attention to the issue or problems in your environment that might benefit from innovative thinking?

DAY 15: ALIGNING ACTIONS AND BELIEFS

To become a credible leader, first you have to comprehend fully the values, beliefs, and assumptions that drive you. You have to freely and honestly choose the principles you will use to guide your actions.

James M. Kouzes and Barry Z. Posner

How many times have you done something in a particular way because someone else has done it that way or because someone told you to do it that way?

We often act without considering whether our behavior is congruent with our own underlying beliefs about what is right. When people assume new leadership roles, existing leaders are often ready to offer advice—for example, one group might tell you to "Be strong, make sure you don't back down. People will be testing you at first, and you will have to be tough." Another might say, "Don't come on too strong right away—you need to get to know everyone and understand what is going on, before you start making changes." What is most important is that you take genuine action that is aligned with what you believe.

Here is a chance for you to determine your basic assumptions about leadership: Do you believe that (a) leaders are born or (b) leaders are made? That (a) leadership is positional (that is, based on their positions, only certain people in organizations are leaders) or (b) everyone in an organization can exert leadership? That (a) leadership exists independently of ethics (for example, Hitler was a leader) or (b) leadership is inherently ethical (for example, Hitler was not a leader)?

Does your behavior indicate that you believe that certain people are blessed at birth with leadership abilities? Or do you act as if everyone can learn to exhibit some degree of leadership if they choose to? Do you see that leadership is vested in people with certain titles, or do you believe in the leadership capacity within all people in an organization? In your belief system, what is the relationship between leadership and ethics? You should be able to tie your behavior to one of the assumptions in each pair. Is your behavior congruent with what you believe, or have you fallen into a pattern of acting inconsistently with what you believe?

Reflection

What are the beliefs operating in your organization? What are the beliefs about who can be a leader? How do these beliefs influence your actions? How might you surface and discuss the beliefs that may be limiting you?

DAY 16: EXAMINING YOUR CULTURE

Any organization that sets out to change its own culture remains powerfully influenced by that culture even as it attempts the change.

Robert Evans

What is the culture of your organization?

Culture in an organization usually evolves over time and is based on assumptions and beliefs. The personalities of the leaders often determine the beliefs, behaviors, and assumptions that eventually become firmly established, although they may not be especially visible. It is much less common for leaders to consciously and deliberately establish the type of organizational culture that serves their needs. As a result, new leaders often inherit a culture that doesn't support changes they want to make in the organization. And they find out quickly that a nonsupportive culture can be very inhospitable to a change initiative.

If you are a leader of a new organization or project, you have the opportunity to build the type of culture you believe works best. If you take over an existing entity, you have the harder task of assessing and changing the culture—a difficult but not impossible task.

If you are a leader in a school, one way to assess the culture is to ask yourself, "What are the current beliefs about who can learn? Do educators in the school believe all students can learn? How genuine are people's actions with respect to this belief?"

For example, while most educators will say all students can learn, the schools are not always organized to ensure that all children learn. Rick DuFour and others (2004) identified four types of schools with different beliefs about who can learn. The "Charles Darwin School" believes students can learn based on their ability. The teachers in these schools see aptitude as relatively fixed and do not believe they can have a great influence on the extent of student learning and they teach accordingly. The "Pontius Pilate School" operates on the belief that all students can learn if they take advantage of the opportunity the school provides and put forth the necessary effort. The "Chicago Cubs Fan School" is based on the belief that all students can learn something and helps students experience academic growth in a warm and nurturing environment. Only the "Henry Higgins School" operates on the belief that all students can achieve high standards of learning as long as they receive enough support and help from the staff (DuFour, DuFour, Eaker, & Karhanek, 2004, pp. 30–31).

Leaders must examine the culture in the organization and ask, "What beliefs and assumptions are operating in our system that makes us act this way?" Most often people are not even aware of the disconnect between their behaviors and their espoused beliefs.

Reflection

If you are in a school or working with schools, which of the four types described most closely matches your culture and underlying beliefs? What are your assumptions about who can and cannot learn? What are your and others' beliefs about teaching and learning? To what extent is there alignment between your beliefs and the existing culture?

Are you in a position to help establish or change the culture? If so, what would be your top three priorities?

DAY 17: BUILDING A TRUSTING CLIMATE

Just bringing good ideas into schools with severely damaged social infrastructure is tantamount to bringing a lighted candle into a wind tunnel.

Charles M. Payne

Take a good look at your organizational structures and systems. How well do they support the people in the organization to achieve their vision and mission?

As leaders work to transform their organizations, they must create structures that are in greater alignment with current expectations for students as well as the organizational visions and goals. They must also build opportunities for meaningful collaboration, and keep a laser focus on student outcomes and other results.

However, even with all of the "right" resources and supports in place, if the organization is characterized by a "climate of pervasive distrust" often the leaders' efforts are to no avail. Charles Payne (2008) found in his work in the Chicago Public School system that the social barriers to school change often override all efforts for improvement. He notes, "I started, like many others, with the notion that there was some particular kind of programming or some particular form of pedagogy that was going to transform the system. It was just a matter of figuring out which one was best and then doing that all over the place" (p. 2). Instead, what he found was that very few of the reform efforts were "taking root" and that the faculty in the schools were distrustful of the system, each other, and their leaders. Efforts to organize teachers into collaborative and collegial teams met with failure due to school norms of isolation and competitiveness and absence of professional dialogue (pp. 32–33).

Over time, Payne and the Consortium on Chicago School Research identified the Five Fundamentals for School Improvement that enabled schools to overcome their climates of pervasive distrust.

1. *Instructional leadership*, including the development of teacher-principal trust

2. *Professional capacity*, including quality professional learning, building the capacity of teachers to dialogue with one another, and a collective responsibility for teaching and learning

3. *Learning climate*, including students' perceptions of teachers' high expectations and their own safety

4. *Family and community involvement*, including communication between parents and teachers and the "level of human and social resources in the community"

5. *Quality of instruction*, including intellectually challenging instruction and academic engagement (Payne, 2008, p. 46)

As you consider how to apply these ideas in your own setting, carefully assess the extent to which a culture of distrust may hinder your efforts and anticipate ways in which to address that distrust.

> **Reflection**
>
> To what extent is your organizational culture characterized by a climate of trust or distrust? In what ways might the climate influence your efforts at initiating and leading improvements? How could you strengthen the areas identified in the list of the Five Fundamentals in your own organization?

DAY 18: COLLABORATIVE LEADERSHIP

> *School leadership needs to be a broad concept that is separated from person, role, and a discrete set of individual behaviors. It needs to be embedded in the school community as a whole. Such broadening of the concept of leadership suggests shared responsibility for a shared purpose of community.*
>
> Linda Lambert

Traditionally, those at the top of organizations set the policies and procedures, and those at lower levels carry them out. If we are to have many, rather than a few individuals, who are leaders, we must see the value and importance of developing leadership skills and responsibilities at all levels of an organization.

Collaborative leadership is one way in which to ensure leadership at all levels. According to Hank Rubin (2009), collaborative leadership "is the skillful and mission-oriented facilitation of relevant relationships" and a collaborative leader is one who accepts "responsibility for building—or helping to ensure the success of—a heterogeneous team to accomplish a shared purpose" (p. 2).

What would it look like to embody collaborative leadership and build the partnerships inherent in this type of leadership? Rubin identifies several aspects of collaborative leadership, including:

- All key stakeholders and decision makers are represented in the partnership.
- Everyone in the partnership is clear about the partnership's purpose.
- Everyone in the partnership is confident that more can be accomplished as a team than as individuals.
- A synergy evolves so that all involved are looking for ways to better contribute to the achievement of the purposes.
- One person needs to have the resources and authority to manage the logistics of the partnership.
- All contribute to the development of an action plan that is aligned with the purpose.
- The partnership targets achievable and ambitious outcomes (Rubin, 2009, pp. 10–11).

Reflection

What does leadership in your organization look like? Are stakeholders and decision makers active participants in leading? To what extent do you perceive your role as one of supporting others within a partnership, focused on specific purposes and outcomes? If your leadership is not collaborative, what steps might you take to move toward a more collaborative and partnership-based approach to leading?

DAY 19: BUILDING RELATIONSHIPS

Relationships are all there is. Everything in the universe only exists because it is in relationship to everything else. Nothing exists in isolation. We have to stop pretending we are individuals who can go it alone.

Margaret Wheatley

If Wheatley (2002) says that relationships are all there is, and Fullan (2001) says that "you can't get anywhere without them," relationships and their cultivation are crucial to successful friendships, colleagueships, partnerships, and organizations.

Whether in organizations or in families or among friends, relationship problems often determine the future and fate of an institution, a marriage, or a friendship. Productive relationships are critical for organizations and the people who make up these organizations to survive.

Think for a moment of the problems you are currently facing. How many involve a relationship problem with a colleague, a friend, or member of your family? Can you pinpoint the underlying cause?

The emotional intelligence (EQ) work of Goleman (1995), Goleman, Boyatzis, and McKee (2002), and Stein and Book (2000) has expanded our knowledge of the importance of strong relationships in human and organizational functioning, the skills essential for forming and maintaining effective relationships, and how to diagnose and heal relationship problems. So what are the components of emotional intelligence? Stein and Book name five:

1. *Intrapersonal:* Self-awareness, actualization, independence, and self-regard
2. *Interpersonal:* Empathy, social responsibility
3. *Adaptability:* Problem solving, flexibility
4. *Stress management:* Stress tolerance, impulse control
5. *General mood:* Happiness, optimism

A high level of skill in these five areas is essential for relationship building and maintenance. As Fullan says, "If relationships are (almost) everything, a high EQ is a must" (p. 74). Your leadership ability—that is, your ability to effectively interact with others—is directly related to your relationship EQ.

> **Reflection**
>
> Look at the five components of emotional intelligence listed. How do you assess yourself on each? Put an *S* next to those that are strengths and a *W* next to those you see as weaknesses. If you are currently experiencing relationship problems, are any of the weaker elements contributing to them? What can you do to strengthen at least one area of weakness (for example, increase your tolerance of stress or become more flexible in your thinking)?

DAY 20: TRYING SOMETHING NEW

The only true insanity is doing the same thing over and over again and expecting different results.

Albert Einstein

Think of a time you felt stymied by your attempts to change a frustrating or irritating situation. Have you found yourself doing the same thing over and over? Or perhaps the same thing with only slight variations? How readily do you change what you are doing to better meet others' needs?

In such situations, we often think that the problem is with the other person, people, or organization. However, we cannot control the behavior of anyone but ourselves. With that as a given, here are two different approaches for breaking the cycle:

1. *Reframe the situation.* You can turn a perplexing problem into a marvelous opportunity for learning by reframing. It is possible to transform what appears to be a failure into a test case, which failed in some ways, succeeded in others, and yielded great learning.

2. *Change your behavior.* There are always myriad things you can do. Use a different approach. Treat the person differently. Be kinder or firmer. Give more help or less help. Talk more or talk less. Be more independent or ask for help. If you are not sure what behavior to change, ask for advice from a trusted colleague.

Either reframing the situation or changing your behavior increases your chance of seeing some behavior change on the part of the other person. It is likely to work better than continuing to do whatever you have been doing that has not been getting the desired results.

Reflection

Think of a time you repeated the same behavior but expected different results. Were you eventually able to break out of the pattern? If so, what happened? How do you recognize when you are caught in a cycle? Which of the techniques described is most useful in helping you respond differently?

DAY 21: COPING WITH AMBIGUITY, CHANGE, AND CONFUSION

> *Entering the era of perpetual unrest means confusion, mixed feelings, and ambiguity are here to stay.*
>
> Daryl Conner

Have you ever found yourself thinking that surely life will slow down when the current crisis or demand on your time is over? We often hope that our lives will be more manageable, slower paced, or less hectic when some major event ends. What happens is that when one event is over, another takes its place. And they keep coming, so that we never experience the respite we wish for.

The reality is that the days of small, incremental changes, which we could not only incorporate but often prepare for, are gone. As Daryl Conner (1998) describes, "The world is inundated with disruptions: unforeseen dangers, unanticipated opportunities, unmet expectations, alarming new statistics, startling twists of fate, shocking innovations, unheralded improvements, unrealistic requirements, overwhelming demands, contradictory directives, staggering liabilities, astonishing results, sudden strokes of luck, and more" (p. vi).

What, then, does it take for leaders to cope with continuous ambiguity, continuous change, and continuous confusion? Here are three major strategies:

1. *Accept ambiguity, change, and confusion as the norm rather than the exception.* The degree to which you experience stress is directly related to your expectations. If you expect your life to move slowly

in a harmonious fashion, you may be upset when a meeting is canceled at the last minute, your car breaks down, or you leave your computer at the security gate. If you know that you are subject to many external forces and that the only thing you have control over is how you choose to react, you are much better equipped to deal with inevitable ambiguity, change, and confusion. Anchoring yourself in your core values and beliefs will give you additional support in weathering change.

2. *Be resilient.* Your ability to deal with the unknown is much greater if you have a high level of resiliency. Your outlook and attitude are important, as well as how you handle the daily stressors. Do you know how to release anger? Relieve frustration? Handle criticism and failure without internalizing? Do you have a support system to rely on? Do you get away from work on a regular basis and take care of yourself physically and emotionally? These are all ways to be a resilient person, one who is capable of maintaining his or her productivity and quality standards along with physical and emotional stability while assimilating change (Conner, 1998).

3. *Act anyway.* Unless you are content to be paralyzed by your fear or to attempt escape to a more peaceful place and time, you have no choice other than to move ahead. Move ahead despite the continuous ambiguity, continuous change, and continuous confusion. Use your best available information and move forward with your fear and anxiety in hand, rather than attempting to repress or escape from your feelings. Do each day the best you can.

Reflection

On a scale of 1 (low) to 10 (high), how do you rate your ability to cope with ambiguity and to assimilate change? Which of the three strategies listed do you rely on to cope with major changes? What can you do to strengthen your capacity to deal with a constant state of flux?

DAY 22: LEADING THROUGH A CRISIS

Denying reality destroys more careers and organizations than incompetence ever did.

Bill George

Tony Antonito couldn't believe it. He had just found out that one of his tenured teachers had been accused of helping her students cheat on the state standards-based assessment. Yes, her students' scores were high, actually higher than last year, but there were plausible reasons. Tony had always seen her as one of his best, and most trusted, teachers. Could this be true?

Sooner or later it happens to most every leader. A crisis erupts. Maybe you saw it coming; maybe it was a complete surprise. But here it is, and you've got to deal with it. Crises in schools have become more and more common. Whether it's a drastic budget cut, a takeover by an outside management group, a closing, or a staff impropriety, a crisis is likely to come up. If so, what do you do?

According to Bill George (2010), the first step is to face reality. Don't try to pretend that something didn't happen or that whatever happened was not that important. Accept your role and responsibility in the crisis. Without your leadership, the crisis won't be fixed. Your accepting reality will go a long way in helping your colleagues who may be in denial.

Next, don't try to solve this crisis by yourself. You may have a natural tendency to turn inward, away from friends and colleagues. Instead reach out to your colleagues as well as friends and family for support. Letting others share the burden will help you resolve your fears, which are almost always worse than the reality.

Determine the root cause before coming up with a plan to fix the crisis. (See Book Five, Day 12 for more on root cause analysis.) There's a natural tendency to want to "fix" the crisis as soon as possible. If you do, you may be fixing the symptoms rather than the cause. Our principal Tony has a lot of data to gather before taking any action. Is this accusation true? Did the teacher actually help students change some answers? If she didn't, why was the accusation made and by whom?

Finally, be proactive; focus on winning. As Bill George says," Look at a crisis as a gift" (2010, p. 28). Use the crisis to make some changes that will strengthen your position. In fact, Charles Duhigg in his book *The Power of Habit* believes that much good can come from a crisis. He says, "Crises are so valuable, in fact, that sometimes it's worth stirring up a sense of looming catastrophe rather than letting it die down" (2012, p. 175).

In this scenario, perhaps Tony can develop a process for reducing the likelihood of cheating on the standards-based assessment. Perhaps he can surface a long-standing grudge and provide one of his best teachers with a safer teaching environment. As a leader, he can find a way of turning a challenge into an advantage.

> **Reflection**
>
> Think of a crisis that you have observed in your career. What did the leader do? Did he or she follow the suggestions above? What was the outcome?
>
> Now think of a crisis that you have been directly involved in. What did you do? Did you follow the suggestions above? What was the outcome?
>
> What might you do differently when the next crisis occurs?

DAY 23: BALANCING LEADERSHIP AND MANAGEMENT

Managers are people who do things right, while leaders are people who do the right thing.

Warren G. Bennis

What is leadership and what is management?

Both are very important in organizational life and shouldn't be confused. Leadership is doing the right thing; management is doing things right. Managers direct the hacking of a new path through the jungle; leaders make sure that they are in the right jungle.

One of the major contributions that a leader can make is to always be able to distinguish between these two important functions. We often become so focused on the day-to-day realities of what we do that we lose sight of whether we are doing the right thing.

Leaders often have to ask the hard questions: Are we getting the best results possible? Where can we improve? Who is not learning and what can we do about it? Are there ethical issues involved? What knowledge and skills does our staff need, and how will they get them? Will the proposed professional learning opportunities give us what we need? Is our strategic planning council effective? These queries will help you challenge the status quo that is often accepted without question.

> **Reflection**
>
> Think about the leadership role you play and ask yourself the following questions:
>
> - Why are you doing what you are doing? What data do you have to show that you are addressing the right problems and doing the right work?
> - How are you spending your time? What percentage of your day is spent on managing tasks? What percentage is focused on setting the course, engaging with others, and providing leadership?

- Are you sure you are "doing the right things" before you set up procedures to "do things right"?
- What beliefs and assumptions drive your leadership approach? Are these consistent with where you want to be?

DAY 24: LIVING WITH PARADOX

The contradictions of life are not accidental. Nor do they result from inept living. They are inherent in human nature and in the circumstances which surround lives.

Palmer Parker

Inevitably, anyone in a leadership role encounters people and circumstances that reflect inherent contradictions. These are called paradoxes. Paradoxes stem from conflicting polarities: the existence of two opposing attributes, tendencies, or principles that are interdependent. For example, in large organizations, there is often tension between the desire to centralize and the desire to decentralize procedures and services. Having both operational in a system is the paradox. Another example is the need to work in teams versus working individually. Polarities and the paradoxes they create are ever present; they never go away.

Leaders in education encounter many paradoxes that they need to thoughtfully balance as they lead improvement efforts. For example, Bybee (1993) identified this set to describe the paradoxes leaders must balance as they carry out change efforts in their organization.

Leaders must:

- Think abstractly and act concretely.
- Have direction and retain flexibility.
- Initiate change and maintain continuity.
- Encourage innovation and sustain tradition.
- Fulfill a national agenda and incorporate local mandates.
- Achieve goals and endure criticism (pp. 164–166).

Successful leaders recognize and work through both sides of the paradoxes. The first step in working with them is knowing one's own biases. We tend to prefer one side of the pole over the other. We must see the validity of both sides, recognizing the simultaneous existence of opposites. The second step is to discuss how to address each one. For example, how will you pursue achieving the goals if you are being criticized? What things will you maintain and which will you change?

If your organization is focusing on one side of a polarity as the solution to a problem, your role as a leader is to alert people to the other. For example, if your colleagues are pushing for a concrete set of action steps to address a problem, work on that together and then ask the team to think abstractly about their plan—what values do they think it represents? What will they look for in terms of results? Likewise, as leaders work with their teams to lay out a direction for the organization, they also must ask what might happen that would cause them to change their direction. How can you remain flexible enough to respond to feedback and changes in the environment? Your role as a leader is to balance both sides of the polarity and not allow one side to dominate to the exclusion of the other (Terry, 2001).

> **Reflection**
>
> What paradoxes do you face in your work? Which side of the polarity are you biased toward? What can you do to make sure that the other side of the polarity is considered and addressed?

DAY 25: PAYING ATTENTION TO LEADERSHIP ACTIONS AND TRAITS

Leadership comes from integrity—that you do whatever you ask others to do.

Scott Berkum

In our Leadership Academy we ask participants to recall a time when they were particularly effective as a leader and to bring to mind their actions as well as the personal characteristics or dispositions they exhibited at the time. As they share their stories and experiences, it becomes clear that leadership actions and personal traits work hand in hand to support quality leadership. They report taking actions such as:

- Developing and communicating a clear purpose.
- Holding high expectations for everyone.
- Anticipating and addressing small problems before they grow into bigger ones.
- Demonstrating a deep understanding of the work.
- Developing others.
- Facilitating change.

But as they take these actions, they are also using personal characteristics that contribute to their success, such as being action oriented, enthusiastic, realistic, caring, committed, and taking risks. They underscore the importance of having integrity and being a listener and a learner and willing to change their minds. What emerges from this exercise is a composite of actions and traits of effective leaders.

Karin Chenowith and Christina Theokas of the Education Trust (2012) found in their research on successful high-poverty schools, that these schools' principals exhibit specific leadership traits and actions, many of which are ones we address with individual reflections in this book, and that also mirror what leaders we work with have found to be true in their own roles as leaders. The traits and actions they identified include:

- Setting the vision that all children will be successful.
- Establishing a climate and culture of respect.
- Focusing on instruction.
- Managing the building to support instruction.
- Inspecting what they expect.

High performance leadership comes from balancing key leadership actions with personal dispositions that strengthen and support leadership results.

Reflection

Think about a time you saw someone demonstrate tremendous leadership skill. What did they do that contributed to their success? What personal characteristics did they possess and how did these support their actions? Think about a time when you were particularly effective as a leader, and make a list of the personal characteristics or dispositions you exhibited. In what ways does your list reflect the characteristics described in this contemplation?

DAY 26: GETTING SUPPORT

The person who tries to live alone will not succeed as a human being. His heart withers if it does not answer another heart. His mind shrinks away if he hears only the echoes of his own thoughts and finds no other inspiration.

Pearl S. Buck

In most of the contemplations in this book so far we talk about what actions effective leaders take to support other people and the organization;

but there are also things you need to do for yourself to feel supported in your leadership role. To keep up your energy, enthusiasm, and sheer will to get things done, you need ample support from and contact with others and to be able to call on them when you need help and inspiration. Leadership comes with a tremendous amount of stress—for example, sometimes things don't work out the way you had hoped, people are resistant to your ideas, and forces out of your control undo your actions. When these situations occur, leaders may feel like they are out there all alone. As one leader described it, "I feel like I am rolling a tremendous boulder uphill—and if I stop for a moment, it will come tumbling down on me and no one else will be there to help me catch it."

One of the participants in our Leadership Academy gets the support she needs by talking with other administrators outside of her district who have been in her shoes. She gets their feedback on what she is trying to do in her own district and asks how they would handle a similar situation—she does the same for them. When she goes to conferences or regional events in her state she actively talks with others in her role to ask them what has worked for them—and then she asks them if she can stay in touch via e-mail or phone. She has put together her own personal network. It is not unusual for us to get a call from her that starts with, "Hello, I am calling 911—here's what happened and I need to think it through with you." Usually, she had thought through what she needed to do, but just needed that extra ear and reassurance that she hadn't missed something. At the end of the call she will say, "Thanks, you are a lifesaver!" Having support like that can be a lifesaver, since it relieves the stress and loneliness of leadership that can wear you out.

Good leaders recognize that they do not have to do it all themselves. It is okay to "dial 911" when you need support—it is not a sign of weakness, but rather a sign that you are aware of what you need for yourself to be an effective leader for others.

Leaders begin to build networks of support by talking with people who have similar roles in their own organization or geographic area. They actively ask others to share their perspectives on different situations and ask for honest feedback from colleagues. Leaders identify what support they need from supervisors and communicate those needs to them.

Reflection

What personal characteristics do you draw on to enhance and support your own leadership skills? How hopeful and positive are you? Do you avoid expressions of doubt and convey confidence in yourself and your team? How do you display enthusiasm for your work? Can people feel your energy, or are you seen as worn out and exhausted by the demands of your leadership position? How can you reenergize yourself?

What have you done for yourself lately to get support? When you feel the stresses of being "the leader" closing in on you, how do you take care of yourself? Who do you talk with? What else can you do?

DAY 27: ASKING GOOD QUESTIONS

The important thing is to never stop questioning.

Albert Einstein

In the Day 2 contemplation in this book, we share five practices effective leaders use to accomplish extraordinary results. One of them—"Challenge the process"—recognizes that leaders today must continuously ask how to get better and improve outcomes. They ask, "Why are we doing what we are doing? Why are we doing it this way? Are there more effective things we can do?" (Kouzes & Posner, 2012).

In today's fast-paced world, leaders can't possibly have all the answers. They need to use good questions to guide others to get to the "right answers." Peter Scholtes (1998) identified "seven basic all-purpose questions" leaders must ask (p. 266):

1. *Why?* When you encounter a problem, ask why. Ask why as many as five times to get to the root cause of the problem. (See Book Five, Day 13 for more about the "5 Whys" strategy.)

2. *What is the purpose?* People love to suggest things and often grab onto new ideas to implement in their organizations without making sure there is a match between the organization's needs and their ideas. Help people clarify the purpose—or the desired outcome—as they plan new projects.

3. *What will it take to accomplish this?* While it is nice to dream, your job as a leader is to support people to implement their ideas. This question gets others to think through the methods they will use to put ideas into action.

4. *Who cares about this?* Ask this question to make sure you are choosing actions that will matter to the right people. If the people you serve notice or care about the action, it should have higher payoff for you.

5. *What is your premise?* Many suggestions and ideas are made without stating the assumptions or beliefs that are guiding them.

When you ask people to state their premise or assumption, you help them gain greater insight.

6. *What data do you have or could you get?* Some suggestions and ideas are based on perceptions and hunches—asking this question pushes people to "ground" their actions in real data.

7. *What is the source of your data?* Before you base decisions on data, make sure it is valid and comes from a reliable source.

Increasingly, a leader's role is to coach colleagues to think through plans, anticipate problems, and get the right things happening. Questioning and demonstration are the basic tools of a good coach. Scholtes (1998) suggests that leaders ask a series of questions when a team is implementing a new project or intervention. For example, *prior to starting the project*, ask, "What could realistically go wrong? How might that be prevented? What should we monitor to see if the problem is occurring? How can we be prepared to react if it goes wrong?" *During the implementation of the project* ask, "What are you doing? Why are you doing it? How do you know this is the right thing to do?" And, *after implementation*, ask, "Are we getting what we wanted? Are we avoiding what we didn't want? Do we need to make any adjustments?" (p. 273)

Reflection

Are you always ready with the answer, or do you help your staff or colleagues think through solutions by asking good questions? How can asking questions help you become a better leader?

Learn to use inquiry and questioning skills as a key part of your leadership style. Choose one of your major goals—for example, maybe it is a goal you have set to enhance student performance. For one week, as you interact with your colleagues, ask them how what they are doing or deciding will influence that one goal. You will see how asking good questions can change the discussion and focus everyone on the key goals.

Copy the seven questions and keep them on your desk or someplace handy. Remind yourself to use them in meetings, as problems arise, and when you are planning and conducting your work.

DAY 28: FINDING WIN/WIN SOLUTIONS

Win/win is not a personality technique. It's a total paradigm of human interaction.

Stephen Covey

How do you usually approach interactions that may involve competition, conflict, and/or negotiation? Do you:

- Fight for an outcome in which you win and someone else loses?
- Give in to a solution in which you lose and the other person wins?
- Settle for a result in which both of you lose?
- State that the solution must be one of win/win, or you will refuse to participate?

At times, any of these outcomes may be appropriate. For example, for a tennis match, a win/lose outcome is a given. It is the nature of the activity. In a situation in which you want to accommodate someone else, you may select a lose/win outcome. Sometimes, a win/win solution is appropriate. The best choice depends on the situation, and your challenge is to know which orientation is best in your situation.

However, according to Covey (1989), most situations "are part of an interdependent reality, and win/win is really the only viable alternative" (p. 211). So, if win/win (what some are now calling "gain/gain") is the most desirable paradigm for most circumstances, what does this require? Integrating a paradigm of win/win requires three character traits: integrity, maturity, and an orientation of abundance mentality (Covey, 1989). *Integrity* is the value placed on self—knowing one's values and making and keeping commitments. *Maturity* is "the balance between courage and consideration" (p. 217). *Abundance mentality* is an orientation to the notion that there is more than enough to go around. Lacking an abundance mentality results in seeing everything as a "zero sum" game. If this is the case, you see resources as limited and feel you must compete with others to get as much as possible for yourself or your programs. To engage in synergistic partnership requires that both parties value sharing their resources toward the greater good.

A win/win approach to collaboration also reflects the 21st century learning skills that contribute to success in the global economy. For example, working creatively with others includes being "open and responsive to new and diverse perspectives" and exercising "flexibility and willingness to be helpful in making necessary compromises to accomplish a common goal" (Partnership for 21st Century Skills, 2011).

Operating out of a win/win paradigm seems easy, maybe even simplistic. In reality, it is actually very complex. Most people tend to think in "either/or" terms, and "both/and" thinking is more difficult. Ask yourself what you have to gain from a situation. What do others have to gain? What does anyone have to lose? Is there a way to minimize the loss and maximize the gain?

Reflection

Think of a recent situation you were in that could have resulted in someone losing and someone winning. What was your position? If you operated from a win/win orientation, what difference did it make? If you did not, how might the outcome have been different if you had? What benefits do you see to integrating a win/win approach to working with others?

Think about a problem that you are now facing, especially a difficult one for which you can envision only a win/lose solution. Maybe budget cuts are forcing you to consider eliminating certain activities. What people share a stake in solving this problem? What conditions are needed to pull these people together and have a productive discussion focused on how to find a win/win solution?

DAY 29: MODELING LEADERSHIP

The best way we can contribute to a culture of integrity in the workplace is to speak and act with integrity ourselves.

Roland Barth

Each day leaders perform thousands of symbolic acts that, regardless of their size, ripple through organizations and have profound effects. The behavior of leaders is always being observed and interpreted.

Sometimes this communication is conscious and intentional. More often, however, it is unconscious and unintentional. Here are some of the different ways leaders communicate:

- Body language (gestures, posture, touch, stance, facial expressions)
- Physical presence, including dress
- Ability and willingness to listen
- Accessibility and openness
- Words (written and spoken)
- Behavior (has a vision, walks the talk, uses good judgment, communicates with the right people)

Organizations need leaders who send clear, coherent, consistent, and appropriate messages. If leaders are vague, inconsistent, or noncommittal, followers are likely to be confused and lose connection with the leader and the organization's vision and mission. People build trust and credibility through observing leaders' behavior more than by reading their policy documents.

A caution, however: Modeling behavior you'd like to see in others doesn't always produce the desired result (Goslin, 2012). Consider the principal who stood outside her office every morning to greet children as they arrived. She had hoped that all of the teachers in the building would also stand outside their classroom doors to great youngsters, but only two did. Since modeling wasn't working, she needed to make explicit the connection between her behavior and her expectations for her faculty.

Reflection

Use the list above to consider how you model leadership. Think of the ways you communicate. Are you readily accessible? Do you have a strong physical presence? Are your words and actions congruent? Are there times when you've deliberately modeled a behavior you wanted to see (but didn't) in others? Did you make your expectations more explicit? What happened? How do you strengthen your communication skills as a leader?

DAY 30: ETHICAL LEADERSHIP

The time is always right to do what is right.

Dr. Martin Luther King

What does it mean to be an ethical leader?

The Interstate School Leader Licensure Consortium (ISLLC) Standards (Council of Chief State School Officers, 2008) states that one of the five standards that school leaders should know and be able to do effectively is to "promote the success of every student by acting with integrity, fairness, and in an ethical manner" (p. 18). Embedded within the standard are five functions, including:

1. Ensure a system of accountability for every student's academic and social success

2. Model principles of self-awareness, reflective practice, transparency, and ethical behavior

3. Safeguard the values of democracy, equity, and diversity

4. Consider and evaluate the potential moral and legal consequences of decision making

5. Promote social justice and ensure that individual student needs inform all aspects of schooling (Council of Chief State School Officers, 2008, p. 19)

Not only are there standards and guidelines for ethical leadership, but educators Zubay and Soltis (2005) provide guidance for leaders who are focused on creating ethical schools, including:

- Encourage identification of and reflection on the ethical principles that underwrite certain school rules and actual decisions made at the school
- Help a diverse, pluralist community come to see those ethical values, moral principles, and virtues that they hold in common as members of the school community
- Create an ethical environment, a morally sensitive community that acts with civility, virtue, and justice in the daily business of living together
- Create a morally nurturing place for students; a school with many adult exemplars of the virtues of honesty, responsibility, courage, and principled behavior (pp. 17–18)

Reflection

Consider the ISLLC's five functions of ethical leaders. On a scale of 1 (poor) to 10 (excellent), how would you rate yourself and the other leaders in your organization on each of the functions? Which one or two of these functions do you want to enhance?

Consider the actions of leaders who are focused on creating ethical schools. Which ones are reflective of your leadership actions? Of the norms and culture of your school? Which ones would you like to emphasize more, and how might you go about doing that?

DAY 31: DOING THE RIGHT THING

You may encounter many defeats, but you must not be defeated. In fact, it may be necessary to encounter the defeats, so you can know who you are, what you can rise from, how you can still come out of it.

Maya Angelou

How do you know you are doing the right thing?

This is a question that haunts leaders. They often have to take action without all the answers and without all the resources and support they need. Sometimes they are subject to criticism and have self-doubt, yet have to press on.

Reflection on what you are doing and why can be very helpful in addressing criticism and resolving doubt. Here are questions that can guide you to assess whether you are doing the right thing in your leadership role:

- Are factors in place that will enable your leadership efforts to be successful? Is your vision clear? Do you have a clear moral purpose? Do you have sufficient resources—both material and human? Is the timing right?
- Are you doing it because it needs to be done for your clients and organization or because it is good for you? Jim Collins (2001) found those companies that achieved great results were led by humble leaders who focused on what the organization needed over their own needs and advancement.
- Is your plan based on best practice? Have you and your team consulted the research and asked others with more experience to inform your thinking? Can you defend your decision based on research and informed professional judgment?
- Do you have sufficient support to accomplish your plan? Throughout history individuals have accomplished remarkable feats alone, but the likelihood of a single person transforming an entire organization is slim. The existing system is set up in a way that makes that very difficult to happen. Therefore, before you can be successful, you need to have a strong base of support.

Reflection

Are you sure that you are doing the right things? Are you having doubt about actions you are trying to take in your organization? If so, what is the source of the doubt? Review the preceding questions. Are any of these areas you need to address?

Feedback from peers, supervisors, and subordinates can provide great insight into whether you are doing the right things. Ask for regular feedback from people around you. You can do this informally by asking a few people after a meeting to give you some feedback and/or sending out an e-mail to a small number of colleagues and ask them to make a list of your strengths and the areas they think need to be enhanced. Discuss what you learn with your coworkers and, if appropriate, be willing to make changes in your plan and actions.

REFERENCES

Anthony, S. (2012). Innovation is a discipline, not a cliché. *Harvard Business Review Blog Network*. Retrieved December 12, 2012, from http://blogs.hbr.org/anthony/2012/05/four-innovation-misconceptions.html

Bybee, R. W. (1993). *Reforming science education: Social perspectives and personal reflections.* New York: Teachers College Press.

Chenowith, K., & Theokas, C. (2012). Leading for learning. *American Educator, 26*(3), 32-33.

Collins, J. (2001). *From good to great.* New York: HarperCollins.

Conner, D. R. (1998). *Leading at the edge of chaos.* New York: Wiley.

Council of Chief State School Officers. (2008). *Educational leadership policy standards: ISLLC 2008.* Washington, DC: Author.

Covey, S. R. (1989). *The 7 habits of highly effective people.* New York: Simon & Schuster.

Covey, S. R. (1990). *Principle-centered leadership.* London: Simon & Schuster.

DuFour, R., DuFour, R., Eaker, R., & Karhanek, G. (2004). *Whatever it takes: How professional learning communities respond when kids don't learn.* Bloomington, IN: National Educational Service.

Duhigg, C. (2012). *The power of habit.* New York: Random House.

Ellis, D. (2002). *Falling awake: Creating the life of your dreams.* Rapid City, SD: Breakthrough Enterprises.

Fullan, M. (2001). *Leading in a culture of change.* San Francisco: Jossey-Bass.

George, B. (2010). Leading in crisis. *Leader to Leader, 55*(Winter), 24–29.

Goleman, D. (1995). *Emotional intelligence: Why it can matter more than IQ.* New York: Bantam Books.

Goleman, D., Boyatzis, R., & McKee, A. (2002). *Primal leadership.* Boston: Harvard Business School Press.

Goslin, K. (2012). Is modeling enough? *Kappan, 93*(7), 42–43.

Hargreaves, A., & Fullan, M. (2012). *Professional capital: Transforming teaching in every school.* New York: Teachers College Press.

Kouzes, J. M., & Posner, B. Z. (2012). *The leadership challenge: How to make extraordinary things happen in organizations, fifth edition.* San Francisco: Jossey-Bass.

Kouzes, J., Posner, B., & Morrow, M. (2010). *The leadership challenge practice book.* San Francisco: Pfeiffer.

Lindsey, R. B., Robins, K. N., & Terrell, R. D. (2003). *Cultural proficiency: A manual for school leaders, second edition.* Thousand Oaks, CA: Corwin.

Marzano, R. J., Waters, T., & McNulty, B. A. (2005). *School leadership that works: From research to results.* Alexandria, VA: Association for Supervision and Curriculum Development, and Aurora, CO: Mid-continent Research for Education and Learning.

Partnership for 21st Century Skills. (2011). *Framework for 21st century learning.* Washington, DC: Author.

Payne, C. M. (2008). *So much reform, so little change: The persistence of failure in urban schools.* Cambridge, MA: Harvard Education Press.

Rubin, H. (2009). *Collaborative leadership: Developing effective partnerships for communities and schools, second edition.* Thousand Oaks, CA: Corwin.

Schoemaker, P., Krupp, S., & Howland, S. (2013). Strategic leadership: The essential skills. *Harvard Business Review, 91*(1-2), 131–134.

Scholtes, P. (1998). *The leader's handbook.* New York: McGraw Hill.

Senge, P. M. (1990). *The fifth discipline.* New York: Doubleday.

Singleton, G. E., & Linton, C. (2006). *Courageous conversations about race.* Thousand Oaks, CA: Corwin.

Stein, S., & Book, H. (2000). *The E.Q. edge.* Toronto: Stoddart.

Terry, R. (2001). *The seven zones for leadership: Acting authentically in stability and chaos.* Palo Alto, CA: Davies-Black.

U.S. Department of Education. (2011). The innovation agenda. Retrieved December 12, 2012 from http://www.ed.gov/oii-news/innovation-agenda

The Wallace Foundation. (2013). *The school principal as leader: Guiding schools to better teaching and learning.* New York: Author.

Wheatley, M. (2002). *Turning to one another: Simple conversations to restore hope to the future.* San Francisco: Berrett-Koehler.

Wojciki, S. (n.d.). Eight pillars of innovation. Retrieved January 19, 2013, from http://www.thinkwithgoogle.com/quarterly/open/note.html

Zubay, B., & Soltis, J. F. (2005). *Creating the ethical school: A book of case studies.* New York: Teachers College Press.

Book 2

Leading Change

Book Two is a collection of thoughts and inspirations on leading change efforts. Often, the principal role of the leader is to recognize that change is needed, design the best map for change, and engage others in the journey. These 31 contemplations contain information about current research and practice on leading change in organizations.

The contemplations explore a number of key questions about change. How does change occur in an organization? Where do changes originate? Why do people experience the same change differently? What are the stages of change? How does one plan for change? What factors in our society contribute to the increasing rate of change? In any major change effort, what aspects of an organization need to remain stable? What motivates people to change? What are the roles of vision, mission, and goals in a change initiative?

And the questions continue. Why is it important to grieve what is lost when a change occurs? Why is resistance to change a natural phenomenon, and how can it be useful in guiding a change effort? Who should be involved in a major change effort? Why is an organization's change history important in determining the success of a current change initiative? Is it possible to determine an organization's readiness for change? What is the leader's role in modeling behaviors that support change? How do leaders protect themselves from burnout during intense change initiatives?

The questions are grouped around four major themes:

- What is organizational change, and how do we approach it?
- What is necessary for a successful change effort?
- What are the challenges of leading a change effort?
- What are the roles of a leader in a change initiative?

These themes are interwoven throughout the contemplations for Days 1 through 31 in Book Two.

DAY 1: CHANGE AS A PROCESS

Change is a process, not an event.

Gene Hall and Shirley Hord

What is the difference between an event and a process? An event is a one-time occurrence. It happens, and it is done. In contrast, a process is ongoing. It takes place over time and may involve developmental stages of growth.

What are some of the common mistakes leaders make when they do not understand the change process? The following are some illustrations:

- Sending out a memo saying that from this point on, this is how things will be done
- Purchasing a new curriculum program and expecting that teachers will automatically be able to use it
- Requiring staff to attend one workshop and expecting them to immediately behave differently
- Enacting a new policy or practice and then announcing it to the staff
- Inviting volunteers to be the first to make the change instead of engaging a more broadly based group of stakeholders
- Expecting to see immediate results from a change initiative

When people treat change as an event, unless the change is one of minimal consequence, it simply won't happen.

What is different when leaders understand the change process? They do the following:

- Involve the people affected by the change in planning for and leading the change
- Consider and plan ahead for the impact of change on the people involved
- Know that any significant change takes time and set expectations accordingly
- Employ professional development over time to ensure that people acquire the right knowledge and skills to implement the change
- Set realistic expectations for implementation
- Build a culture of support for the change that avoids blaming people for past mistakes
- Apply a monitoring procedure to track key benchmarks

Viewing change as a process increases the likelihood of obtaining the desired results.

> **Reflection**
>
> Recall one or more examples in your organization in which change was treated as an event. How did that occur? What was the end result? How did people feel about what happened?
>
> Are there examples from your organization in which a change effort was well managed? What was different?
>
> As a leader, what actions can you take that model change as a process rather than as an event?

DAY 2: CHANGE HAPPENS IN PEOPLE FIRST

Things do not change, we change.

Henry David Thoreau

It is very easy to refer to an organization as an entity separate from its people. We talk about how an organization fails to value individual initiative. Or we may discuss how resistant it is to change. We treat the institution as if it were a being in and of itself.

In reality, every organization is made up of its people—the employees or members—and the structures—policies, practices, and culture—that organize them. When we say that our organization fails to value individual initiative or is resistant to change, we are really talking about the individuals in the organization and/or the organization's policies, practices, or culture.

Successful change requires that leaders focus on people as well as on the change itself. A leader must be able to assess who is making the change and how well they are enacting the innovation. They need to understand what motivates people to change and adopt a personalized approach. What works for some people won't work for others. "Since change is made by individuals, their personal satisfactions, frustrations, concerns, motivations, and perceptions all contribute to the success or failure of a change initiative" (Loucks-Horsley & Stiegelbauer, 1991, p.18).

> **Reflection**
>
> Think of the last two major changes you have been involved in for your organization. Who was involved and to what degree? How were people "invited" and supported to make the change? How did you monitor who was involved and how? Were some individuals seen as the early adopters, while others were just expected to come along later? How has your organization managed the people side of change?

DAY 3: THE IMPACT OF CHANGE

Whether people perceive a change as positive or negative depends not only on the actual outcomes of the change, but also on the degree of influence they believe they exert in the situation.

Daryl Conner

Different people perceive change differently.

And the same change can affect people very differently. For some, the change may have little impact. For others, the impact may be great. Factors such as prior experience, level of knowledge and skill, individual resiliency, and the degree of influence a person has can affect how he or she experiences a change.

Here is an example. Which of the following would be hardest for you to do? Easiest?

- Move to a rural area
- Relocate to midtown of a large city
- Move to a foreign country
- Buy a different home in the same neighborhood

All things being equal, most people would probably say that remaining in the same neighborhood would be easiest for them. But then, things are never equal when decisions such as those must be made. Some people feel very comfortable moving to a rural area or to the heart of a major metropolis, especially if that is where they grew up. A military family that once lived in Japan might welcome a return. People's prior experiences greatly influence how they approach change. Usually, the greater the familiarity and comfort with a new situation, the greater the sense of control people feel.

If the impact of the change on individuals is small or slight, implementing the change is often a simple matter. For example, filling out a different time sheet or using a new procedure for ordering supplies are minor things for most people.

But if the change has a significant potential impact—especially if it affects people's self-confidence, their span of control, their comfort, or their competence—then expect it to be more difficult and to possibly generate some resistance. With rare exceptions, it is human nature to resist anything new that has a major impact on us—even something we really desire.

Recognize, too, that individual reactions to a change effort may in part be related to background and life circumstances. For example, an organizational move may affect one group more than another if the move is to an area where there is less access to services, food, churches, or other resources with which they wish to affiliate. People who use public transportation would be disadvantaged by a change that required them to travel to places not on the public transportation route. Or if a change requires extensive professional development, sessions may need to be scheduled at different times to accommodate people with small children who have limited daycare coverage. As a leader, you must be alert to how the change will affect different people and address their concerns to help them to be successful.

> **Reflection**
>
> Think of a change effort in your organization that you have experienced. Recall how individuals responded to that change:
>
> - Did some people implement the change with seemingly little effort? Were there any commonalties among these individuals?
> - Did some people experience more difficulty? If so, did the change affect their competence, control, comfort, and/or confidence?
> - Did race, ethnicity, gender, disability, age, or life circumstances affect how people reacted to the change? If so, how?
>
> Was the change successfully implemented or not? Why or why not? Can you relate success or failure to how different people responded to the change?

DAY 4: MOVING THROUGH THE STAGES OF CHANGE—CONCERNS

There is still and will always be a critical place for consideration of the individual in the change process.

　　　　　　　Susan Loucks-Horsley and Suzanne Stiegelbauer

Everyone involved in a change has a somewhat different set of perceptions, expectations, feelings, motivations, and frustration points that evolve over time. We call these concerns. These concerns need to be addressed throughout the change process or people will fail to fully implement the new initiative.

The Concerns-Based Adoption Model (Hall & Hord, 2011) provides tools to assess people's concerns about change in a way that enables leaders to know, and even predict, what concerns people have and to respond appropriately.

The Concerns-Based Adoption Model (CBAM) delineates seven stages that people move through as they implement a change (see Table 2.1). Response to the change is developmental in nature; although people may differ in the pace at which they move through these stages, their concerns at each stage are similar.

The research on the model has revealed how people grow and develop through the stages. For example, individuals with limited experiences related to the change are likely to express concerns at Stages 0, I, or II (awareness, informational, or personal). As they become more involved and start using the practices associated with the change effort, their concerns are likely to be at Stage III (management). As they gain confidence and start noticing their impact on learners, their concerns move to Stage IV (consequences). With experience, their concerns may shift to wanting to collaborate (Stage V) or searching for better approaches (Stage VI). Levels 0, I, and II are concerns that are focused on *self*; Level III is focused on *task*; and Levels IV, V, and VI are concerns about *impact.*

Thus, the model predicts the development of individuals within a group and enables us to assess where a group is at any moment. Knowing where people are enables the leaders of any change effort to target their interventions more effectively. For example, there is no point in focusing on use and management issues when the group isn't even familiar enough with the proposed change to identify what management issues they might encounter.

Table 2.1 The Concerns-Based Adoption Model: Stages of Concern

Stages	*Expressions of Typical Concerns*
VI: Refocusing	I have some ideas about something that would work even better.
V: Collaboration	How can I relate what I am doing to what others are doing?
IV: Consequence	How is my use affecting learners? How can I refine it to have more impact?
III: Management	I seem to be spending all my time getting materials ready.
II: Personal	How will using it affect me?
I: Informational	I would like to know more about it.
0: Awareness	I am not concerned about it.

SOURCE: From Gene E. Hall, Shirley M. Hord. *Implementing Change: Patterns, Principles, and Potholes.* (3rd ed.). © by Pearson. Reprinted by permission of publishers. Pearson, Saddle River, NJ.

> **Reflection**
>
> Think about a change initiative in your organization.
>
> Are you aware of the different concerns people have about using the initiative? Do they encompass the entire continuum described, or are they concentrated in the self, task, or impact levels? How does the support and/or professional learning opportunities that you are providing directly relate to people's specific stages of concern?
>
> How can knowing more about people's stages of concern help you better lead your change effort?

DAY 5: MOVING THROUGH THE STAGES OF CHANGE—BEHAVIOR

They always say time changes things, but you actually have to change them yourself.

Andy Warhol

The Concerns-Based Adoption Model (Hall & Hord, 2011) delineates the levels of use that individuals typically go through in implementing an innovation. This model lists seven levels of use and common behaviors associated with each level (see Table 2.2).

Table 2.2 The Concerns-Based Adoption Model: Levels of Use and Behavioral Indices

Levels of Use	Behavioral Indices
VI: Renewal	The user is seeking more effective alternatives to the established use of the innovation.
V: Integration	The user is making deliberate efforts to coordinate with others in using the innovation.
IVB: Refinement	The user is making changes to enhance outcomes.
IVA: Routine	The user is making few or no changes and has an established pattern of use.
III: Mechanical	The user is using the innovation in a poorly coordinated manner and is making user-oriented changes.
II: Preparation	The user is preparing to use the innovation.
I: Orientation	The user is seeking out information about the innovation.
0: Non-use	No action is being taken with respect to the innovation.

SOURCE: From Gene E. Hall, Shirley M. Hord. *Implementing Change: Patterns, Principles, and Potholes.* (3rd ed.). © by Pearson. Reprinted by permission of publishers. Pearson, Saddle River, NJ.

Obviously, for any organization to change, the individuals must implement the change effort, and their leaders must support them in this process and often make the change themselves. Leaders must identify the level of use of the change for each person and supply relevant support to match their levels.

> **Reflection**
>
> Go back to the organizational change effort that you recalled for the previous day's contemplation and answer the following questions, this time thinking about the levels of use:
>
> - What level of use do you think most people are at now? Are they in preparation—just starting to use the innovation? Or, have they reached higher levels of use?
> - Given this knowledge of the levels through which individuals move, what might you do differently in leading your next change initiative? How can you make sure the assistance you provide is directly tied to people's needs?

DAY 6: CHANGE AS CONTINUOUS IMPROVEMENT

Change is a double-edged sword. Its relentless pace these days runs us off our feet. Yet when things are unsettled, we can find new ways to move ahead and to create breakthroughs not possible in stagnant societies.

Michael Fullan

The pace of change is so great these days that organizations are continuously bombarded with one change after another. The concept of continuous improvement used to be an ideal, something that the most effective organizations strived for. Today continuous improvement is necessary for survival. Organizations that move through a loop of action-reflection-action create a continuous enhancement of culture and performance.

If organizations engage in continuous improvement, people will come to see change as a normal component of organizational life. They will regard the everyday state of their organizational and personal lives as being "permanent white water" (Vaill, 1992). A continuous improvement perspective may help to create an orientation of "polishing the stone" rather than repairing a defect.

One approach to continuous improvement is the Plan-Do-Check-Act (P-D-C-A) cycle (Senge et al., 1999), from the total quality management model. This approach provides a vehicle for carrying out the overall plan for a change effort, from initiation to implementation to institutionalization. In the "Plan" phase, the organization collects and analyzes data, determines the vision and/or desired outcomes, and creates an initial plan and actions. In the "Do" phase, the organization prepares people, builds the supportive environment, and implements the plan. The "Check" phase is for examining results and methods. This stage is also often called "Study." In the "Act" phase, the organization takes appropriate actions to improve, maintain, or correct the plan and actions. Repeating this cycle results in a well-managed process and supports the concept of continuous improvement.

If people realize that change is inevitable and that it can be managed effectively (as long as leaders remain flexible and in tune with the complexities and changing circumstances along the way), they are more likely to feel some degree of control and be more open to and less frustrated by change efforts. And if they believe that they possess some measure of control, they are more likely to support the change (Block, 1991), and a culture of continuous improvement is more likely to become a reality.

Reflection

What have you done (or can you do) to promote a broader view of change as a process of continuous improvement that can be built into the culture of your organization? How are you helping everyone participate in continuous improvement of programs and practices?

DAY 7: SPEED OF CHANGE

The rate of change is not going to slow down anytime soon. If anything, competition in most industries will probably speed up even more in the next few decades.

John Kotter

Change in all aspects of society, including education, now moves at a startling rate and with a complexity that is unknown in the history of civilization. As Ed Houle and Jeff Cobb (2011) write, "There will be at least as much change in the fifteen years from 2010 to 2025 as there has been in the thirty five years since 1975" (p. 39).

Early on, Daryl Conner (1993) previewed seven factors that explain why change in today's world is so complex and rapid:

1. Faster communication and knowledge acquisition

2. A growing world population

3. Increasing interdependence and competition

4. Limited resources

5. Diversified political and religious ideologies

6. Constant transitions of power

7. Ecological distress (p. 39)

Most of these factors have their counterparts in the educational system. These include the rapid rate at which knowledge is changing; technology that promotes instant access and collaboration; the need to do more with less; the increasing diversity of the nation and the press for personalization; and the growing interconnections of schools and their communities. Each of these factors creates change independently of and in conjunction with the others.

We are in one of the most dynamic periods of change in human history, a time that Houle and Cobb call the "Shift Age," an age when we "come to terms with what it means to be globally connected and master the opportunities that connectedness brings" (p. 41). In this new age, rapid and pervasive change is an integral part of everyday life. We need new skills and dispositions to succeed in this new frontier. These authors suggest that all of us will need to be masterful in the areas of creativity, collaboration, critical thinking, and have the ability to adapt rapidly to the new circumstances in which we find ourselves (Houle and Cobb, 2011).

This illustrates why change must be regarded as a journey and not a blueprint. There are too many unknowns and unknowables; it may be impossible to determine the solution in advance. There are always unexpected events; rarely can they be fully predicted, but leaders can be prepared.

> **Reflection**
>
> How are Conner's seven factors relevant to the rate and complexity of change in your organization? Which are the most significant? Are there other factors that contribute to the rate and complexity of change that you experience?
>
> Think about some of the fundamental changes you experienced in just the last few years, e.g., in banking, entertainment, technology, and publishing. How have these influenced you? What can you do now that you couldn't do just a decade ago?
>
> How are changes like these affecting and enhancing the work you do? What new innovations do you expect based on this? How can you help others in your organization anticipate and prepare for such change?

DAY 8: THE MISSING PIECE IN CHANGE

> *The sequence of change is not ANALYZE-THINK-CHANGE but rather SEE-FEEL-CHANGE.*
>
> John Kotter and Dan Cohen

The reason why so many large change initiatives fail, according to John Kotter and Dan Cohen (2002) in *The Heart of Change*, is that leaders miss the most important piece. They focus on strategy, structure, culture, or systems and ignore the role of emotions. In Book Two, Day 4, we raise the idea that change happens with individuals, and leaders must be attuned to people's concerns as they make changes in practice. Kotter and Cohen also believe that change occurs when people change, and for people to change, their feelings must be addressed.

Why is that? Chip Heath and Dan Heath (2010) in their book *Switch* describe the phenomenon well:

> The conventional wisdom in psychology, in fact, is that the brain has two independent systems at work at all times. First, there's what we call the emotional side. It's the part of you that is instinctive, that feels pain and pleasure. Second, there's the rational side, also known as the reflective or conscious system. It's that part of you that deliberates and analyzes and looks into the future. (p. 6)

All too many change efforts address the rational side, ignoring the emotional side, and then wonder why they fail. Let's take a look at something that's pretty commonly used in education and other fields: SMART goals. SMART stands for Specific, Measurable, Actionable, Relevant, and

Timely. A typical SMART goal might be something like, "By next year increase the retention rate of rising freshman by 10 percent." Or, "By the end of this year, increase by 15 percent the number of fourth graders scoring proficient on the state assessment." These goals appeal to our rational side, but change leaders must also consider how to capture people's emotions and engage them in the change required to reach the goal. Unless there are strategies that generate motivation on the part of the teachers and students, chances are that the goals will remain unmet. One strategy might be establishing teacher mentors for every ninth grader in danger of failing or dropping out of school. The teacher-mentors would be responsible for collaborating with students to draw on their strengths and to find ways to meet academic, social, financial, health, or other needs.

> **Reflection**
>
> Think of a change initiative going on in your organization. Has the appeal been made largely on the basis of analysis of data, logic, and cost, and imposed top down? Or have the individuals affected by the initiative been involved, and do they connect emotionally with the need for the change? Is the change good for children? Will it have a positive impact on the quality of teaching and teachers personally? What will ultimately happen? Will the change survive, be reversed, or just fade away? As a leader, think about how you can take people's feelings into account when proposing a major change. What would you do differently?

DAY 9: BALANCING CONSTANTS AND CHANGE

The art of progress is to preserve order amid change and to preserve change amid order.

Alfred North Whitehead

Change, change, change! We hear that word so much these days. So much, in fact, that we may forget that change is just one side in one of the fundamental dichotomies of life. The other choice is to stay the same. As discussed in Book One, Day 24, one paradox leaders must balance is "initiating change while maintaining continuity."

In many change efforts, the parts that stay the same are overlooked. The entire focus is on the changes going on—not the elements that remain stable, stationary, and strong in the midst of change.

Dichotomies (centralization versus decentralization, holding on versus letting go, and staying the same versus changing) are best viewed as "both/ands" rather than "either/ors."

In any successful change effort, considerable attention needs to be given to what remains constant. Without this balanced view, the daunting perception of change can overwhelm a system and the people in it.

So, how do you balance staying the same and making changes at the same time? You deliberately and thoughtfully designate some things that will not change during a certain period. For example, your school will implement a new curriculum in mathematics and science for K–6 over the next three years, but the reading and social studies curricula will remain stable. Balance can also be achieved by conducting a change priority inventory (Kaser & Horsley, 1998), so that competing change initiatives do not negate each other in their struggle for resources. A change inventory does the following: documents how many people are affected by the change and who they are; estimates the impact and potential outcomes of the change; provides a timeline for full implementation of the change; and lists all of the resource requirements. Such an inventory can identify what is not being changed along with the changes that are planned.

The areas of stability need to be highlighted in written and oral communications and supported by leaders in the organization. This assures the staff that the leadership is committed to balanced change and to keeping what is good and what works well within the organization. For example, one of the authors recently met a principal new to her school. Her first act as principal was to interview each teacher, asking two questions: (1) What are the three things that I should not "touch" or consider changing? and, (2) What are your top three priorities for things that need to change to enhance teaching and learning in this school? The principal's communication with each teacher and the targeted questions clearly sent the message that she was intent on keeping what worked well and balancing change with stability.

Reflection

Jot down some of the change initiatives going on in your organization. Can you balance each change effort with some parallel aspect of your organization that is remaining stable? If you can't, people are likely to feel overwhelmed by all the changes.

If your organization is not emphasizing stability sufficiently to balance the desired change, what can you do?

DAY 10: RECOGNIZING ASSUMPTIONS

The inertia of deeply entrenched mental models can overwhelm even the best systemic insights.

Peter Senge

Another requirement for an organization to respond successfully to change is awareness of what Senge (1990) calls *mental models*. Mental models are the assumptions people carry with them, and they run the gamut from simple generalizations or stereotypes about people and things to complex belief systems about how the world works. Our assumptions influence how we think and act and how we interpret information and experiences. Leaders need to understand the assumptions held by people in their organizations and, at times, work to change the assumptions.

One example of a firmly entrenched assumption in education was the belief that schools were responsible for teaching versus learning. Historically, educators have looked upon their role as that of providing education; whether children and youth actually acquired the education was primarily the students' responsibility. However, today in many places this assumption has changed. The emphasis has shifted to the belief that all students should learn. Following from this, if students are not learning, then educators need to ask what they need to do differently to help all children succeed.

Another mental model being challenged by contemporary thought is that of leadership. Rather than leadership being vested only in the mid-level and top management of an organization (the firmly entrenched model again), we are shifting to models where all staff have as much leadership responsibility as possible. But if that is the case, we have to set up different structures in our organizations to accommodate, support, and encourage this broader concept of leadership. Old structures don't mesh with the new assumptions.

We act on the basis of our assumptions continually, so it is important to surface them in conversations and develop a shared awareness of what they are. When encountering a problem, ask yourself, "What about my beliefs or assumptions is contributing to this situation?" "How am I looking at this problem, and is there another way to interpret it?" When we decide, we act on our assumptions, and the assumptions usually remain implicit. Making our assumptions or mental models explicit helps us better understand why we make the choices we make and can lead to great insights. In turn, those insights can result in better communication and more effective decision-making and problem solving.

> **Reflection**
>
> What are some of the basic assumptions operating in your organization? Perhaps start with views of leadership. What are the assumptions you and others hold about who should be a leader and what traits leaders should possess? What are your views on other important issues?
>
> Do you assume all can succeed, or do you think some must fail? Do you believe that individuals must have certain prerequisites or follow a certain path to be successful, or can education be more tailored and personalized? Do you view your organization as impervious to change? What could happen if you changed the way you look at these issues? How might changing assumptions affect the outcome of a change initiative?

DAY 11: CRAFTING A SHARED VISION

Leadership isn't about imposing the leader's solo dream; it's about developing a shared sense of destiny.

James M. Kouzes and Barry Z. Posner

As discussed in Book One, Day 6, a true vision is never imposed. It evolves through people having a similar picture of what they want to achieve and knowing that they can achieve it most effectively by their collective, not individual, actions. Reaching shared vision of a change you are implementing starts with individuals understanding how the new vision connects to their work and to their personal visions. "If people don't have their own vision, all they can do is 'sign up' for someone else's" (Senge, 1990, p. 211). It is the personal vision that motivates. People with their own personal visions can form a powerful group to create what they want for themselves and for their organization.

In the education field there are fundamental shifts underway propelled by new visions of what it means to be educated for the 21st century. For example, educational institutions are shifting away from a vision in which all students are provided with the same learning experiences to a vision of education as more personalized and student-centered. They are shifting to systems in which student learning can happen not only in the classroom during the regular school day, but virtually anywhere and anytime—in the community, at home, or via the Internet. Staff who previously worked alone and with great autonomy are being asked to collaborate and to use consistent practices.

As leaders plan change efforts like these that fundamentally change the vision of the organization, they must spend the time to help everyone in the community commit to and share in the new vision. A litmus test of the power of a vision is whether people know it and live it. There are likely to be different emphases from person to person, but the similarity should be apparent. Enacting changes to create a 21st century institution on top of old visions designed for a 20th century institution will not work.

As leaders plan and carry out major change initiatives, they need to proactively plan how they will enlist everyone—staff, community members, and other stakeholders—in the new vision. One school district we have worked with in New Hampshire achieved this by engaging its staff and community members in crafting a comprehensive 21st century vision for its schools, for the students and adults in its community, and for its graduates. All change efforts underway are carefully aligned to this vision, and ongoing communication helps everyone stay connected to the district's purpose and goals.

A leader's role in leading a change effort is to help people connect the desired change to their own personal visions and to make sure these personal visions are aligned with the organization's overall vision.

Reflection

Consider a change initiative in your organization that you are involved with. Does it have a compelling vision? Is it aligned with the overall organization's vision?

As a leader, what will you do with others to build a consistent vision of the change effort, including why you are making the change and how it ties to your organizational vision, mission, and goals?

DAY 12: MISSION AND GOALS

The greatest satisfaction you can find in life comes from discovering and courageously following your mission.

Richard Barrett

When making changes in an organization, leaders need to help people see the connection between the change effort and the organization's mission and goals. The organization's mission provides a common sense of direction and describes what the organization is and its purpose. Trying to make changes that disrupt or are dissonant to the mission and goals of the organization has been likened to rolling a boulder uphill or rowing a boat against the incoming tide.

Although there is usually just one shared vision for an organization, different parts of an organization may have their own mission statements and goals that are aligned with the vision. In some organizations, individuals write personal mission statements that are compatible with their organizational role. This results in a staff that has a common sense of direction. For example, a school may have as part of its vision that the staff are continuous learners. A mission statement that states that the school provides ongoing quality learning opportunities for children and adults, in turn, supports the vision. Different departments may have their own goals in support of continuous learning; for example, improving student engagement or using formative assessments. However, all staff support the vision of the school.

For leaders, having a clear and compelling mission and specific goals are essential parts of change management. Together, these serve as a compass for organizational action.

Reflection

Are you clear about your mission and goals? As a leader of change, how do you communicate with others about how the change effort is aligned to and supports your overall mission and goals?

If the change you are attempting to make is not in line with your mission, what modifications are needed?

DAY 13: MOTIVATING OTHERS

> *There is only one way under high Heaven to get anybody to do anything. Did you ever stop to think of that? Yes, just one way. And that is by making the other person want to do it. Remember, there is no other way.*
>
> Dale Carnegie

What is motivation to change? Is it simple or complex, one dimensional or multidimensional?

What sustains motivation to achieve a goal? What keeps us going even when our chances of success seem remote?

According to Richard Barrett (1999; 2003), motivation has four dimensions: physical, emotional, mental, and spiritual. The physical and emotional dimensions are satisfied primarily by external conditions. For example, financial reward is an example of the physical component; open communication is an example of the emotional. Physical and emotional aspects can be fulfilled by either positive external incentives (for example, promotions) or negative external incentives (for example, loss of status). The efficiency of external rewards declines over time and so must be increased to remain motivational.

Many organizations provide only extrinsic rewards or punishments as they lead change. They promise increased pay, good annual evaluations, or bonuses in exchange for asking employees to make the required change. Yet intrinsic rewards almost always work better and motivate more. In a meeting with a staff member several years ago, one of the authors listened as the staff member listed all the work she "had to" do. Through probing it became obvious that the employee was not doing substantial work that she valued personally. She was unclear about how her work connected to a greater purpose. The author asked the employee to consider what work she truly wanted to do and listened carefully. This small intervention resulted in the employee reshaping her work and her attitude. Effective leaders carefully consider what motivates people, and they recognize that motivation is different for everyone. They actively engage their colleagues in seeing how their work connects with the work of their co-workers and clients and to a greater purpose.

Although all four dimensions will motivate individuals, the most sustainable level of commitment comes when mental and spiritual needs are satisfied. The mental dimension is met through opportunities for professional and personal growth or opportunities to use new knowledge and skills to solve real problems. The spiritual dimension is met through having work that is meaningful, that matters, and that makes a difference in the world.

Reflection

Think about your role in leading change. What dimensions of motivation are you addressing? Are your key people motivated to make the changes needed? Are there incentives or disincentives for them doing so? Are you making the case for the change and communicating feedback and progress on the change effort?

Do staff find the work meaningful? Do they have a sense of making a difference? If the rewards are more external than internal, what can you as a leader do to address the mental and spiritual aspects and strengthen commitment?

DAY 14: PLANNING FOR CHANGE

We think in generalities, but we live in detail.

Alfred North Whitehead

The prior contemplation raised the importance of motivation among people making change. Effective planning is central to motivating people. The people in your organizations need to know the plan and where they fit into it.

How concrete are the details regarding your change initiative? Are these details set forth in a written plan?

Are the people involved in formulating the change initiative aware of what is happening and when? Is there a timetable? Do people know what is expected of them and are they committed to carrying out their roles? Have benchmarks been set to gauge progress? Are organizational supports in place for institutionalization? Are there criteria for success?

And most important, is the plan flexible? Can it be adjusted in response to unanticipated events and feedback? Is it reviewed and adjusted regularly? Are revisions to the plan communicated to others involved in the change initiative?

Managing successful change requires having a plan for each stage of the change. It is important to consider the organization's readiness to make the change and to factor that information into the plan. For example, change leaders can assess the readiness of the organization for the change. Fixsen, Naoom, Blasé, Friedman, and Wallace (2005) point out that there are instruments available that measure organizational readiness for change (Lehman, Greener, & Simpson, 2002; Simpson, 2002). These collect information on: "motivational readiness (need for improvement, training needs, pressure to change), institutional resources (space, staffing, training, computers, e-communication), staff attributes (growth, efficacy, influence, adaptability), and organizational climate (clarity of mission and goals, cohesiveness, autonomy, openness to communication, stress, openness to change)" (p. 9). A good implementation plan takes such contextual factors into account.

Your plan details what steps will be taken, by whom, at what point, and to what end. A plan has the following purposes or dimensions:

- Sets forth desired outcomes
- Serves as a guide for achieving those outcomes
- Identifies the benchmarks that will be used to monitor how well the intervention is progressing
- Documents the degree of alignment that exists among the vision, missions, goals, and activities
- Serves as a means for aligning the intervention throughout the organization

A plan for any stage is not cast in stone. As change efforts evolve, the plan is revised; that is the nature of organizational change. Overall direction and guiding principles are always more important than the details. However, as each next step comes closer in time, the details become more important. Flexibility is the key. A dynamic plan continually serves as a guide for all to follow.

One final caveat: Make sure that far more energy goes into carrying out the plan than in developing it. Avoid becoming so focused on planning that implementation does not occur.

> **Reflection**
>
> How prepared is your organization to make the changes you are planning? Are the motivations and resources in place? Does the change fit with your climate/culture? If not, how will you create the necessary conditions to make the organization ready for the change? Does your organization have a documented plan (or plans) for its change initiative? Is it a working document that the staff uses and regularly updates? Who is the custodian of the plan? Who knows about the plan and has access to it? Do evaluation and reflection activities inform revisions to the plan?
>
> If you answered any of these questions "No," what will you do to encourage your organization to develop a working plan?

DAY 15: ORIGINS OF CHANGE

Both top-down and local, or bottom-up, approaches are needed. The challenge is finding the right balance.

Jim Clemmer

How many times have you heard people (maybe even yourself) debating about whether organizational change comes from the top or the bottom and where it should actually originate? It's an age-old argument.

A typical conversation may sound something like this: "You can't impose change from the top. I don't care how many edicts leaders issue, change can't be mandated. If the people don't want to change, there are all kinds of ways to undermine any initiative. Any real change has to come from the staff—not the leaders. Let me tell you about what happened in my organization . . ."

Another counters: "People at lower levels rarely have the power, authority, or resources to bring about any kind of major change on their own. Quit kidding yourself. Organizations can squelch a budding initiative just by firing a person or two or denying them resources. Any real change has to have the sanctions and support of leaders. Let me tell you about what happened in my organization . . . "

And so the arguments go. If you have found yourself caught up in such discussions, vow right now that you won't repeat such a conversation. The question itself is a spurious one, posed as either/or: Change comes either from the top or from the bottom.

In reality, it is both. Both the leaders and the staff must be active players in a change initiative if it is to succeed. Either one is capable of subverting a change, so both must be working in concert to ensure success.

Reflection

Think of a change effort in your organization that succeeded. What role did the leaders play? What was the staff's role? How was the change initiated? Was it lodged more in the top, or the base of the organization, or was it spread across the organization? Did the leaders support the change effort? (Many change efforts fail because leaders don't provide sustained support.)

How did the staff come to implement the change effort? (Change efforts can also fail because the staff is not supported to develop the interest, knowledge, or skills to carry out the new initiative.) How were people informed? Did the change effort expand to include more people? How did this happen? What can you learn from this effort that would help you in your role of leading change?

DAY 16: ACCEPTING LOSS

He that lacks time to mourn lacks time to mend.

William Shakespeare

In some way, all significant change involves giving up something of your former self, and all losses must be grieved.

Whenever a major change takes place, we lose something. It may be the loss of a relationship, an office, or a lesson we loved to teach. Even if we want the change (perhaps a better relationship, a nicer office, or an improved curriculum), we still feel a loss. The loss may be a pattern of interaction, a convenient working environment, or the joy of helping others learn something important to us; or it may be the loss of that which was comfortable and familiar.

A loss that remains ungrieved keeps us anchored in the past, unable to fully commit to the present. The work of Dr. Elisabeth Kübler-Ross (1970) identified five stages of the grief process:

Stage 1: *Denial.* We pretend that nothing has happened. Things will be just the way they have always been. Perhaps we are having a bad dream. We'll wake up, and everything will be fine. We may enter into a robot-like stage in which we suppress our anger and become depressed. Because we are in denial, we don't tell other people. In fact, we haven't even told ourselves.

Stage 2: *Anger.* Feeling angry about a loss is normal and necessary. We may feel angry at another person, maybe even at the world. Why did this have to happen to us? Life isn't fair. Or: Why did this have to happen now? The timing is not good.

Stage 3: *Bargaining.* In this stage, we seek to make amends. What do we have to do to restore conditions to what they were? What can we trade or give up? What can we promise to do or never do again?

Stage 4: *Letting go.* This stage is the final letting go of the old. It is, in one sense, the darkness before the dawn. It may be characterized by deep sadness. It is a reflective stage in that we ask deep questions, such as "What is the meaning of this experience?" "What do I truly want for myself?" "What have I learned over the past weeks or months?" Rarely does letting go occur at a single instant. Rather, it occurs incrementally.

Stage 5: *Acceptance.* Here, we have moved beyond our emotional attachment to the loss and have relinquished our investment in the past. We are now ready to move and to accept whatever new situation is awaiting. We are reenergized and hopeful about the future.

Movement through the stages is similar to that of an organization going through systemic change. Progress is not linear, and it is possible for people to become stuck in a stage or skip a stage completely. Some may even work backward or appear to move in circles. However, for the grieving process to be most effective, grievers need—at some point—to experience each stage.

In organizations, resistance may come from losses ungrieved. According to Garmston and Wellman (2009), "Endings must be marked concretely and symbolically" (p. 154). In the absence of grieving, the staff may hold on to elements of the old and not be able to fully embrace the new.

> **Reflection**
>
> Again, think of a major change going on in your organization. What is the loss that the staff may be feeling? Maybe they have given up a planning period to collaborate with colleagues or have lost some sense of autonomy that was important to them. In what ways can you recognize these "losses" and help people get to acceptance?

DAY 17: DEALING WITH DISAPPOINTMENT

You may be disappointed if you failed, but you are doomed if you don't try.

Beverly Sills

In spite of your good intentions and actions, you may fail in your attempts to bring about a major change in your organization. The reasons are manifold: a budget cut, a change in top leadership, the lobbying of an opposing group. Or maybe you chose the wrong plan, or the timing was wrong. Or perhaps the loss is more personal: You didn't get the promotion, or you were given another assignment and couldn't follow through with your plans.

Leaders who take on the job of making great changes will experience some failure and disappointment along the way. If you don't occasionally fail, you're probably not acting boldly enough. In today's rapidly changing world, organizations are inventing and adapting all the time. To do so they experiment and take calculated risks to discover new ideas and solutions. In this context, leaders will likely experience more "failures" but they are only true failings if nothing is learned or gained.

Learning from failures is accepting disappointment, a natural reaction to falling short of our goals; discerning what you can about the failure; and then trying again with new knowledge. Your approach to dealing with your own disappointment sets a tone for your organization. According to Cini (2004), here are five things that you can do:

1. *Don't take disappointments personally.* Perhaps analyze the situation as if it had happened to someone else. That will likely give you a different perspective.

2. *Know yourself. Especially, know your values.* Perhaps this organization is not the right place for you at this time. Perhaps you need to make a move.

3. *Take full responsibility for yourself and your actions.* Don't blame others, bad luck, bad timing, or other external factors for the failure. Acknowledge your role fully and move on.

4. *Think beyond your own situation.* How did this failure impact your colleagues and the organization as a whole?

5. *Explore this situation with your boss. You and your supervisor need to be clear on what happened.* Just as you don't want to blame others, you want to avoid being blamed, too.

> **Reflection**
>
> How does your organization handle failures? Are people supported to take reasonable risks and learn from them? When things go wrong, is blame cast, or are staff asked to examine and learn from what happened?
>
> What is your typical pattern of handling disappointment? Do you blame others or yourself? Are you clear about the difference between blaming yourself and taking responsibility for your behavior? Are you a positive role model for dealing with disappointment? What might you do differently?

DAY 18: CHANGE AND RESILIENCE

What one has to do usually can be done.

Eleanor Roosevelt

How well equipped are people to handle change? How do you know their potential for responding to change?

Daryl Conner (1998) sees each person as having an individual *speed of change*. He defines this as the rate at which you can move through the adaptation process with a minimum of dysfunctional behavior—the pace at which you can bounce back from the confusion caused by uncertainty and grasp the opportunities that the new environment presents (p. 189).

According to Conner, the single, most important factor that affects one's speed of change is resilience. Highly resilient individuals are able to operate at a higher speed of change than those who are less resilient.

Conner (1998) identified five characteristics that constitute resiliency:

1. *Positiveness:* Resilient individuals effectively identify opportunities in turbulent environments and have confidence in their ability to succeed.

2. *Focus:* Resilient individuals have a clear vision of what they want to achieve, and they use this as a lodestar to guide them should they become disoriented.

3. *Flexibility:* Resilient individuals draw effectively on a wide range of internal and external resources to develop creative, malleable strategies for responding to change.

4. *Organization:* Resilient individuals use structured approaches to manage ambiguity, planning, and coordinating effectively in implementing their strategies.

5. *Proactivity:* Resilient individuals act in the face of uncertainty and take calculated risks rather than seeking comfort. (p. 189)

Although these five factors are interrelated to some extent, they are separate attributes. One change initiative may draw principally from one or two factors, whereas another may tap a different factor. This led Conner (1998) to view resilience as "the ability to draw effectively on whichever characteristic, or combination of characteristics, is called for in a particular situation" (p. 193).

Conner (1998) also sees a link between resiliency and physical health. The higher the resiliency, the greater the likelihood of excellent physical health and vice versa. He has also identified a similar link between the level of resilience and leadership. Leaders in organizations are more likely to have higher levels of resilience, and those with high resilience are more likely to be leaders.

> **Reflection**
>
> Using Conner's five factors (positiveness, focus, flexibility, organization, and proactivity) plus overall physical health, how would you rate your own resiliency? How about key staff you work with in your change effort? Which of these factors stand out?
>
> Although resiliency is personal, it can be affected by what goes on in an organization. As a leader, what can you do to bolster people's positiveness, focus, flexibility, organization, proactivity, and overall physical health?

DAY 19: FACING PROBLEMS

Problems are our friends.

Michael Fullan

Sounds a little scary, right? This is especially true given the complex nature of the problems that organizations and society as a whole face today. How can problems have any kind of positive connotation?

Problems in the broadest sense are inevitable. Given the increasing complexity of our society and the rapid rate of change, we are going to experience new kinds of problems, most of which will be complex and not easily resolved. These are often referred to as adaptive challenges (Heifetz, Grashow, & Linsky, 2009). It is our reality—whether we like it or not. If we confront our fears, we have a better chance of resolving them. Rather than trying to avoid a problem or pretend it doesn't exist, we are better off facing it directly.

It is through solving problems, often by trial and error, that we learn. One of the characteristics of adaptive organizations is an acceptance of failure as inevitable and valuable. We often learn more from a failed attempt than a successful one. In today's organizations, however, failure is not carte blanche. It is balanced with accountability. What Garmston and Wellman (2009) call *failing forward* is the way people learn from their mistakes. In failing forward, we advance by the way we respond to a situation. Instead of reacting to the event and attempting a quick fix, we dig deeper to determine the root cause of the problem and to correct what organizational policies, programs, or practices are at the core. In that sense, problems are opportunities for us to broaden our attitudes, knowledge, and skills while moving our organizations forward.

Reflection

What is the prevailing attitude in your organization toward problems? Are they ignored? Seen as troublesome interruptions? Looked on as opportunities to improve your operation and your results and to advance knowledge in the organization?

What is your organization's attitude toward failure? Are people able and willing to take risks without fear of recrimination? Do people learn from their mistakes, and does that learning become part of the organization's common knowledge?

As a leader, what can you do to help people in your organization see problems as friends rather than enemies? What can you do to establish a climate supportive of failing forward?

DAY 20: NEUTRALIZING RESISTANCE

One cannot hope to implement change without persuading people that it is necessary. This is a task of daunting proportions that must often start by challenging people's view of themselves, their performance, and their clients.

Robert Evans

Getting people to feel some sense of urgency for a major change is an art form. Lowering resistance involves increasing the tension of not supporting the change effort and reducing the tension related to trying it. Both drive behavior in the direction of the change.

What are some ways of decreasing resistance to change?

1. *Increase the tension of not supporting the change*

    - Provide evidence that documents the need for the change.
    - Make it clear that all are expected to make the change.
    - Make sure that all key opinion leaders support and model the change. Ask them to garner the support of others.

2. *Decrease the tension related to trying the new way*

    - Determine the concerns of the resisters. Are they afraid they will fail or have too little time to learn a new approach? Find out what they are worried about and respond with the appropriate interventions.
    - Help resisters see how the change initiative connects to their personal visions and missions.
    - Set up a timetable that allows adequate assimilation time.

In describing what often happens in organizations, John Kotter (2012) says:

> I've seen people start by building the change coalitions, by creating the change vision, or by simply making changes. But the problems of inertia and complacency always seem to catch up with them. Sometimes they quickly hit a wall, as when a lack of urgency makes it impossible to put together a powerful enough leadership team to guide the changes. Sometimes people go for years—perhaps with an acquisition fueling growth and excitement—before it becomes apparent that various initiatives are flagging. (p. 49)

One way that leaders keep people out of the "complacency zone" is to identify and celebrate milestones in the implementation of the change effort. As we point out in the very first contemplation in this book, effective leaders keep attention and energy focused on the success of the change effort. They recognize and celebrate milestones, which gives people a sense of control and accomplishment.

A caution: If the degree or extent of resistance seems greater than would normally be expected, leaders should look at the change initiative itself. Perhaps it is not the appropriate initiative for the culture of your organization or circumstances. Maybe there is a better solution waiting. Knowing people's specific objections can help you determine if you need to reconsider what you are proposing.

> **Reflection**
>
> As a leader of change, what do you do when you face resistance? What are the factors that fuel people's resistance? Have your strategies focused both on decreasing disincentives and increasing incentives? What is your evidence of decreasing resistance? If your change requires a long time for implementation, is there a danger of people becoming complacent? If so, how can you keep people engaged and motivated and reduce complacency? How are you recognizing contributions and celebrating accomplishments with all?

DAY 21: CAPITALIZING ON RESISTANCE

Understand that resistance can be a gold mine!

Carol Bershad and Susan Mundry

When you hear the word *resistance*, does it conjure up a positive or a negative reaction?

Most people will think negatively: that resistance is an obstacle and something to be overcome.

What would happen if you reframed the notion of resistance? What if you saw it as an indicator of where people were in relation to a change? What if you saw resistance as an opportunity for you and others to learn? How might this change your perspective?

The level of resistance to change in an organization often gives us insight into the potential impact of the change. The greater the impact of the change, the more resistance it is likely to encounter. For example, substituting one textbook for another is not likely to have great impact, and therefore minimal resistance is likely to appear. However, moving from a textbook to an activity-based curriculum or an e-book is likely to have much greater impact and therefore give rise to greater resistance. Resistance is normal and natural. If there is no resistance, you can assume that the impact of change is minimal or that people are indifferent.

When leaders understand that resistance stems from feelings they are better able to determine the source of resistance. And once we know the source of the resistance, addressing it becomes much easier. Here are 12 common sources of resistance divided into different categories:

Sources Related to Not Having the Ability to Change

1. Lack of knowledge and skills in the content
2. Lack of knowledge and skills in the process

Sources Related to the Lack of Willingness to Change

3. Lack of support for the change because of poor communication
4. Lack of ownership, seeing no need
5. Lack of alignment between the change and the culture or mission of the organization
6. Lack of resources of time, materials, and/or facilities
7. Having an oppositional nature (either individuals or a group); disliking the mandated change
8. Lack of leadership or positive role models
9. Lack of trust in the system or in the leaders

Sources Related to Special Circumstances

10. Style differences that are misinterpreted as resistance
11. Having a sincere and accurate belief that the proposed change is wrong or that it is being implemented the wrong way
12. Personal reasons unrelated to the change (for example, focusing on another challenging work project or change effort, impending retirement, pregnancy, or serious illness.) (Kaser & Horsley, 1998, pp. 1–2)

Reflection

How much resistance do you encounter to your current change effort? Can you identify the sources of the resistance? What steps are you taking to overcome the resistance? What can other people do?

Can you think of at least one antidote for each one of the 12 sources of resistance? There are actually several for each one of the sources, so if you can come up with more than one, you are thinking in the right direction.

Here are just a few ways that leaders address resistance to change:

- Build relationships among all
- Practice communicating the negative aspects of the change as well as the positive
- Gather and share data about how the change is working and people's concerns (See Day 4)
- Address people's concerns directly with support and assistance, e.g., coaching
- Build a shared vision of what you are trying to accomplish and how it will benefit everyone
- Communicate high expectations for everyone to make the change (Mundry & Bershad, 1998)

DAY 22: KNOWING YOUR CONSTITUENTS

Unless you regularly account for all your stakeholders, your organization will likely not survive.

Stephen Covey

Who is involved in your change effort?

It's a rare organization today that doesn't have several stakeholder groups to consider. Take a public school, for example. In addition to employees and a governing body, there are children and youth, parents and community members, unions, businesses, other institutions such as colleges and universities, and perhaps even some special interest groups. All of these groups need to be considered in any organizational change, as they are likely to have a vested interest.

Implementing any kind of major change is so difficult that your instinct may be to limit involvement. However, ignoring some group or not keeping key people properly informed and engaged is likely to backfire and may derail your initiative later. If you only occasionally reach out to stakeholders, you are likely to raise their expectations and have them experience frustration if their involvement does not lead to change.

Covey (1992) points out that real change happens when organizations begin to problem solve around data gained from stakeholders. He recommends a "stakeholder information system—a feedback system or database on what shareholders, customers, employees, communities, suppliers, distributors, and other parties want and expect" (Covey, 1992, p. 258). He suggests that if a stakeholder information system is set up properly, data can be highly accurate as long as they are obtained "systematically, scientifically, anonymously, using random sampling of the population" (Covey, 1992, p. 258).

Here is an instance of a school administrator who failed to consider his stakeholders: His elementary school was slated to be closed, and students would be moved to a much larger, more modern school across town. He went on record as fully supporting this decision. The school they were leaving was old, lacked a gym and adequate wiring for computers, and was not accessible to persons with disabilities. The parents were outraged. They saw the smallness and character of the old school, the individual attention it afforded children, and its proximity and community school atmosphere as benefits that far outweighed the negatives. In a public forum, the principal was shown to be out of touch with one of his most important stakeholder groups.

Using Covey's idea of establishing a stakeholder information system, how could this situation have been avoided?

> **Reflection**
>
> Who are the stakeholders affected by the change your organization is proposing? What assumptions are you making about how they will react to the change? Have you verified your assumptions with members of the group?
>
> How are you involving them in your reform effort? Has anyone been left out? If so, why? How will you bring them on board?
>
> Do you have a stakeholder information system established? If not, how could you establish one?

DAY 23: MANAGING MULTIPLE CHANGE EFFORTS

Q: How can executives manage 29 change projects all at once?
A: They can't. In successful transformations, executives lead the overall effort and leave most of the managerial work and the leadership of specific activities to their subordinates.

John P. Kotter

The nomenclature used in Book Two (that is, the use of the terms that describe change initiatives) may be misleading. Expressions such as "developing a mission" or "data-based decision making" may lead a reader to believe that change occurs in a linear fashion, one initiative at a time.

Nothing could be farther from the truth. It would be rare for an organization to have a single change effort going on. It is not uncommon for a school district, for example, to identify 50 or more changes going on at the district level simultaneously.

One of the major reasons change efforts fail is that they are overshadowed and sometimes overrun by others that have more support and resources. Unless leaders attend specifically to each change effort and its relationship to the vision, mission, and goals of the organization, some inevitably stave off others. *Attending* means (1) knowing what resources each reform effort needs to be successful and delivering them, and/or (2) prioritizing the various change efforts so that each has a different ranking over a specific period of time. Such determinations cannot be haphazard.

Attending to each change effort independently is critical for another reason. Each has its own goals, staffing, resource requirements, and timetable. Sponsors and supporters, including stakeholders, are likely to be different. The impact of the change varies from one initiative to another, and it is the impact of change on people that determines how easy or difficult implementation will be. If you are gathering data about your change effort, they must be collected separately for each initiative so that you understand the particulars for each one. The National Implementation Research Network provides links to helpful implementation measures that can be used to monitor implementation of change efforts (http://nirn.fpg.unc.edu/learn-implementation/measures).

Just as you need to treat each change initiative individually, you need to see each in relation to the others and support appropriate coordination and integration. A major organizational paradox exists: treating each change effort individually while seeing each as part of a larger whole. As a leader, you need to keep the big picture in mind, looking across the different initiatives to coordinate and integrate as needed.

Reflection

Make a list of the changes you have initiated or implemented this year. (You might ask a colleague to do the same thing and then compare your lists.) How many did you come up with? Did the number surprise you? Why?

Now consider who is involved in these initiatives. Do you see any patterns? Are some people overburdened? Are some left out? Do any of these change efforts compete with each other for resources? How are you monitoring the progress of each effort? To what extent is implementation progressing and how do you know? What can you do to salvage change initiatives that are stalled or threatened?

> Is each change effort being treated independently and at the same time being seen as part of a larger whole? If not, what can you do to make sure that each change initiative is seen from this dual perspective? Can you identify linkages between and among the various change efforts?
>
> Are the change efforts aligned with the organization's vision, mission, and goals, and with each other?

DAY 24: SYSTEMS THINKING

Today, systems thinking is needed more than ever because we are becoming overwhelmed by complexity.

Peter Senge

What is systems thinking, and how does it relate to organizational change?

Systems thinking is a particular form of analysis that, rather than breaking a problem down into discrete components, helps people examine the big picture, looking for interrelationships among interactions, causes, and effects. Developed by Jay Forrester at MIT in 1956, the ideas were not widely used until the expansion of total quality management in the United States and in the 1990's with Peter Senge's identification of systems thinking as the missing ingredient for effective organizations in the 1990s.

In his book *The Fifth Discipline,* Peter Senge (1990; 2006) outlines 11 "laws" that are characteristic of systems thinking. Three of these are especially relevant to bringing about change in organizations:

1. *"Today's problems come from yesterday's 'solutions'"* (p. 57). Although we usually hope that solving a problem takes care of a situation, in reality, solving one problem often creates another. For example, the high school that instituted a high minimum grade point average for all athletes found that its dropout rate increased. Instead of motivating students to study harder and get good grades, the rule had the effect of pushing a certain group of students off the teams and out the door. Solving problems in a system without simply transferring a problem from one part of the system to another is a delicate business.

2. *"Cause and effect are not closely related in time and space"* (p. 63). In simple situations, seeing a direct and timely relationship between cause and effect is common. For example, children learn very quickly that if they don't share their toys and play nicely, they are likely to be removed from their playgroup. But direct cause-and-effect relationships like these are

uncommon in complex systems such as organizations. For example, in the high school example just given, cause and effect were not what this well-intended group of educators expected them to be and it took time for the unintended consequence to happen.

3. *"Small changes can produce big results—but the areas of highest leverage are often the least obvious"* (p. 63). In systems thinking, the most obvious solutions often don't work. Setting a grade point average cutoff for participation might be the most obvious solution for student athletes who are not doing well academically. The only problem is that it doesn't have the desired effect (pp. 57–67). A powerful example of a small change that led to a dynamic impact is that of Rosa Parks, in 1955, in Montgomery, Alabama. She refused to give up her seat for a white man and move to the back of the bus. Her act sparked the civil rights movement across the United States.

Chaos theory suggests that small, insignificant actions strategically placed can result in significant and lasting improvements. These are called *high-leverage* changes. The challenge for change leaders is with finding these high-leverage moves since they are not obvious and not closely connected in time and space to the problem at hand.

Senge (1990) recommends that learning to see the underlying structures, patterns, and assumptions that drive thinking and action in organizations—instead of simply reacting to events—points us in the right direction.

Reflection

Think of a problem you would like to solve. What is its root cause? To get at the root cause, ask yourself why you have the problem. Then ask why again and again in response to your answer. (Take as much time as you need to do this.) Then ask yourself and others what else might be contributing to this problem. Now ask what about your current systems and structures could be contributing to the problem and what about your own thinking and beliefs and assumptions play a role? This deeper inquiry will help you get at the underlying causes of the problem.

Consider what solutions would address the underlying cause and then play out the implementation of these solutions. Who would be affected? How? What would be the costs and benefits across the system? Would implementation inadvertently cause harm or unintended consequences in the system?

DAY 25: EXAMINING CHANGE HISTORY

Those who do not remember the past are condemned to repeat it.

George Santayana

One factor often overlooked in systemic change efforts is an organization's history of change. Change history refers to how the organization has handled changes in the past and is important for two reasons. First, staff members have recollections of how the organization responded in the past. If change efforts have been successful, the staff will expect new attempts to enjoy success. If the track record shows many failed attempts, then the mindset of the staff will be that the next change will similarly be doomed to failure.

Second, the staff's expectations are likely to be accurate and on target. Success breeds success; past failure suggests future failure unless people believe that something will be different on this occasion.

How do you know what to look for in your organization's change history? Here is a list of questions to ask yourself:

- Did leaders support prior change efforts?
- Were prior change efforts well communicated?
- Did staff become champions for the change?
- Did leaders anticipate and plan for the impact of the changes on staff?
- Did the leaders adequately address the needs of individuals?
- Did the leaders commit the resources necessary to implement the change fully?
- Did the leaders model the behaviors they wanted to see in others as the result of the change?

A typical organization pattern is to initiate a major change but fail to provide support for its full implementation. As a result, a change remains only partially implemented, dies out after 2 or 3 years, or is displaced by some other change.

For example, we often hear from people in our Leadership Academy that lack of full support derails their change efforts. A typical scenario: Leaders and staff within a school adopt a new science or mathematics curriculum, but the supporting structures are never fully provided nor offered over time. Teachers may attend a summer workshop to learn about the new materials, but sustained professional learning isn't forthcoming. Teachers new to the school or grade-changing teachers do not have ongoing opportunities to learn about the curriculum. After a few years, the curriculum is abandoned, and full implementation is never achieved. This pattern can plague any new initiative.

If this has been the pattern in your organization, then staff and stakeholders are likely to be skeptical of the latest effort. Leaders have to overcome the effects of prior failures and the lingering institutional history to ensure current success. There may be skeptics who won't commit until they see whether this attempt is going to be different. As a leader, you must negotiate for the resources you need in order to implement the changes for which you are responsible.

Reflection

What do you know about your organization's change history? If you don't know about it, how can you find out?

If you know the change history, what does it suggest you need to do to make your current change initiative successful? How will you signal to everyone that the unproductive patterns of the past will not dictate your future?

DAY 26: THE DOWNSIDE OF CHANGE

> *In order to make things substantially better, you often have to make things worse in the short run.*
>
> Jeffrey Pfeffer

Hmmm, not good news, you say. But it is true. Sometimes the right action that you need to take will make things worse in the short run. That's why leaders will often avoid taking action, or they pursue an alternative, although ultimately ineffective, course. Who wants to turn things upside down anyway?

But that's the job of a leader: to see emerging problems and take corrective action to avoid a worsening situation. Not doing so is a failure of leadership, according to the Leader to Leader Institute (2005). Many of such instances are what Bazerman and Watkins (2004) call *predictable surprises:* situations that could be forecasted but are not addressed until they occur. Their classic example is, of course, the terrorist attacks of September 11, 2001. Although not all emerging problems are of such catastrophic magnitude, all organizations have their equivalents. Perhaps it's an impending budget shortfall, plummeting test scores in a school, or rapidly decreasing or increasing participation or enrollment.

There are several reasons why leaders don't respond to a mounting crisis. They may be in denial, hoping the problem will dissipate. Correcting the situation now will be costly, and the long-term benefits are unknown. There is a natural human tendency to resist change and maintain the status quo that affects all humans, including leaders. Also, maintaining the status quo will often benefit some group that will usually lobby on its own behalf (Leader to Leader Institute, 2005).

Bazerman and Watkins (2004) suggest three critical steps for heading off predictable surprises: recognition, prioritization, and mobilization. In *recognition*, leaders take steps to recognize an impending problem earlier. They may do so through studying their past crises or developing scenarios of what might happen in the future, including strategies for addressing problems posed by these various scenarios. In *prioritization*, leaders can participate in structured dialogue (see Book Four, Days 12 and 13). An organization may also provide incentives to help leaders reorder their priorities. In *mobilization*, an organization needs to overcome its natural inertia, neutralize opposing factions, and resolve conflicting priorities.

Averting predictable surprises is one of the hardest jobs that a leader has. It requires gathering evidence and rallying people to deal with emerging problems. This is not magical, but it is the hard work of responsible and courageous leaders.

> **Reflection**
>
> Recall at least one example of a predictable surprise that has occurred in your organization. What evidence existed that was ignored? How long was the situation developing? What happened when it became a crisis? What should have been done earlier to avert this crisis?
>
> What crises do you see on your organizational horizon? What is your evidence? What can you do to alert others and take action to avoid another crisis situation?

DAY 27: BUILDING OWNERSHIP FOR CHANGE

> *Organizational effectiveness depends upon the sharing or distribution, not the hoarding, of power and influence.*
>
> James M. Kouzes and Barry Z. Posner

Major changes must involve people at all levels of an organization. If people feel no ownership in the change initiative, they are not likely to support or implement it. As a leader of a major change initiative, how do you help everyone develop ownership for the change and get everyone to share responsibility? One way is to build an ownership culture where everyone is expected to contribute to new initiatives and developments. Leaders support such a culture when they recognize the staff for taking initiative and moving new ideas ahead and when they coach and support colleagues to make the needed changes.

Leaders also can build ownership by helping everyone discover what their self-interest is in making the change. For example, be sure to discuss how the change benefits them or their stakeholders. Help them see how their work can be facilitated or how they can be more productive or successful if they make the change. Discuss how your clients or stakeholders will be better off in some way. Once you've clarified self-interest, here are four steps to enable people to develop responsibility and feel more in control of what is happening to them (Kouzes & Posner, 2012):

1. Make sure that they have a sense of power and influence within the organization.

2. Let them know that they have choices, the latitude, and discretion to effectively carry out their tasks.

3. Provide skills and/or attitude training so that they develop more competence and confidence.

4. Make sure that they take personal responsibility for themselves and their actions.

Reflection

Consider the people involved in your organization's change effort. On a scale of 1 (low) to 10 (high), how much ownership do you think they feel in your initiative? Are there ways you can clarify their self-interest and increase their sense of control, ability to take action, and level of responsibility?

Are you working to build an ownership culture? If so, what has been your experience? What more do you want to do to enhance staff ownership?

DAY 28: INDIVIDUALS AS AGENTS OF CHANGE

I decide. I do. Me.

Frank Hague

What can one person do?

So much of Book Two stresses that change is a collaborative effort. It is highly unlikely that a single individual can carry out a major change initiative alone. Organizations are far too complex for one person to exert that degree of influence.

Does that mean there is nothing an individual person can accomplish? Not at all. As a leader, you can serve as a catalyst for change and in that process, serve as a model for others.

At minimum, here is what you can do:

- Commit to being the best you can and pursue a path to high performance.
- Dedicate yourself to being a continual learner and to see problems as opportunities for learning and change.
- Acknowledge your failures and what you have learned.
- Willingly share your knowledge and resources with others who are interested in what you are doing.
- Organize and convene teams to address problems and suggest improvements.
- Offer to coach others.
- Use evidence and data to inform decisions, and let others know the basis of your decisions.
- Articulate your vision, mission, and goals clearly and concisely.
- Actively support change efforts you believe in.

Essentially, you are exhibiting the attitudes and behaviors that are supportive of systemic change. Moreover, you are taking on a leadership role, even though your position may not be one of institutional leadership. If you do these things in a way that is respectful of your colleagues and the organization as a whole, you will make a difference. In fact, you may be the catalyst for starting a change effort or implementing one.

Reflection

How do you see yourself functioning in your organization? Are you having all the influence that you possibly can? On a scale of 1 (low) to 10 (high), where do you rate yourself on influence? Are there ways you can be more influential?

Of the preceding list, which of the following are you doing now? Which could you do? What would be the likely result?

DAY 29: SELF-ASSESSMENT AS A CHANGE LEADER

Ninety percent of the world's woe comes from people not knowing themselves, their abilities, their frailties, and even their real virtues. Most of us go almost all the way through life as complete strangers to ourselves.

Sydney J. Harris

Leaders increase their credibility and their likelihood for success if they have experienced what they expect others to do. It is very important for leaders of change to go through major change initiatives themselves. They need to experience resistance firsthand and work through it so they can help others do the same. They need to understand and be committed to personal mastery and exhibit behavior congruent with its principles.

As a leader, you convey what you think and feel more by your actions than by your words. Your colleagues judge you more by what you do than by what you say. Therefore, you need to assess your own personal experience base in dealing with change as part of expanding your leadership role.

Reflection

Here is a list of questions for you to consider as part of your expanding ability to lead change in your organization. It is intended to get you started on your self-assessment.

- Think of two or three changes you have experienced—either personal or professional. What was the impact of the changes on you? Was the impact similar for others? If the changes had a differential impact, to what do you attribute that?
- When you are experiencing a change, what needs to remain stable in your life? How much change can you handle? How do you know your limit?
- Have you had the experience of grieving for losses when a change has taken place? If so, how have you done that? What works best for you?
- What is your commitment to high performance? Do you have a vision for your work and personal life? Do you view yourself as a continuous learner? Why or why not? Are you committed to stating the truth about your current reality? Can you recall instances in which you have denied the truth about what was currently happening?

- Think of some of your recent leadership decisions or actions. Can you identify what beliefs were influencing you? What assumptions were you making? Did you share these with others so they understood your decision or action better? Are the underlying assumptions you have the ones you want? What could you do to change beliefs that no longer work for you?
- How do you use data and evidence in your work and life? What are your most reliable sources of information? Are they diverse enough? Can you recall instances in which you ignored data? What were the consequences?
- What is your typical reaction when you discover some problem that you need to address? How might you respond if you regarded a new problem as an opportunity for learning?
- What personal vision do you have for your professional work? How committed are you to this vision? What would make you more committed to it? Is your mission in line with your vision? If not, what do you need to do to make it more so?
- Do you have plans for achieving your vision? What is your plan?
- What is the speed at which you respond to change? How do you assess your speed in relation to the speed of other people? How resilient are you? What would make you more resilient?

Based on your answers to these questions, how comfortable do you feel in leading a major change initiative? What could increase your level of comfort? What kind of experiences are you lacking? How can you get the experience you need?

DAY 30: SUSTAINING INDIVIDUAL LEADERSHIP

> *Leaders are the stewards of organizational energy. . . . They inspire or demoralize others first by how effectively they manage their own energy and next by how well they mobilize, focus, invest, and renew the collective energy of those they lead.*
>
> Jim Loehr and Tony Schwartz

Recall a time when you felt overwhelmed by all of the changes going on in your organization, your personal life, or both. You probably wanted to call a time out, but there was no slowdown in the flow of events and your need to respond to them.

How does a leader keep going without burning out? Michael Fullan (2005) sees the key to sustaining oneself over time as *cyclical energizing*. This term refers to alternating periods of intense engagement with regular breaks and other energy-regaining methods.

We draw energy from four sources: the physical, emotional, mental, and spiritual (Loehr & Schwartz, 2003). (See Day 13, Motivating Others.) We grow when we stretch ourselves in one or more of these dimensions. If we don't push our limits, we're not likely to expand our capabilities in any of these four areas. However, too much stretch can cause fatigue, burnout, and illness.

The secret to individual sustainability is knowing when and how to conserve and create physical energy, emotional energy, mental energy, and spiritual energy when we need to do so. It's also knowing how to relax and recover after periods of intense challenge and exertion.

Loehr and Schwartz (2003) recommend two specific routines for managing energy. One is the incorporation of rituals into our daily lives; the other, a change of venue, especially one that provides solitude. According to the authors, the power of rituals stems from the fact that they conserve energy. Examples could be morning meditation or a 15-minute walk at lunchtime. One of the reasons we know these rituals are energizing is that we tend to feel worse if we don't do them. "The power of rituals is that they insure that we use as little conscious energy as possible where it is not absolutely necessary, leaving us free to strategically focus the energy available to us in creative, enriching ways" (p. 14).

A great source of personal renewal is going to another venue for a period of time. This is especially valuable when there are opportunities for being alone. An extended period of reflection can lead to heightened self-awareness, greater clarity, more creative thinking, and a stronger sense of self.

Reflection

Choose a recent time period, perhaps the past week or month; chart the energy demands that you experienced during that time. How would you assess those demands—were they high, medium, or low? If high, how did you respond? How did you feel at the end of the time period? Were you exhausted, or did you find ways to balance your energy intake and expenditure?

What is your normal pattern of "cyclical energizing"? How balanced is it? What can you do to balance your most intense times with downtimes when you can reenergize?

What are the specific ways that you generate physical, emotional, mental, and spiritual energy? Where are you most effective? Where could you improve your skills?

What rituals do you employ to help you conserve energy? How effective are those? Are you able to escape from the crowd and spend time alone? If so, how and how often?

DAY 31: INITIATING, IMPLEMENTING, AND INSTITUTIONALIZING CHANGE

> *Today's successful . . . leaders will be those who are most flexible of mind. An ability to embrace new ideas, routinely challenge old ones, and live with paradox will be the effective leader's premier trait. Further, the challenge is for a lifetime.*
>
> Tom Peters

How do you know if your organization is ready to embark on a major change initiative and be successful over the long haul? Organizations that are prepared to do so have leaders and staff who use a wide range of behaviors to initiate, support, and sustain changes, including the following:

1. Involve the appropriate stakeholders
2. Think systemically
3. Have a compelling vision that is shared throughout the organization
4. Cultivate a high level of urgency for change
5. Think and act in terms of "both/and" rather than "either/or"
6. Challenge assumptions and beliefs that are getting in the way of success
7. Use evidence to inform decisions
8. Regularly take time for reflection
9. Consciously manage personal energy
10. Empower people at all levels
11. Create structures with minimal hierarchy, fewer layers, and just the essential rules
12. Regularly conduct environmental scans and/or customer surveys to determine changes in external influences that may have an impact on the organization
13. Exhibit a high level of risk taking, courage, and avoidance of blame
14. Identify what remains the same and what changes
15. Clearly define and monitor the key elements that will be implemented as part of the change

16. Value continuous improvement
17. Commit the appropriate level of resources to support the change
18. Promote resiliency in people and the organization
19. Designate benchmarks and recognize their achievement
20. Celebrate successes and reward progress
21. Have a process for orienting new personnel and securing their support
22. Evaluate the outcomes and use results to inform future planning

Organizations today don't have the luxury of being able to reject or accept the opportunity to change. They must change, or they will cease to exist. The only open question is how successful they will be with whatever change initiatives they undertake.

> **Reflection**
>
> How often do you engage in the behaviors on this list? Some single items (Numbers 1, 4, 7, and 17, for example) can instantaneously stall a change initiative if they are not attended to properly.
>
> If your organization is in the midst of a change initiative, how well is it going? What has worked? What needs improvement?
>
> What is the likelihood of your change initiative being sustained? If it's low, what needs to happen to increase its chances? Look over the list of behaviors above, which ones would help you sustain the use of your new practices?
>
> If your organization isn't ready to take on a major change effort but needs to, what can you do to increase the organization's readiness to embrace change?

REFERENCES

Barrett, R. (1999). The power of purpose. *Inner Edge, 2*(4), 20–22.

Barrett, R. (2003). *Training, developing and motivating people.* Cheltenham, UK: Nelson Thomas Ltd.

Bazerman, M. H., & Watkins, M. D. (2004). *Predictable surprises: The disasters you should have seen coming and how to prevent them.* Boston: Harvard Business School Press.

Bershad, C., & Mundry, S. (2000). Playing to learn: Systems change game challenges and teaches. *ENC Focus, 7*(1), 24–27.

Block, P. (1991). *The empowered manager: Positive political skills at work.* San Francisco: Jossey-Bass.

Cini, J. (2004). *Kingmaker: Be the one your company wants to keep—on your terms.* Upper Saddle River, NJ: Prentice Hall.

Conner, D. R. (1993). *Managing at the speed of change: How resilient managers succeed and prosper where others fail.* New York: Villard Books.

Conner, D. R. (1998). *Leading at the edge of chaos.* New York: Wiley.

Covey, S. R. (1992). *Principle-based leadership.* London: Simon & Schuster.

Fixsen, D. L., Naoom, S. F., Blasé, K. A., Friedman, R. M., & Wallace, F. (2005). *Implementation research: A synthesis of the research.* Tampa, FL: National Implementation Research Network.

Fullan, M. (1993). *Change forces: Probing the depths of educational reform.* London: Falmer.

Fullan, M. (2001). *Leading in a culture of change.* San Francisco: Jossey-Bass.

Fullan, M. (2003). *The moral imperative of school leadership.* Thousand Oaks, CA: Corwin.

Fullan, M. (2005). *Leadership and sustainability: System thinkers in action.* Thousand Oaks, CA: Corwin.

Garmston, R. J., & Wellman, B. M. (2009). *The adaptive school: A sourcebook for developing collaborative groups* (2nd ed.). Norwood, MA: Christopher-Gordon.

Hall, G. E., & Hord, S. M. (2011). *Implementing change: Patterns, principles, and potholes* (3rd ed.). Upper Saddle River, NJ: Pearson.

Heifetz, R.A., Grashow, A., & Linsky, M. (2009). *The practice of adaptive leadership.* Boston: Harvard Business School Press.

Heath, C., & Heath, D. (2011). *Switch: How to change things when change is hard.* New York: Random House.

Houle, E., & Cobb, J. (2011). *Shift ed: A call to action for transforming K-12 education.* Thousand Oaks, CA: Corwin.

Kaser, J. S., & Horsley, D. (1998a). *Description of a change inventory process.* Albuquerque, NM: Kaser and Associates.

Kaser, J. S., & Horsley, D. (1998b). *Sources of resistance.* Albuquerque, NM: Kaser and Associates.

Kotter, J. P. (2012). *Leading change.* Boston: Harvard Business School Press.

Kotter, J. P., & Cohen, D.S. (2002). *The heart of change: Real-life stories of how people change their organizations.* Boston: Harvard Business School Publishing.

Kouzes, J. M., & Posner, B. Z. (2012). *The leadership challenge.* San Francisco: Jossey-Bass.

Kübler-Ross, E. (1970). *On death and dying.* New York: Macmillan.

Leader to Leader Institute. (2004, Summer). From the front lines: Practical wisdom: Dealing effectively with disappointment. *Leader to Leader, 33,* 60–61.

Leader to Leader Institute. (2005, Winter). From the front lines: Executive challenges: Tough talk about leadership failure. *Leader to Leader, 35,* 53–54.

Lehman, W. E. K., Greener, J. M., & Simpson, D. D. (2002). Assessing organizational readiness for change. *Journal of Substance Abuse Treatment, 22*(4), 197-209.

Loehr, J., & Schwartz, T. (2003). *The power of full engagement.* New York: Free Press.

Loucks-Horsley, S., & Stiegelbauer, S. (1991). Using knowledge of change to guide staff development. In A. Lieberman & L. Miller (Eds.), *Staff development for education in the '90s: New demands, new realities, new perspectives* (pp. 15–36). New York: Teachers College Press.

Mundry, S., & Bershad, C. (1998). *Systems thinking/systems changing: A simulation game.* Andover, MA: The NETWORK.

Senge, P. M. (1990, 2006). *The fifth discipline.* New York: Doubleday.

Senge, P. M., Kleiner, A., Roberts, C., Ross, R. B., Roth, G., & Smith, B. J. (1999). *The dance of change.* New York: Doubleday.

Simpson, D. D. (2002). A conceptual framework for transferring research to practice. *Journal of Substance Abuse Treatment, 22*(4), 171-182.

Vaill, P. B. (1992). *Managing as a performing art.* New York: Villard Books.

Book 3

Leading Learning Communities

Book Three is a collection of thoughts and ideas on leading professional learning and building learning communities. The leader's role is to carefully design and nurture the conditions that promote learning for all—individuals, teams, and organizations. The 31 contemplations herein provide information to help leaders promote learning for themselves and the individuals with whom they work.

Leading learning communities requires knowledge of current research and best practice on learning communities, the roles of leaders within those communities, how adults learn and under what conditions, and how to create and sustain environments that focus on continuous learning and improvement. In the first 10 contemplations we engage leaders in thinking about several questions: What is a learning community? How do individuals within these communities learn? What constitutes powerful learning? What do we know about how adults learn? How do adults transfer learning from one context to another? Why is developing expertise within a community valuable?

With Day 11 we begin a focus on what we know from research and best practice about the process of designing professional development experiences and programs for adult learners. Some of the questions explored include: How do we design professional development programs that align our beliefs and assumptions with our behaviors and actions? What roles do vision and a commitment to standards play in designing professional development? How can we best use data to assess our needs and guide our learning designs?

We prompt leaders to address questions such as: How do we select learning opportunities for teachers that have an impact on student learning? How do we sustain adult learning programs? What should we consider when expanding programs? How do we know if our anticipated outcomes have been achieved?

The contemplations for Days 30 and 31 ask leaders to explore the ways in which they lead learning by example and what steps they can take to become more effective leaders of learning communities.

The questions in Book Three are grouped around four themes that are interwoven throughout the 31 contemplations:

1. What are the characteristics of learning communities? What are culturally proficient communities? What role do leaders play in developing learning communities?

2. What do we know from research about how people learn? What are the contexts that support effective learning?

3. What is effective professional development? What are the inputs into designing professional development? How do we evaluate program effectiveness?

4. What are the strategies for professional learning? How do we align strategies with outcomes and results?

DAY 1: LEADING COMMUNITIES OF LEARNING

To cope with a changing world, any entity must develop the capacity of shifting and changing—of developing new skills and attitudes; in short, the capability of learning.

Arie De Gues

Communities of learning, professional learning communities, communities of practice, self-renewing organizations, learning organizations—what do these phrases convey about organizations and the people within them?

Clearly, *learning* is at the core of each one. The implication is that not only do the individuals within organizations have opportunities to learn, but also that the organizations learn. For example, given that we live in a world where new knowledge is continuously discovered and one that is constantly changing, it follows that organizations, and the people within them, cannot remain static. In order to adapt and evolve, organizations need structures and processes for obtaining, sharing, and learning from the information that most directly impacts them and their clients. As Michael Fullan (2001) writes, "Leaders commit themselves to constantly generating and increasing knowledge inside and outside the organization" (p. 6) and "make knowledge building a core value" (p. 90). To support and enact their commitments they initiate and sustain ways in which to engage people in generating and sharing knowledge (see Book One, Day 10).

With knowledge and learning at the core of an organization's values, there is a parallel need for collegial and collaborative processes to enable people to engage in learning together and to share what they have learned from external sources. Nowhere is this more critical than in schools. In writing about "professional learning communities" (PLCs), Richard DuFour and others (DuFour, DuFour, Eaker, & Karhanek, 2004) state that there are six key characteristics that distinguish a school organized in PLCs from more traditional schools. In combination, these six characteristics can provide the organizational values and structures for becoming a learning community:

1. Shared mission, vision, values, and goals
2. Collaborative teams
3. Collective inquiry
4. Action orientation and experimentation
5. Continuous improvement
6. Results orientation

The way to create an environment for individual and organizational learning, according to Lindsey, Roberts, & CampbellJones (2005), is through face-to-face relationships among people in the organization. These relationships influence individual learning, which leads to change, and creates the organizational knowledge that can transform the organization.

Reflection

Recall a situation where you were encouraged to learn continuously and the organization valued new knowledge as a source of information for adapting and changing. How did the organization manifest its commitment? How did you and your colleagues feel? What difference did this make in the organization? In what ways did the organization change as a result of new information or knowledge? What characteristics of a community of learners did this organization have?

What about the organization you are part of now? To what extent do your colleagues see learning as a value and an explicit goal of the organization? What can you do to promote a community of learning and knowledge generation and sharing? Do you personally value, model, and contribute to a community of learners?

DAY 2: LEADING LEARNING IN ORGANIZATIONS

Experience is not what happens to you; it's what you do with what happens to you.

Aldous Huxley

Leaders of learning organizations apply knowledge on how people learn to establish structures and processes within their organizations. That knowledge is drawn from research and best practice (Bransford, Brown, & Cocking, 1999, 2000; Donovan & Bransford, 2005; Owen, Cox, & Watkins, 1994) and is reflected in Owen et al.'s 12 principles of knowledge acquisition:

1. People are born learners. Notice the natural curiosity of children. All humans are born with an intrinsic motivation to learn.

2. People seek to understand new information and experiences by connecting them to what they already know. New knowledge must be connected to prior knowledge for effective learning to occur.

3. People learn in different ways. Research has documented the fact that people have inclinations toward learning through particular styles or approaches.

4. Thinking about one's own thinking improves performance and the ability to work independently. The ability to stand back and observe one's own thought process is an important skill of effective learners.

5. An individual's stage of intellectual, social, and emotional development affects how he or she learns.

6. Although people may naturally make connections as they learn, they often need help to transfer knowledge or apply it in different contexts. Unconnected knowledge is rarely retained.

7. Having a repertoire of strategies enhances learning. Learning is essentially a process of problem solving. The greater the variety of strategies for achieving a goal that a learner has, the more successful he or she is likely to be.

8. Certain predispositions, attitudes, and habits of mind facilitate learning. Qualities such as flexibility, open-mindedness, reflection, and empathy promote learning. Rigidity, bias, tunnel vision, and impulsiveness are barriers to learning.

9. Working with people who have different learning styles and perspectives enhances learning. Working in a diverse group can stimulate members to engage in higher-order cognitive skills.

10. Those who do the work do the learning. Effective learners create knowledge for themselves, own it, know why they learned it, and how they learned it.

11. A resource-rich environment facilitates learning. For learners to actively construct knowledge, they need access to a wide variety of materials. These include ideas, books, visual and auditory media, technology, artifacts, and opportunities to interact.

12. Developing shared understandings about what constitutes quality work fosters learning. Effective learners integrate their internal goals with external expectations (Owen et al., 1994, pp. 16–29).

Reflection

Reread each of the 12 principles. As you do so, think of an implementation strategy that exists in your organization for each. For example, a strategy for Number 9 (working with people who have different learning styles) could be having groups follow the norms of collaboration (see Book Four). Which principles are reflected in your organization? Which are not being honored? What can you do to make sure all of these principles are an integral part of your organization's culture?

DAY 3: BUILDING CULTURAL PROFICIENCY

In the end, we will remember not the words of our enemies, but the silence of our friends.

Martin Luther King Jr.

As leaders, we have a moral responsibility to increase our own and our learning community's cultural proficiency by engaging others in conversations about equity, diversity, and culture.

We work within multicultural organizations and schools; and as facilitators and leaders of communities of learners, we often face the challenge of engaging our colleagues in dialogue about race, diversity, and culture. People may fail to see the diversity that exists among the different people they work with or how it is going to increase as our population diversifies. Or they may mistakenly believe that being blind to color, race, gender, or disability is desirable.

What is *cultural proficiency*? According to Lindsey, Robins, and Terrell (2003), "Cultural proficiency is a way of being that enables both individuals and organizations to respond effectively to people who differ from them" (p. 5). Lindsey and his colleagues (Lindsey, Robins, & Terrell, 2003; Lindsey, Roberts, & CampbellJones, 2005) describe a continuum that reflects individuals' and organizations' "healthy and destructive" behaviors, including:

- *Cultural destructiveness:* The elimination of other people's cultures by negating, disparaging, or purging cultures that are different from your own. "See the difference, stomp it out."
- *Cultural incapacity:* Believing in the superiority of one's culture and cultural values and engaging in behaviors that disempower or suppress cultures that are different from your own. "See the difference, make it wrong."
- *Cultural blindness:* Acting as if the cultural differences you see do not matter or do not exist, or not recognizing that there are differences among and between cultures. "See the difference, act like you don't."
- *Cultural precompetence:* Recognizing that the lack of knowledge, experience, and understanding of other cultures limits your ability to effectively interact with them. "See the difference, respond inadequately."
- *Cultural competence:* Interacting with other cultural groups in ways that recognize and value their differences, motivate you to assess your own skills, expand your knowledge and resources, and, ultimately, cause you to adapt your relational behavior. "See the difference, understand the difference that *difference* makes."
- *Cultural proficiency:* Honoring the differences among cultures, seeing diversity as a benefit, interacting knowledgeably and respectfully among a variety of cultural groups, and knowing how to learn about individual and organizational culture. "See the differences, respond positively and affirmingly."

Reflection

Think about each level of the cultural proficiency continuum. Where do you believe that you personally lie on the continuum? What behaviors do you engage in that support your perception? Where do you believe the people in your organization or school lie on the continuum? What collective behaviors or practices do people in the organization engage in that support your perception?

> Think about a recent experience in which another person's values reflected cultural destructiveness, incapacity, or blindness. How did you respond? Does your awareness of the continuum change the way you might respond to this person in the future? As a leader, what responsibility do you believe you have to confront and challenge others' destructive behaviors concerning cultures different than their own?

DAY 4: POWERFUL LEARNING EXPERIENCES

Epiphany—any sudden and important manifestation or realization.

Oxford English Dictionary

Whether we call it an "aha!" experience or the moment when "the light goes on," we have all had powerful learning experiences. These experiences often occur when we connect new information to something we already know and understand, and it takes us farther in our thinking.

An analysis of our "light bulb" experiences can give us insight into how we learn best, what learning is most important to us, and the circumstances in which the learning occurs (Owen et al., 1994). Let's see whether this is the case for you.

Reflection

> Think about a learning experience in your life that had a powerful impact. It could have been an event from your formal schooling or any aspect of your life. It could be something that happened recently or a long time ago. You may recall it as being either pleasant or unpleasant.
>
> First, recreate this experience in your mind. Imagine being in the situation again. What happened? What did you do? What were you feeling? What did others do? What was the impact? Did the influence of this experience occur immediately or later?
>
> After you have a clear picture of the event, write a brief description of it.
>
> Now, answer the following questions about your powerful learning experience:
>
> - Where did your experience occur?
> - What were the characteristics of the learning? Think in terms of the connections, the conditions, the environment, and the resources available.

- Was there a teacher of some sort present? If so, what role did this person play? What role did you play in this experience?
- If your experience was positive, what would be necessary for it to be duplicated either within or outside of formal schooling?
- If your experience was negative, is this something that should be avoided? If so, what would be necessary to make sure that others did not have this same experience?

Relate your awareness of what makes learning powerful to efforts that you are currently implementing within your organization. How can you strengthen learning experiences for your colleagues or clients? How can you communicate high expectations and provide needed support? As a leader, how can you make sure that others have the most powerful learning experiences?

DAY 5: HOW PEOPLE LEARN

Learning is not attained by chance, it must be sought for with ardor and attended to with diligence.

Abigail Adams

Knowledge of how people learn is a critical input into the design and implementation of adult learning experiences. Think for a moment about how you learn new information. What do you know about how others learn?

Summaries of research on cognition (Bransford et al., 2000; Donovan & Bransford, 2005) have helped to explain more about how people learn. This knowledge can be instrumental in designing both student and adult learning opportunities and includes the concepts that:

- New knowledge is built on the learner's prior knowledge.
- Learning is an active process.
- Knowledge is constructed through a process of change.
- New knowledge comes from experiences and interaction with ideas and phenomena.
- Learning needs to be situated in meaningful and relevant contexts.
- Learning is supported through interaction among learners about the concepts and ideas of the new knowledge.

Opportunities for learning that embody the research on cognition pay attention to creating four types of learning environments (Bransford et al., 2000; Donovan & Bransford, 2005):

1. *Learner-centered environments* encourage attention to preconceptions and initiate learning based on what people currently think and know.

2. *Knowledge-centered environments* focus on what is to be learned, why it is important to learn it, and what mastery of the knowledge looks like.

3. *Assessment-centered environments* emphasize frequent and ongoing assessment of what the learner knows and thinks in order to guide and inform instructional next steps.

4. *Community-centered environments* respect the social nature of learning and foster a culture of questioning, respect, risk taking, and interactive engagement.

Reflection

Think about your own educational organizations and ask yourself the following questions:

- To what extent do the adult and student learning activities you are involved in reflect the research on how people learn? In what ways do you create the four environments for learning? What areas need more emphasis?
- In what ways do you as a leader promote and provide opportunities that value the ways that people learn?
- As a leader, what could you do to enhance your colleagues' awareness of the research on how people learn and the environments that support that learning?

DAY 6: TRANSFORMATIVE LEARNING

We cannot solve problems with the same thinking that created them.

Albert Einstein

What implications does the knowledge base on how people learn have for the ways in which leaders design and implement adult learning experiences?

One implication is that adult learning experiences must transform current thinking and practices rather than simply adding new skills and ideas on top of the old. In *additive learning*, the goal is to acquire new skills and incorporate them into an existing repertoire. The goal of *transformative learning* is to change deeply held beliefs, knowledge, and habits of practice. Additive learning alone will not suffice when new ways of thinking about something are also needed (Thompson & Zeuli, 1999).

Thompson and Zeuli (1999) describe five distinguishing characteristics of transformative learning:

1. It creates cognitive dissonance, a disruption in someone's thinking, causing him or her to struggle to make sense of something that doesn't fit with their current ideas.

2. It provides time, contexts, and support for adults to resolve this dissonance by engaging over time with facilitators who have had experience in coaching and mentoring.

3. It ensures that the dissonance-creating and dissonance-resolving activities are relevant to the participant.

4. It provides a means for adults to develop new practices that are congruent with the new ideas they are constructing.

5. It ensures adults of continuing help in the cycle of surfacing the new issues and problems they will encounter, gaining new understandings from these experiences, translating new understandings from them, and recycling through the process.

In education, cognitive dissonance can occur when teachers engage with student thinking and assess how well their current methods address the students' learning. Teachers are likely to discover that using the same old approaches to teach more challenging content just is not effective. They see the need to rethink what they do and how they interact with students. These experiences produce discomfort with current practice and the need to adapt to create better outcomes.

Both additive and transformative adult learning experiences may be necessary. Additive learning is appropriate for developing new skills. However, learners must understand the assumptions and beliefs that guide the skill, or they may learn the skill well but lack the understanding of why they are using it. Transformative learning focuses more on making shifts in assumptions and beliefs and helping learners understand why a new approach might be necessary. The emphasis of education today is moving toward integrating both transformative and additive learning.

> **Reflection**
>
> Think of a learning experience that created cognitive dissonance for you. What were you thinking and feeling? How did you resolve the dissonance? We often resolve dissonance by rejecting the new idea and holding fast to our prior beliefs. Without challenge and support to get to the other side of the dissonance, learning will not occur.
>
> Think about the adult learning that has transpired in your organization. Would you describe it as more additive or transformative, or as both? Give some examples to support your answer. If you think that your organization needs adult learning experiences that are more transformative, what can you as a leader do to help make that happen? If you think both additive and transformative learning are needed, how might you integrate them?

DAY 7: TRANSFERRING SITUATIONAL LEARNING

Successful knowledge transfer involves neither computers nor documents, but rather interactions between people. If you want me to absorb your knowledge, then spend time with me, work with me, do my job, and let me do yours.

Thomas H. Davenport

Ideally, the learning experiences we engage in apply to real-life situations and help us to be productive workers, responsible citizens, competent parents, and to have rewarding relationships. However, even if we are provided with transformative learning opportunities, not all our learning experiences ensure that we will successfully transfer the knowledge to new situations or contexts.

What promotes knowledge transfer? What impedes it? Bransford et al. (2000) reported the following:

- Knowledge and skills must be beyond the narrow context in which they are first learned. As an example, knowing how to solve a mathematics problem in school doesn't automatically mean that one can solve similar problems in real life.
- Learners must understand when it is appropriate to apply what they have learned. The conditions of applicability must be made

clear; it cannot be assumed that the learner will necessarily see the connection.
- To be widely applicable or transferable, learning must be based on generalized principles. For example, what is learned by rote memory can rarely be transferred. On the other hand, understanding general principles, which can be applied to a variety of situations, promotes transfer.
- Transfer is more likely to occur if learners have conceptual rather than just factual knowledge. For example, conceptual knowledge includes an understanding of part-whole relationships and similarities and differences.
- Individuals who see themselves as both learners and thinkers are better at transfer. They are better able to monitor their own level of understanding and its application.
- Learners need to have sufficient time on task to adequately process information. Learning can't be rushed if the ability to transfer is to develop.
- Prior experiences can help or hinder new learning and, as a result, transfer. Some "unlearning" of misconceptions may have to take place or adjustments made to accommodate new knowledge.

Reflection

Recall one or two adult learning experiences that you have designed or facilitated. To what extent did they result in the ability to transfer learning into other contexts and real-world examples? What was designed into them to ensure that such transfer would occur? What evidence do you have that transfer took place?

DAY 8: DEFINING EXPERTISE

> *I wish we could understand the word expert as expressing an attitude of mind which we can all acquire rather than the collecting of information by a special caste.*
>
> Mary Parker Follett

Learning communities not only value continuous learning, but also the development and nurturing of expertise within the system. Effective leaders have expertise, and truly collaborative communities have experts at all levels of the system. In fact, a goal within learning communities, especially schools, should be to develop expertise among all members (Stiles & Mundry, 2002).

What is an *expert*? Why is it important to develop everyone's expertise? Is *expert* a general term used to describe someone who knows a lot about a specific subject? Exactly what makes someone an expert? Is there a line that one crosses to move into expertise?

Interestingly, recent research has revealed clear distinctions between novices and experts. Expertise is not just the possession of general abilities, such as memory or intelligence, nor is it the use of general strategies. Instead, experts have extensive knowledge that affects their perceptions and how they process information. This affects what they remember, how they reason, and how they solve problems—all very important attributes of leaders and of every member within a learning community.

Recent research shows that experts:

- Notice features and meaningful patterns of information that novices don't detect.
- Have acquired a great deal of content knowledge that is highly organized. Their organization of information reflects a deep understanding of the subject matter.
- Have knowledge that cannot be reduced to sets of isolated facts or propositions, but instead, reflects contexts of applicability.
- Are able to retrieve important aspects of their knowledge with little effort.
- Are not always able to instruct others about the topic although they may know their disciplines thoroughly.
- Have varying levels of flexibility in their approaches to new situations. (Bransford et al., 1999, p. xiii)

All learners—both students and teachers—can profit from practice with identifying patterns, understanding problems in terms of underlying concepts or big ideas, using models of how experts approach and solve problems, recognizing relevant versus irrelevant information, determining conditions under which information is important, and being able to retrieve the right information with ease. Teachers who develop these skills as experts also consciously incorporate learning experiences for their students that provide opportunities to develop students as experts.

School-based adult learning programs need to more frequently embed what we know about developing experts into their programs. As Learning Forward's *Standards for Professional Development* (2011) states:

> Effective designs for professional learning assist educators in moving beyond comprehension of the surface features of a new idea or practice to developing a more complete understanding of

its purposes, critical attributes, meaning, and connections to other approaches. To increase student learning, educator learning provides many opportunities for educators to practice new learning with ongoing assessment, feedback, and coaching so the learning becomes fully integrated into routine behaviors. (pp. 41–42)

Reflection

Do you consider yourself an expert in one or more areas? If so, to what extent do these research findings apply to you? Do you see yourself as needing additional knowledge and/or skills to become an expert? If you want to grow in your expertise, what steps can you take?

Does your organization or school recognize the value of experts and encourage the development of expertise? As a leader, what can you do to help others develop expertise?

DAY 9: CHARACTERISTICS OF EFFECTIVE PROFESSIONAL LEARNING

In most schools, a large gap exists between what is known about professional learning that affects teaching and improves student achievement and the professional development that teachers and principals regularly experience. The solution to [this] problem, I believe, is high-quality, school-based professional learning and collaborative work that affects all teachers virtually every day.

Dennis Sparks

What did professional learning in education used to look like? How is it changing?

Historically, in the field of education, most adult learning was provided through in-service workshops. Rarely did teachers have a voice in the types of learning opportunities that would best meet their emerging needs. Too often, these workshops did little to help teachers connect new learning with their own teaching practices or provide follow-up experiences to deepen and extend learning and practice.

Today, professional learning in schools has moved in a different direction. Due to the emphasis on continuous improvement and developing schools that are communities of learning and practice, teachers and other educators have opportunities to plan, lead, and engage in learning experiences that are more directly related to their needs and those of their students. This new emphasis on practice-based professional learning has several distinguishing characteristics, including:

- Directly relating the learning opportunities to the school's goals, students' learning needs, and the teachers' needs in meeting those goals
- Supporting teachers in making explicit connections between what they do and what their students learn
- Building a learning community in which all take responsibility for learning and working collegially to share knowledge, insight, and experience
- Empowering teachers to design, conduct, and follow through on their own learning, with multiple learning experiences provided over time and with greater depth
- Promoting practice, reflection, and refinement in a safe environment in which teachers can take risks and explore new practices
- Requiring accountability for learning and outcomes
- Continuously monitoring and evaluating the successes and challenges within the context
- Is driven by an image of effective classroom learning and teaching
- Is designed to address student learning needs identified through data analysis
- Provides opportunities for teachers to build their content and pedagogical content knowledge and critically examine practice
- Is research based and engages teachers in learning approaches they will use with their students
- Provides opportunities for teachers to collaborate with colleagues and other experts
- Supports teachers to serve in leadership roles
- Provides links to other parts of the educational system
- Is continuously evaluated and improved

Reflection

Reflect on the types of professional learning experiences most organizations offered just 10 or so years ago. Write a list of about a dozen words that describe those experiences. Then, generate a list of about a dozen words that describe your more recent learning opportunities. What differences do you see? What accounts for these differences? If you don't see changes, why not? In what ways are new technologies changing our learning experiences? What new changes do you foresee?

> In what ways does your current professional learning reflect what is known about effective professional development? Which principles are reflected in your experiences? Which ones are missing? In what ways would you like to enhance your professional learning programs?

DAY 10: ALIGNING BELIEFS AND BEHAVIORS

The thing always happens that you really believe in, and the belief in a thing makes it happen.

Frank Lloyd Wright

Alignment is one of the key words used in educational change. For example, we talk about curriculum and professional development being aligned with standards. Likewise, we encourage organizations to align structures with their visions and missions.

Another area of alignment is ensuring the congruency between what we believe and how we behave. It means identifying our underlying assumptions and determining whether our behavior is consistent with our beliefs. For example, if leaders believe that the ideas reflected in the preceding days' contemplations are critical for professional learning, do they act upon those beliefs? When you examine what is going on in schools today, several inconsistencies may stand out (see Table 3.1).

These inconsistencies may have several different causes:

- Organizations lack norms and structures for examining their own practices and planning for improvement.
- Staff do not reflect on whether espoused beliefs match day to day behaviors and decisions.
- Leaders do not see the lack of alignment as a problem that needs to be addressed.
- Changes in organizational culture normally lag behind other types of institutional changes; adopting a new curriculum is much easier than getting everyone to become proficient in teaching it.
- Existing resources are insufficient to support desired changes.

> **Reflection**
>
> Examining individual and organizational beliefs and behavior is a critical first step for ensuring that we provide effective and powerful professional learning opportunities. Think about your own organization. Generate a

list of "what we say" beliefs and then the corresponding "what we do" actions. What incongruities exist in your own context? What other incongruities not listed in Table 3.1 can you identify? What are the causes for these discrepancies? How can you engage your colleagues in looking for and surfacing misalignments and inconsistencies?

Table 3.1 Examples of Misalignment

What We Say	What We Do
Teacher learning is the centerpiece of effective change.	Provide a few hours of in-service each year.
Students should be independent, self-directed learners.	Give teachers little say regarding the content or process of their own professional development.
Teaching is a complex process of decision making requiring a wide range of instructional strategies to meet individual learner needs.	Limit the instructional strategies teachers experience in professional development to courses and workshops.
Every child, every teacher, and every organization is in some ways unique, and programs need to be tailored to meet individual needs.	Reduce professional development to "one size fits all."
Change is long term.	Direct professional development resources to "one-shot" workshops without follow-up support.
Change is system wide.	Work with volunteers, the early adopters, which produces pockets of change rather than system-wide change.

DAY 11: DESIGNING PROFESSIONAL DEVELOPMENT

A bridge, like professional development, is a critical link between where one is and where one wants to be. A bridge that works in one place almost never works in another. Each bridge requires careful design that considers its purpose, who will use it, the conditions that exist at its anchor points . . . and the resources required to construct it. Similarly, each professional development program . . . requires a careful and unique design.

Susan Loucks-Horsley

The key ideas raised in many of the previous contemplations reinforce the need for leaders to design and implement professional learning experiences that build on beliefs, assumptions, and knowledge. However, knowing what we believe and acting in accordance with those beliefs is not the only important step. Leaders also need to thoroughly understand their context, the learning needs and goals of the people within that context, the issues that may be critical for success, and how to evaluate whether specific outcomes have been achieved.

As the quotation above points out, each context is different. There is no one right way to approach the design and implementation of professional development; each bridge is unique. There are, however, frameworks for designing learning experiences based on what we know to be effective.

Leaders of learning are often in the position of designing, or suggesting that others design, professional learning activities for individuals or groups. Effective professional development addresses a number of important and fairly specific issues or factors. It isn't cobbled together; it isn't cookie cutter; it isn't the innovation du jour. It is consciously and deliberately designed.

Figure 3.1 presents one framework for designing professional development for both individual and group learning (Loucks-Horsley et al., 2010).

Figure 3.1 Professional Development Design Framework

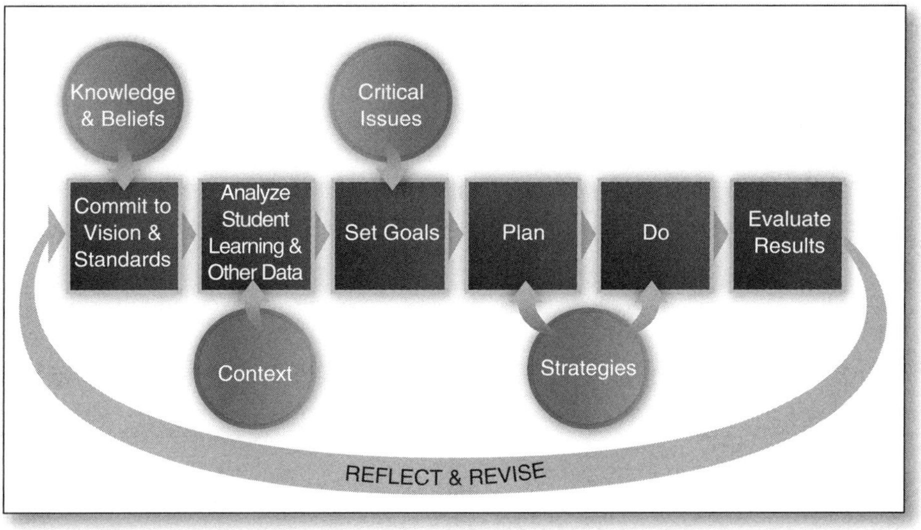

SOURCE: Loucks-Horsley, Stiles, Mundry, Love and Hewson, Copyright 2010. *Designing Professional Development for Teachers of Science and Mathematics, third edition* (p. 18). Thousand Oaks, CA: Corwin. Reprinted with permission.

The framework includes several components and processes, including:

- A commitment to vision and the standards.
- An analysis of student learning needs and other school-wide data.
- A set of clearly defined goals and intended outcomes.
- A plan that includes a combination of professional development strategies aligned with the goals and outcomes.
- An articulated and sequential design for taking action.
- A process for gathering data, reflecting on learning, evaluating effectiveness, and making adjustments based on that information.

Reflection

Think about a professional development program that you have been a part of and answer the following questions:

- What was the vision that drove the need for and design of the program?
- What student learning or adult learning needs were identified prior to the design of the program?
- What were the goals and desired outcomes?
- In what ways were the strategies aligned to meet those goals and outcomes?
- How did you know if the goals and outcomes had been met?
- What changes in the program did you make based on continuous learning and evaluation?

DAY 12: COMMITTING TO VISION AND STANDARDS

Zip codes might be great for sorting mail, but they should not determine the quality of a child's education or success in the future workforce. With common standards and assessments, students, parents, and teachers will have a clear, consistent understanding of the skills necessary for students to succeed after high school and compete with peers across the state line and across the ocean.

Former Gov. Bob Wise, West Virginia

What is your school's or organization's vision? To what extent is that vision an extension of the standards that guide your work?

In education, educators rely on standards to guide almost every aspect of schooling, from adopting curriculum and selecting instructional materials to guiding best practice in the classroom. These documents serve as both a banner for reform and a template for guiding decisions about policies and practices (*Common Core State Standards*, 2010; *A Framework for K-12 Science Education*, 2012; *Next Generation Science Standards*, 2013). In addition, the professional development standards (Learning Forward, 2011) articulate a vision of what we need to know and do in professional development to provide all educators with high quality and effective adult learning experiences.

Included in the standards are images of the college and career ready students of the future who will be critical thinkers and doers able to use practices of analysis, evidence based decision making, and other skills essential for life in the 21st century. Contemplations that appear in Books One and Two describe the importance of leaders developing, building, and sustaining vision. In designing professional development, leaders need to facilitate dialogue among teachers, administrators, parents, students, community members, and other stakeholders to ensure a common vision of who and what the school wants to become. To have coherent professional learning programs, your professional development design should be firmly grounded in the vision your community creates.

Reflection

What is your vision for teaching and learning and for your organization? How was that vision developed? What do teachers need to know and be able to do to create learning experiences that align with this vision?

As a leader, what role have you played in developing this common vision? To what extent is that vision based on educational standards?

DAY 13: USING DATA TO GUIDE PROFESSIONAL DEVELOPMENT DESIGNS

> *In a rush to "do" something, schools may latch onto popular or simplistic solutions to resolve complex problems. Data help school staff dig deeper, consider the local context, and more fully understand a problem before jumping into action.*
>
> Nancy Love

How close is your current reality to your vision? How do you know?

Gathering and analyzing school or district-wide data can provide you with the information necessary to determine where you are in relationship to the vision you have developed. Leaders can then guide the development of an effective program that ensures they are addressing the critical areas most in need of improvement.

Today's schools and districts are inundated with data and are constantly given the message that data-driven decision making is essential for meeting accountability standards. Often, the data that schools have access to are not the most relevant for understanding individual student's and teacher's knowledge or skills (see Book Five, Day 8). It is exactly this type of data that is needed to guide the design of a professional development program that meets all learners' needs.

The data that are most relevant for informing professional development programs consist of:

- Demographic data about students and teachers.
- Multiple measures of students' achievement of standards.
- Student learning data disaggregated by race and ethnicity, economic status, English language learners, students with special needs, and gender.
- Data about classroom practice and students' opportunity to learn.
- Data about results of past professional development, the school culture, and leadership (Loucks-Horsley et al., 2010, p. 34).

Reflection

Think about the data you have access to and the ways in which you use those data to guide school-wide improvement efforts. In what ways do you use data to determine existing student learning needs? How have you used data to identify what teachers need to know and be able to do in order to meet student learning needs? To what extent is examining data a regular, school-wide, and collaborative effort? What data do you not have that would better inform your design for school wide improvement? How could you obtain such data?

DAY 14: INPUTS INTO PROFESSIONAL DEVELOPMENT DESIGN

Many locally developed programs have been enormously successful in improving student achievement. However, successful replication across sites suggests that a program's accomplishments are less dependent on the characteristics of an individual school and more related to the design of the staff development effort.

Joellen Killion

Designers of adult learning opportunities must consider four important inputs into the design process (see Day 11, Figure 3.1).

1. *Knowledge and beliefs:* The design must reflect the knowledge base on learning, teaching, the nature of the subject matter, professional development, the change process, and the fundamental beliefs that will guide you.

2. *Context:* The design must suit the context in which the learning will take place and the teaching will occur. The context includes learners, teachers, practices (for example, curriculum, instruction, and assessment), the learning environment, organizational culture, leadership, policies, available resources, and stakeholders, such as families and community members.

3. *Critical issues:* The design must take into account those elements that will affect—either positively or negatively—the success of the overall program. These elements include building capacity for sustainability, making time for professional development, developing leadership, ensuring equity, building professional culture, garnering public support, and scaling up.

4. *Strategies:* The design must reflect the different approaches to learning that are most appropriate given the purposes and context. Examples include strategies within four clusters: immersion in content, standards, and research; examining teaching and learning; aligning and implementing curriculum; and the structures for professional development (Loucks-Horsley et al., 2010).

Reflection

Think about a professional development program that you have been a part of and answer the following questions:

- What assumptions did the learning program make about the nature of teaching, learning, the content, and the change process? How were they guided by research?
- Did the learning program take the context of the school or district into account? If so, how?
- What strategies of teaching and learning did the program employ? Were they the right ones for the situation? Would you have chosen different strategies? If so, describe what and why.
- How successful was the learning program? How do you know? Were there any critical issues that the program did or didn't address that affected the outcome?

DAY 15: KNOWLEDGE AND BELIEFS IN SCIENCE AND MATHEMATICS

The opinion prevailed among advanced minds that it was time that belief should be replaced increasingly by knowledge; belief that did not itself rest on knowledge was superstition, and as such had to be opposed.

Albert Einstein

Effective professional learning draws upon the credible knowledge and beliefs of the discipline or content area the learning is addressing. In the education field there is a rich body of knowledge that should inform the design and conduct of professional development.

Knowledge refers to information that is supported by and grounded in research. *Beliefs* are what we think we know (Ball, 1996) based on current information. Beliefs also inform our perspective on and interpretation of new knowledge—beliefs serve as our personal filters for how we deal with new knowledge.

According to Loucks-Horsley and colleagues (2010), five distinct, but related, knowledge bases inform the work of professional developers and include what we know about:

1. Learners and learning.
2. Teachers and teaching.
3. The nature of science and mathematics.
4. Adult learning and professional development.
5. The change process.

Nature of the Disciplines

Every discipline or content area has its own set of standards or frameworks. The discipline of science is dynamic and produces new knowledge that either expands upon existing knowledge or, in some cases, negates prior understanding. The practices of inquiry, modeling, and argument based on evidence are examples of the nature of this discipline. In the world of mathematics, mathematicians, engineers, and others actively engage in problem solving and practice mathematics.

Likewise, adult learning experiences in science and mathematics education should be designed to reflect the essential characteristics or nature of the disciplines. Teachers learning how to teach science need to engage in science investigations and use the science and engineering practices recommended in the *Framework for the Next Generation Science Education Standards* (NRC, 2012) as they learn. In turn they need to create the same kind of learning experiences for their students that reflect the true nature of the discipline of science. If science teachers do not believe that students learn through active exploration and engagement, then you have valuable information to guide where you might initiate adult learning, such as with an in-depth examination of research on student learning or of video images of classroom practice.

On the other hand, your teachers may be curious about the research that reports that students are most likely to learn—regardless of the type of instruction—if they are encouraged to think about ideas; if the ideas are aligned to specific learning goals; and if the ideas are related to real-life experiences (Banilower, Cohen, Paisley, & Weiss, 2010). If so, you may start with short demonstration lessons or videos of different modes of instruction that meet the criteria cited in the research. Knowing the existing knowledge base and beliefs of the teachers and other adults in the program guides the design and sequence of the learning experiences.

> **Reflection**
>
> As a leader, what do you currently know and believe about the teaching and learning of science and mathematics? What about teachers of these disciplines? What do they know and believe? In what ways can you use existing knowledge and beliefs to design adult learning experiences? How can you more effectively embed the knowledge base into your professional development designs?

DAY 16: PROFESSIONAL DEVELOPMENT IN CONTEXT

> *We are learning that professional development that increases teacher knowledge is more likely to occur when such development . . . respects local knowledge (i.e., problems and practices that attend to the particulars of a context).*
>
> Ann Lieberman and Lynne Miller

When it comes to professional development programs, "off the shelf" and "one size fits all" simply do not work for everyone. And there is a reason why these programs don't work. It is called *context*. Professional learning programs and policies are best when they are designed based on a thorough understanding of the context on the ground where they will be used.

Here are the major factors that constitute context that need to be considered:

- *Students and their learning needs:* Who are our students? What are their cultural backgrounds? What standards are in place for student learning? How are students performing in relation to the standards? What achievement gaps exist? Given these student factors, what needs to be addressed in our professional learning goals?

- *Teachers and their learning needs:* Who are our teachers? What are their cultural backgrounds? What are their prior learning experiences? How well prepared are they to teach challenging and rigorous content? What goals do they have for their own learning? What are their beliefs and perceptions of teaching and learning? How are new teachers inducted and supported? Given our teachers' backgrounds and needs, what priorities should we address in our professional learning goals?

- *Curriculum, instruction, assessment practices, and the learning environment:* To what extent are the written, taught, and assessed curricula aligned? How are content standards reflected in the curriculum? To what extent do teachers use multiple assessment strategies? To what extent do all students have equitable opportunities to learn? Are learning environments respectful of students and their diversity? What work might be needed on our curriculum, instruction, and assessment practice; and how is this reflected in our professional learning goals?

- *Organizational culture and professional learning communities:* Do teachers meet and work together to solve problems? Are all school staff members focused on student learning? Do teachers collaborate and value each other as sources of expertise? Does the school embody and value the concept of a community of learners? Given our professional climate, what changes might be needed to support professional learning to occur?

- *Leadership:* Do teachers and other school staff have opportunities to develop their own leadership skills and abilities? How do the actions of leaders at the building and district level support professional development? How knowledgeable are leaders regarding teachers' learning needs? Do they understand the relationships among actions of leaders, school improvement, and student achievement? How dedicated are they to supporting professional learning?

- *National, state, and local policies:* What policies impact professional development? How strong is the link between the educator evaluation system and professional learning? What accountability systems are in place? How do policies impede or support collegial learning?

- *Available resources:* What time do teachers have available for professional development and collegial work? Does professional development happen mostly during the school day? What is the allocation of funding for professional development? What internal and external resources do teachers have access to? What community supports are available? What instructional materials, equipment, or supplies are available for professional development?

- *Families and communities:* What are families' and the community's interests and concerns about teaching and learning? To what extent do they support the school's vision of teaching and learning and adult learning? How effective are the policies for involving them in the school's functioning, management, and professional learning? How well prepared are teachers and leaders to communicate with all community members? (Loucks-Horsley et al., 2010, pp. 79–116)

> **Reflection**
>
> Think of a professional development program in your school or district that worked well and one that didn't. What role did context play in the success or failure of the programs?
>
> Think of a program that is in the planning stage. To what extent are factors in your context being taken into account? What can you as a leader do to ensure that the program being designed addresses the real needs and works within the constraints of your context?

DAY 17: CRITICAL ISSUES TO CONSIDER

Ignore the critical issues at your own peril.

Susan Loucks-Horsley

The critical issues are the "tough nuts to crack" in designing professional development; they defy easy solutions. However, leaders and professional developers can be one step ahead simply by knowing to anticipate that these issues will at some point, in either the design or the implementation, play a role in determining the effectiveness of the overall program. An appropriate point to begin thinking about how to address these issues is during the goal-setting phase of the professional development design process.

The seven critical issues are presented here:

1. *Building capacity for sustainability:* Would you know capacity if you saw it? Do you develop people who can work with teachers to support their learning and teaching? Do you build support systems for professional

development providers? Do you recognize, study, and apply the knowledge base of professional development theory and practice, and help others do so? Do you work to create and influence policies, resources, and structures that make professional development a central rather than a marginal activity?

2. *Making time for professional development:* How do you find ways to make more effective use of the time currently available for ongoing teacher learning? How can you work toward influencing state and local policies and public perceptions that more readily support time and resources for professional development?

3. *Developing leadership:* Is leadership development a goal of the program? What do you mean by a "leader" and what roles do leaders play? What specific teacher leadership roles are important to develop? What plans do you have in place to develop and support leadership roles? What other leadership roles are important for the success of your program?

4. *Ensuring equity:* Does the content of the professional development experience include opportunities for teachers to examine and challenge their beliefs about who can learn and how diverse groups of students best learn? Does the content include the issues of equitable opportunity for all students to learn? Is access to the professional development experiences equitable? Does the design invite full engagement and learning by participants?

5. *Building a professional learning culture:* Does the organizational culture focus on creating effective learning environments (for example, ones that are learner centered, knowledge centered, assessment centered, community centered)? (See Day 5.) What do you actively do to build professional communities among staff?

6. *Garnering public support:* How have you built public awareness of and support for the importance of professional learning? How have you engaged the public as participants or providers in the professional development? How have you engaged the public in understanding and contributing to your vision of teaching and learning?

7. *Scaling up:* Is the professional development program clearly defined and based on a sound foundation? Do you provide professional development opportunities to large numbers of people? Does each teacher have sufficient support to learn and to change his or her practice? What mechanisms are in place for quality control of the professional development? Is there a plan at each level of the implementation for ongoing use, support, and institutionalization? (Loucks-Horsley et al., 2010, pp. 117–155)

Reflection

Think about a professional development program that you have been part of in the past year. How well did the design of the program attend to each of these critical issues? What lessons did you personally learn about the role of each critical issue in the overall program? At what points in the implementation of the program did different issues arise? In what ways did you address the issues?

DAY 18: ENSURING EQUITY

> *Students in low-income schools who need the best are getting the least qualified teachers. Closing the gap requires high-quality teaching and underscores the need for leaders to examine system policies, contracts, and practices that continue to perpetuate conditions of underachievement.*
>
> Ruth Johnson

One of the most critical issues that professional developers must consider is ensuring equity. Given the growing diversity of the population in this country and the mobility of our society, understanding and appreciating diversity is an essential adult competency. Equity, in terms of access to professional development for all staff, is equally important.

There are normally three concerns related to equity that need to be addressed in any professional development effort. One relates to the staffing and curriculum of the professional development itself, another to the participants, and the third to the content of the professional development.

1. *Staffing and curriculum:* Is the professional development staff diverse in terms of race, ethnicity, gender, disability, and other factors that may be important to the professional development (for example, a mix of staff with experience at different grade levels)? Does the professional development staff reflect the diversity within the participant group? Are the content, pedagogy, and materials employed in the professional development free of bias and stereotyping? Does the staff use inclusive language and promote the interaction of all participants? (See Book Four, Day 15.)

2. *Participants:* What is the racial or ethnic composition of your participant group? Do both women and men participate? Are people with disabilities included? Are the populations that the participants work with represented? Are there data regarding participants' needs and interests in professional development?

3. *Content:* This aspect of equity is especially important when your program focuses on teaching content. For example, does the curriculum of your professional development address equity issues in either the content or pedagogy, or both? Here are some possible questions to explore:

- Which students enroll in the classes the teachers teach? Are they representative of the entire student body? If not, what limits access?
- How do teachers accommodate the diverse learning styles of students?
- Are there instances of bias or stereotyping in the texts or other instructional materials that teachers use? If so, how do teachers use these instances as teaching points? Are there bias-free materials available? If the materials are free of bias, to what extent do they reflect diversity? What types of diversity?
- How does the content affect diverse groups of students? Are there aspects of the content or the pedagogy that might be culturally inappropriate?
- What equity issues exist in assessment? Is one group likely to excel because of some factor or factors, such as bias in the test or testing procedure?

In education, additional equity issues focus on when and where the professional development is held, whether teachers in schools in poorer neighborhoods have adequate access to professional development, which teachers get to attend, and whether released time and/or compensation are provided.

> **Reflection**
>
> What are the key diversity and equity concerns within your organization? How does your professional development address (or not address) these concerns? Does your professional development include opportunities for teachers to openly discuss issues of equity and diversity? What do you think your professional development programs could do better in supporting equity and diversity? How can you make that happen?

DAY 19: STRATEGIES FOR PROFESSIONAL LEARNING

New forms of professional development are needed for teachers at all stages of their careers—forms that can affect teachers' actions and interactions in the classroom and lead to improved learning outcomes for all students.

Margaret Schwan Smith

Leaders need to have a diverse repertoire of adult learning strategies. Gone are the days when we automatically turn to the after-school workshop or hire an expert to come into the school and "train" our teachers. Currently, effective professional development is characterized by thoughtful and deliberate consideration of the existing needs, knowledge and beliefs, contexts, goals, and critical issues to inform the selection and combination of strategies.

Following are 16 different strategies (Loucks-Horsley et al., 2010) for professional development of teachers of science and mathematics, organized into four clusters that offer a broad view of the strategies available for professional development:

Immersion in Content, Standards, and Research

This first cluster has three strategies that focus on deepening teachers' understanding of and engagement with mathematics and science content and process:

1. *Curriculum topic study* is a highly structured activity that deepens teachers' understanding of key curriculum topics in science and mathematics that are found in national and local standards.

2. *Immersion in inquiry in science and problem solving in mathematics* engages teachers in experiencing science or mathematics content and processes as learners.

3. *Content courses* enable teachers to focus intensely on science, mathematics, or related topics for a substantial period of time.

Examining Teaching and Learning

The seven strategies in this cluster focus on teachers examining their teaching practices and the impact of their practices on student learning:

1. *Examining student work and thinking* engages teachers in a shared, collaborative discussion based on student work to reflect and improve teaching practices. This strategy has become very popular in the last few years, especially in using formative assessments to identify what students understand and how to move them to the next levels of learning.

2. *Demonstration lessons* are opportunities for teachers to engage in practice-based learning where the focus is on groups of teachers observing each others teaching lessons and engaging in pre- and

post-discussions focused on a clear purpose to learn from the demonstration.

3. *Lesson study* is a sequential and structured process for developing and refining lessons that are designed to address specific goals or standards.

4. *Action research* is an on-going, systematic study of a teacher's teaching and students' learning. Teachers either define or assist in defining the research questions to be tested and collect and analyze data from their classrooms or schools.

5. *Case discussions* give teachers the opportunity to examine narrative stories or videotapes to reflect on a teaching or learning situation.

6. *Coaching* provides one-on-one learning opportunities for teachers to improve their practices through reflection, dialogue, and feedback. More experienced teachers work with less experienced ones.

7. *Mentoring* is a long-term, teacher-to-teacher relationship usually between an experienced and highly regarded teacher and a less experienced teacher.

Aligning and Implementing Curriculum

This cluster has two strategies:

1. *Instructional materials selection*, the process of selecting materials to use in the classroom, is an opportunity for teachers to broaden their understanding of effective curriculum, Common Core State Standards and science education standards, content, pedagogy, and assessment.

2. *Curriculum implementation* focuses teachers on learning the content and pedagogy necessary to teach the new curriculum, how to teach it, how to assess student learning, and how to incorporate the new curriculum into their overall instruction.

Professional Development Structures

This last cluster includes four strategies that are vehicles or mechanisms into which the other 12 strategies are often embedded.

1. *Study groups* are collegial, collaborative groups of teachers who convene to mutually examine issues of teaching and learning.

2. *Workshops, institutes, and seminars* are structured opportunities for educators to learn from leaders or facilitators with expertise on a particular topic as well as learn from one another.

3. *Professional networks* are professional communities that come together around a specific topic or theme. Their purpose is to share their knowledge with one another.

4. *Online professional development* uses technology and the Internet as a means of facilitating professional learning. Options are manifold, including online and hybrid courses, Webinars, wikispaces, virtual environments, digital video tools, and social networking sites. This option has grown exponentially in the past few years (Loucks-Horsley et al., 2010, pp. 157–278).

Reflection

Consider the current professional development in your school or district. Does it implement any of the strategies listed? Which ones?

If your school or district has a more narrow definition of professional development, could any alternative strategies help you achieve your goals? Which ones would work in your setting? What would you like to try and why? As a leader, what can you do to broaden the concept of what constitutes professional development?

DAY 20: SELECTING AND COMBINING STRATEGIES

Educators diminish organizational creativity when they distort current reality through denial and minimizing and then they select strategies based on wishful thinking rather than a rigorous assessment of the strategies' ability to produce the desired results.

Dennis Sparks

Professional development strategies are not selected or implemented in isolation or in a vacuum. The professional development design framework (Day 11, Figure 3.1) depicts the selection of strategies as the main influence at the "Plan" phase. However, all other inputs—knowledge and beliefs, context, critical issues—have continuous influence throughout the design process. Additionally, what leaders and designers have learned about student learning, standards, and the vision and goals for the program also influences the selection of strategies. Every effective program or plan relies on a variety of strategies in combination to ensure that teachers' professional learning is in direct support of student learning. It's the only way to ensure that multiple needs, contexts, and outcomes are addressed.

How do professional development designers and leaders know which strategies to use? And in what combinations?

Often, four interconnected outcomes (Loucks-Horsley et al., 2010) drive the design of professional development programs and the strategies selected:

1. Enhancing teachers' knowledge
2. Enhancing quality teaching
3. Developing leadership capacity
4. Building professional learning communities (pp. 161–162)

In selecting, combining, and implementing strategies, there are four factors to keep in mind (Loucks-Horsley et al., 2010, pp. 164–166):

1. Any group of teachers will have different learning needs. Moreover, at any time they will be in different learning stages. (See Book Two, Days 4 and 5.) A strong professional learning program needs to be ongoing and include strategies that address teachers' needs at the various stages of their learning.

2. No one or two professional development strategies (e.g., just a course or workshop) can produce the four outcomes mentioned above along with increased student learning. Instead, what will make a difference is the combination of different strategies offered at different times during a teacher's career.

3. Some strategies may be better offered on an intermittent basis; others may be institutionalized as regular ongoing options. For example, weeklong inquiry institutes might be offered every other summer while examining student work and coaching are available on a regular basis.

4. Professional learning experiences for teachers need to be led by facilitators with expertise in adult learning and the subject area. However, this does not mean that the facilitators must be external to the system, but rather, that teacher leaders are often the ones in the best position to enhance their knowledge and skills as leaders of their colleagues' learning. This is especially valuable for professional development strategies that are ongoing, such as coaching, and within professional learning communities.

Reflection

Think about the professional development program in your own school or district and ask yourself the following questions:

- What are the desired outcomes of your professional learning program? How do they align with the four mentioned above?

- To what extent does your professional development program incorporate a variety of strategies?
- Does your professional learning program address teachers' needs and concerns? For example, does the program include awareness-raising strategies for teachers new to the program? Opportunities to reflect on practice for teachers who may have been more experienced in the program?
- What changes would you like to see in your professional development program so that it offers ongoing learning? How can you help bring about these changes?

DAY 21: PROFESSIONAL DEVELOPMENT FOR STUDENT IMPACT

American teachers say that much of the professional development available to them is not useful.

Professional Learning in the Learning Profession:
A Status Report on Teacher Development
in the United States and Abroad

You have a choice to make. Your school's professional development plan calls for teachers to prepare to implement a new mathematics curriculum. Which of the following opportunities would most likely increase teachers' skill and expertise in teaching this new curriculum?

Opportunity A: Attend a full day workshop on the topic followed by participation in three 2-hour meetings during the year to discuss with other teachers their experiences in using the curriculum.

Opportunity B: Attend a three-day workshop in the summer to thoroughly review the curriculum and determine implementation strategies. Teachers meet in grade level teams once a month to discuss progress and then with the larger group twice during the year. One feature of the large group meetings is reviewing videotapes to critique and reflect on practice. Also, each team member is observed and observes another colleague monthly during the year. The curriculum developer provides an online network for teachers from all schools implementing the same curriculum to report experiences and to pose questions anytime during the year's activities.

The field of professional learning has been plagued for years with a lack of solid research on its ability to demonstrate that professional development can change teacher practice that in turn increases student learning and performance. Various factors have contributed to the limited evidence base; for example, the lack of knowledge and funds to design and conduct what we believe to be effective professional development as well as the lack of well-designed research studies that can capture our desired outcomes.

However, that's beginning to change. Research reports the following: Although studies are still limited, there is evidence to show that "sustained and intensive professional development for teachers is related to student achievement gains" (Darling-Hammond, Chung Wei, Andree, Richardson, & Orphanos, 2009). Yoon, Duncan, Lee, Scarloss, & Shapley (2007) found that teachers who participated in substantial professional development (an average of 49 hours) significantly increased their students' achievement. Unfortunately, much of the professional development provided to teachers does not meet the criteria of effective professional learning that will impact student learning.

Reflection

Go back to Day 9. There you'll find 15 characteristics of effective professional learning. Determine which of these 15 characteristics is represented in Opportunities A and B, which is missing, and which is unknown from the information given. From your analysis, why is Opportunity B more likely to yield positive outcomes? If your school or district were to undertake a program designed to prepare teachers to implement a new mathematics curriculum, would the professional learning be more similar to Opportunity A or B? What could you do to make the learning correspond more to B than A?

DAY 22: BALANCING PHILOSOPHY AND PRAGMATISM

The professional development designer faces many dilemmas and decision points.

Susan Mundry and Susan Loucks-Horsley

One of the basic dilemmas within professional development is whether to focus efforts on changing participants' philosophy about something or on pragmatic how-to issues (Mundry & Loucks-Horsley, 1999). As with most dilemmas, there is value in addressing both.

The *philosophical approach* focuses on learning theory and gathering evidence of learning. The *pragmatic approach* emphasizes new materials and practices, such as guides, methods, and curriculum, and other more practical matters.

If a program focuses exclusively on philosophical issues and research on learning, it is likely to ignore the day-to-day reality of making a new program work and may not be relevant enough for teachers who have immediate classroom needs. If it emphasizes the daily how-to's, it shortchanges learners by focusing excessively on surface elements or the mechanics of doing something new without developing an understanding of the intent for the change and promoting real change in beliefs and behavior. Obviously, professional development needs both, especially as designers move toward sustaining a new program or approach and adapting it to the constantly emerging needs and changing beliefs of those involved.

How are professional development designers able to be sensitive to both needs?

First, there must be an infrastructure that supports a dual approach. Flexibility in scheduling is necessary so participants have time to reflect and interact with their colleagues to understand the rationale or philosophy for the program or approach and see examples of practice and gain practical ideas. Second, recognition of the need for integrating both the philosophical and pragmatic approaches is necessary. Many participants are more likely to embrace professional development that directly helps them do something specific. In our Leadership Academy we find it is most helpful to start with a specific example from practice; such as engaging people in learning a particular lesson from the new curriculum, looking at real student work, or cases from the classroom. This focuses teachers on thinking about their practice and student learning from a very practical point of view. Then facilitators can help to guide the discussion to the philosophy or approach to learning that is embodied in the materials and the student work example. This raises the important discussion of philosophy of teaching but grounds it in the realities of practice and student learning.

In anticipation of sustaining a professional development program that incorporates both approaches, it is important to do the following:

- Maintain a balance between philosophical and programmatic approaches and be responsive to changing needs in participants and the context. For example, combine time for teachers to work through specific materials they will later use in their classrooms and then stop and reflect on what beliefs about teaching and learning are embedded in the materials.
- Gain agreement among participants about the focus for the professional development and continuously determine whether the focus remains on track as the professional development initiative proceeds. For example, at the beginning of a teacher learning program, the teachers may want 70 percent of the time focused on the practical aspects of implementation and 30 percent

focused on the philosophy and beliefs supporting the new approach. As time goes on, those percentages will flip, with teachers wanting more time to focus on why they are teaching a particular way and what they are learning and how their students are responding to the new approaches.
- Build an infrastructure (funding, schedule, and varied approaches) to support both philosophically and programmatically focused professional development. For example, workshops and mini-courses can lead teachers to learn the materials they will use with their students; but they also need ongoing communication mechanisms, such as grade-level planning meetings and study groups, to have the conversations about how they are teaching, the impact they are having, and the philosophy behind it.

Reflection

How do you design for and assess the balance between philosophical and pragmatic matters in the professional development for which you are responsible? Do you see substantially more of one approach than the other in your current professional learning programs? If so, how can you create a better balance?

DAY 23: INCORPORATING REFLEXIVE PRACTICE

How we learn is what we learn.

Bonnie Friedman

One of the key characteristics of effective professional development is that it is *reflexive*. That means it is true to itself. It is internally consistent in its content and process. For example, lecturing about the qualities and characteristics of investigative mathematics teaching and learning does not stay true to the intent or nature of the content. Rather, participants should be immersed in learning mathematics by actively engaging in problem solving as learners.

Professional development that is reflexive contributes to the overall adult learning experience and is characterized by the following:

- Participants who take the learning seriously
- An instructor or facilitator who is seen as credible
- Learners who regard the experience as practical and real-world oriented

- Teachers who have opportunities to apply their learning in their classrooms
- Participants who have the opportunity to practice new behaviors

Reflection

Following are three professional development strategies. For each one, list what it requires to be reflexive. In other words, how would the learning experience be true to itself? (For example, professional development on outdoor education should involve some outdoor activity.)

1. Using various kinds of technology, such as computers, telecommunications, video, and online virtual learning environments, to learn content and pedagogy

2. Using structured opportunities outside the classroom (courses, seminars, institutes, or workshops) to focus on topics of interest

3. Working one-on-one with teachers in a coaching or mentoring role to improve teaching and learning through a variety of activities

DAY 24: REACHING EVERYONE OR SCALING UP

Many things can wait. Children cannot. Today their bones are being formed, their blood is being made, their senses are being developed. To them we cannot say "tomorrow." Their name is today.

Gabriela Mistral

As described in Day 17, one of the critical issues to consider and grapple with early in the design of a professional development program is scaling up or reaching everyone and building a culture for learning.

Who participates in professional development activities? All teachers and staff? Those who volunteer? A smaller number who are hand selected? Who should come? These are not easy questions to answer.

In the past, one of the usual characteristics of change was that the staff generally had the option of adopting the change or not. Often, they could say, "No, thank you" to the new curriculum or new teaching approach. With current improvement efforts, accountability issues, and teacher evaluation processes, there is a much greater focus on scaling up interventions to reach all teachers and their students.

The challenge of scaling up goes beyond providing the same experience to a greater number of participants. We know from the Concerns-Based Adoption Model (Hall & Hord, 2011) that people experience different needs surrounding the adoption of an innovation (see Book Two, Days 4 and 5). Providing for all these different needs in a single professional development event is very difficult. The "one size fits all" approach just doesn't work.

Mobility is also a problem. A core group of teachers can go through a professional development experience, and within a year or two, many of them may be working elsewhere or teaching a different grade-level of students. The result is very uneven implementation of the new program or practices.

What is needed to reach all teachers and their students is an organizational infrastructure and culture that supports a focus on continuous improvement. This includes a vision, mission, clear direction, flexibility in scheduling, and adequate resources. There also needs to be a human infrastructure built around a culture of learning, which encourages development of a community of practice. This is how a school culture both encourages and supports the entire staff to continue learning.

To have a professional development program that affects most people in an organization, planners need to do the following:

- Build an articulated culture that embraces change and ensures supportive policies and practices
- Hold high standards for learning and work to build a shared commitment to those standards
- Develop structures that assure new and newly reassigned grade-changing teachers the opportunity to engage in the professional development program (Mundry & Loucks-Horsley, 1999)

Reflection

Is your professional development designed to involve all the teachers it needs to reach? What do you need to do to reach others? How can you begin to make changes in organizational infrastructure or human infrastructure to support a totally inclusive professional development program? For example, do staff set annual or more frequent learning goals tied to their annual performance reviews? What steps can you take to encourage the development of these infrastructures needed to ensure professional learning for all staff in your setting?

DAY 25: TEAM LEARNING

Team learning is not "team building" and shouldn't be taken on lightly.

Peter Senge

Within a professional learning community that focuses on continuous adult learning, people often work and collaborate in teams. Whether these are teams of teachers engaged in professional development experiences such as examining student work, or leadership teams facilitating dialogue about student learning data, there are specific skills and abilities that can enhance the teams' effectiveness. Leaders need to understand how to set up and support such learning environments.

Although *team building* is a common expression and is well understood, the concept of team learning is different. Traditional team building focuses on improving individual team members' skills as a means for working with each other. It leads to improved communication, contributes to more efficient and effective task performance, and builds stronger relationships among the members.

Team learning refers to a team's ability to "think and act in new synergistic ways, with full coordination and a sense of unity" (Senge, Kleiner, Roberts, Ross, & Smith, 1994, p. 352). It is about getting a team to function as a whole rather than as a collection of individuals. Team learning begins with a high level of self-knowledge and progresses toward developing understanding of and aligning with other team members. It encompasses the traditional goals of team building but extends far beyond. It is one of the critical factors in building communities of learners.

The primary approach to team learning is improved conversation through dialogue and skillful discussion. These differ from normal conversation or group discussion in that they follow rules that allow team members to understand and appreciate the different forces at play. Because they don't necessarily come naturally, people need to learn these ways to communicate (Garmston & Wellman, 2009).

For team learning to occur, the following components need to be in place:

- *A task on which to focus and a reason for the group to work together:* This task becomes the practice field on which the team develops.
- *A facilitator to aid learning:* Team members become so engrossed in their own dynamics that there is no way for them to objectively analyze how they are functioning. A trained observer who can be impartial is often the best person to facilitate and give feedback.

- *A set of ground rules for their conversation:* For example, teams might develop ground rules that include telling the truth, sharing only pertinent information, limiting airtime, maintaining confidentiality, and avoiding blaming statements. There should also be ground rules for making decisions and for handling violations of the ground rules.

Reflection

Think about a team that you are part of. Write down several words that describe how your team currently functions.

- *Words that describe my team:* Does your team have a commitment to team learning? How do you know? What is the evidence? If it doesn't, how might you help influence such a choice on your team's part? What do you think your team could accomplish if it focused on team learning?
- *What my team could accomplish:* Does your current focus need to change to make the team learning more effective? How can you help your team move forward? Consider meaningful tasks for all members and processes to guide your work.

DAY 26: SHARING KNOWLEDGE AND CAPTURING LESSONS LEARNED

> *A great cartoon in* The New Yorker *some years back showed two venerable men, obviously scientists, sitting back to back at their respective desks. One says to the other, "It's just come to my attention that we've both been working on the same problem for the last twenty-five years."*
>
> Nancy M. Dixon

One of the ways to institutionalize communities of learning is for an organization to share knowledge and capture lessons learned. Lessons learned are key individual and organizational discoveries—documentation of what works and does not work in a field—captured over the years. The lessons learned can come from research and evaluation efforts, action research, the work of experienced teachers, or the purposeful, collaborative work of a community of learners.

Often, neither the individual nor collective lessons learned in an organization are documented and shared. Education has been noted as the "closed door" profession, where teachers shut their doors and go about teaching and learning as each sees fit. Even when some sharing of knowledge does take place, reorganization and teacher reassignment or turnover can disperse those who possess institutional memory. Under time constraints, teachers may not seek out those with more experience. New teachers may not be sufficiently oriented toward the school's way of doing work. Michael Fullan (2001) points out that one of the key traits of today's professional is his or her willingness to share knowledge with others in the organization. The push for greater accountability has ended the era of the closed door.

Since capturing lessons learned can be difficult if a school is not oriented to the practice, here is an example that might help you get started:

Imagine that you are responsible for providing new staff orientation each fall. Over the years, you have kept a lessons-learned file that has several headings. One heading is "Scheduling and Logistics." Another is "Staff Benefits." Another is "Content," subdivided by subject (for example, District Disciplinary Policies and Procedures, Classroom Management, District Standards, Parent Involvement, Multicultural Issues, and so on).

A staff member who is responsible for setting up the orientation checks the "Scheduling and Logistics" file. There she finds some valuable information: The facility normally used is currently under renovation and is not available; in previous sessions, the staff preferred starting at 8:00 rather than 9:00 so they could get out earlier; and Chef du Jour has consistently provided the best food at the lowest price. Each file has similar information about what has and hasn't worked in the past—valuable information to those planning the orientation, especially those who are new to this function themselves. All files are electronic and open to everyone and are updated after each new orientation.

Another example of capturing lessons learned and sharing those lessons with others is when teachers engage in the analysis of data to guide instruction and student learning. Initial data analysis can help teachers identify students' learning needs and, after implementing interventions, data can inform the extent to which student learning increased. Documenting and sharing what was learned from the results of the intervention can be critical when other teachers encounter similar student learning needs and are looking for appropriate approaches to enhance students' understanding.

Reflection

In your current role, are you sharing knowledge and capturing lessons learned? If so, how? Is this knowledge being used? How is it being documented? Are you sharing only logistical lessons learned or also instructional and school improvement lessons learned? How could you improve your efforts to make both categories of learning accessible to everyone?

If you're not sharing knowledge and capturing lessons learned, how might you do so? What would your process look like? How would you be sure that staff review lessons learned before undertaking a task?

DAY 27: USING PROGRAM LOGIC MODELS

If you don't know where you're going, how are you gonna know when you get there?

Yogi Berra

How do you know that the professional development you plan will bring about the results you desire?

One way to get the results you want is to develop a program logic model. A *logic model* is a picture of how your professional development program works—the theory and the assumptions underlying your program. "It is a conscious process that creates an explicit understanding of the challenges ahead, the resources available, and the timetable in which to hit the target" (W. K. Kellogg Foundation, 2001).

Although logic models vary somewhat in their conceptualization, here's an example of a classic model:

Under intended results are the program's desired results: outputs, outcomes, and impact. *Outputs* are the direct products of program activities. For example, an output of a professional development activity is 50 people who have been immersed in using an inquiry approach to teaching science. *Outcomes* are the specific changes in program participants' attitudes, knowledge, and behavior expected either short term or long term. Following our example, an outcome might be that 45 out of the 50 teachers are skillfully

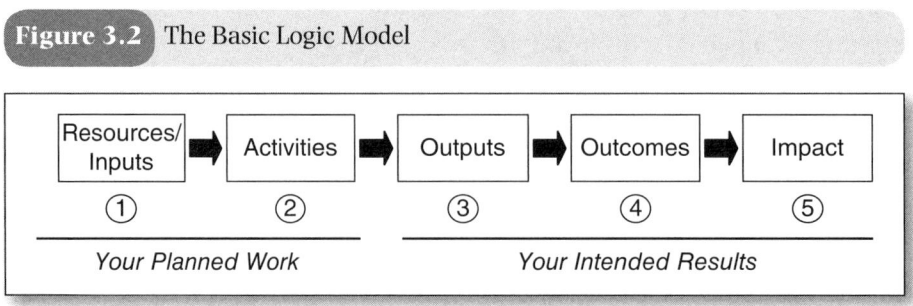

Figure 3.2 The Basic Logic Model

SOURCE: W. K. Kellogg Foundation, Copyright © 2001. *Logic Model Development Guide* (p. 1). Battle Creek, MI: W. K. Kellogg Foundation. Reprinted with permission.

using an inquiry approach to science instruction. *Impact* refers to the basic changes that occur from the program. Impact may be noticeable quickly or not for a long time, even well after a program has ended. Using our example again, an impact would be that more students demonstrate greater achievements in understanding of the science concepts.

Embedded in a program logic model is a *theory of change*. It says, in brief, that if you have these resources that you use in this way, you will produce certain results that will benefit teachers and ultimately students in certain ways.

> **Reflection**
>
> Although making you a skilled user of logic models is beyond the scope of this book, here is a brief exercise.
>
> Select a professional development event that has been scheduled, and develop a logic model for this event. Identify your resources or inputs and the major activities. Then list your outputs, outcomes, and impact. (You could ask a colleague to develop a logic model for the same event, but ask this person to list the outputs, outcomes, and impact before identifying the resources and major activities. Do you notice a difference in the resulting logic models? If so, what influenced the way in which the models were developed?)
>
> What did you find? Are your resources sufficient to conduct the planned activity? Do you think the activities will produce the desired changes? Are they of sufficient quality, intensity, and duration to get you to where you want to be? Was it difficult to distinguish between, for example, outputs and outcomes? If so, don't worry, that will come with practice. What are the weak links in your logic model? For example, are you claiming to impact changes in policies without having a major activity that will engage policymakers in making such changes? What research supports your logic? What needs to be strengthened? What is the theory of change embedded in your model? How sound is it? For example, is it based on research and best practice?

DAY 28: ACHIEVING REALISTIC OUTCOMES

> *I have become convinced that it makes a considerable difference if you do the outcomes before planning the activities. . . . I find that people come up with much more effective activities when they do. Use the motto, "plan backward, implement forward."*
>
> Beverly Anderson Parsons

How do you know what reasonable outcomes to expect for any professional development program? Outcomes are synonymous with a program's results or effects. For individuals, outcomes may include changes in knowledge, attitudes, skills, and/or practice. For an organization, outcomes may be evident in changes in policy, goals, operations, or structures. (See Book Five, Day 18 for more on outcomes.)

Sometimes, distinctions are made among short-term, intermediate, and long-term outcomes to designate when a particular outcome is expected to appear. Achieving intermediate and long-term outcomes is always more difficult because of the interaction between the program and its environment. There can be numerous intervening variables that can support, reduce, or nullify the anticipated outcomes.

One of the most common flaws of professional development planning is a mismatch between activities and desired outcomes. Usually the activity is not of sufficient quality, intensity, or duration to achieve the desired outcomes. Or to state it differently, planners overestimate the magnitude and number of outcomes that the activity will produce. You're more likely to be on target if you start with your desired outcomes and then work backward to design the activities that will produce the outcomes.

Keep in mind, however, that the process of identifying outcomes and strategies often becomes iterative. For example, once you clarify your intended outcomes and attendant strategies, you may find that additional outcomes may in fact be achieved through those strategies. Similarly, you may find several strategies could result in the same outcomes, leading you to condense or modify the strategies you offer in your overall program.

In most cases, acquiring new knowledge and skills and changing attitudes and behaviors require a sustained intervention. Having an impact on services or products requires even more time and effort. And regardless of how good a program is, the intervening environmental factors influence the outcomes, especially the intermediate and long-term outcomes (Kaser & Bourexis, 1999).

Reflection

Think of a professional development program going on in your school or district. What is the specific activity or activities planned? What are the anticipated outcomes? For each anticipated outcome, ask yourself the following questions:

- Is the outcome best described as short-term, intermediate, or long-term?
- Is the activity likely to result in the desired outcome? How do you know?

- What is an estimated time frame for achieving the outcome?
- What intervening factors could influence whether or not the outcome is achieved?
- How might you anticipate and address these intervening factors?

DAY 29: GATHERING EVALUATION DATA

One of the great mistakes is to judge policies and programs by their intentions rather than their results.

Milton Friedman

Leaders are accountable for results. Leaders who organize and support professional learning in schools need to assess what the learning is and how relevant and transferable it is to the mission of the school or district.

There are seven levels of accountability that leaders can consider when evaluating educational programs' effectiveness. They are:

1. *Reach:* How many and what types of people were involved in the program?

2. *Quality:* Does the program's design and implementation reflect best practice in teaching and learning?

3. *Reaction and intended actions:* Were the participants satisfied with the program, and what actions do they intend to take as a result of their experiences?

4. *Learning:* What changes in participants' knowledge, skills, and attitudes took place as a result of the program?

5. *Application:* What changes have occurred in participants' practice and behavior during and after the experience?

6. *Impact:* What sustained actions have occurred over time that support changes in participants' behavior?

7. *Institutionalization:* What permanent changes in the learning conditions of the organization have occurred that support the continuation of the new practices? (Bourexis, Kaser, & Raizen, 2004)

More recently, however, a shift has occurred. In addition to examining reach and reaction and intended actions, program evaluations have also focused on measuring impact and institutionalization. This has been the result of a focus on accountability and a desire to improve student performance. The problem, of course, is that the program evaluators have skipped a few steps. These levels are sequential. One cannot expect changes in student performance until teachers' behaviors have changed. Program evaluations need to take all seven levels into account to ensure the quality of their program and its potential results.

> **Reflection**
>
> Think about the typical evaluation of your professional development programs. Using the schema outlined, what levels are evaluated? Which are generally omitted? How would you redesign your program evaluation to document its quality and to gather the evidence you need to document the program's effectiveness?

DAY 30: LEADING LEARNING BY EXAMPLE

> *Learning as a way of being is a whole mentality. It is a way of being in the world. . . . Learning as a way of being is a whole posture toward experience, a way of framing or interpreting all experience as a learning opportunity.*
>
> Peter B. Vaill

An organization is committed to learning insofar as its leaders model continuous learning themselves, along with having organizational policies and procedures that support learning for all employees.

Such policies represent an organizational commitment to investing in human capital and being a learning organization in all aspects. This covers a range of topics, starting with a philosophical statement on individual, team, and organizational learning, to specifics such as employees taking reflection time for themselves; orientation for all new and newly promoted employees; and the sources and financial support for ongoing learning.

Regardless of what any written policy says, the behavior of the leader of an organization is the most important yardstick for determining what an organization truly values. If the policy says one thing and the leader does another, the stronger message comes from the leader's actions.

Here is what you as a leader can do to model your commitment to learning:

- Say you don't know when you don't know; don't pretend to have all the answers, but be committed to supporting others to work together to find answers.

- Listen attentively and be open to what others have to say.
- Regularly seek out the opinions of others.
- When challenged, listen carefully and deal with the facts; try not to be defensive.
- Insist that all new and newly promoted employees go through orientation; do so yourself, if and when that is applicable. Know what the orientation of your staff entails and discuss that with them, as appropriate.
- Set aside reflection time for yourself and expect your staff to do the same. Also schedule reflection time for your group or team.
- Read and share what you read with others, as appropriate.
- Have learning goals for yourself and let others know what these are.
- Attend conferences in your field and encourage others to do the same.
- Support quality professional development for your staff and others in your organization.
- See mistakes and failures as opportunities to learn.
- Value staying on top of research in your field.
- Value expertise and call on experts.
- Adopt a "problems are our friends" orientation.

Reflection

Reread the preceding list and check off those behaviors that you routinely do.

How many and which ones did you check? Based on your assessment, how strong is your commitment to learning for yourself and for your organization? If you believe that it needs to be strengthened, what additional behaviors do you wish to adopt? How can you help others demonstrate these continuous learning behaviors?

DAY 31: TAKING RESPONSIBILITY FOR LEARNING

Words mean nothing. Action is the only thing. Doing. That's the only thing.

Ernest J. Gaines

Modeling the way for others goes a long way toward contributing to a community of learners. Those who are leaders (and those who aspire to be leaders) are more likely to be successful if they take responsibility for their continuous learning.

Here is a 10-step plan (Reynolds, 2000) to guide you in taking responsibility for your own learning and, in the process, flatten your learning curve:

1. *Acknowledge what you want to learn and why you want to learn it.* Sometimes, you want to learn something because it is new, exciting, and offers certain benefits. Other times, you decide to learn something because you realize that you need to know it. To get to this place, you may need to work through some denial and acknowledge that you must obtain certain knowledge and skills that you don't currently have.

2. *Identify any negative feelings you have about learning something new.* Perhaps you are lucky to feel only excitement and anticipation about learning what you have chosen to learn. However, adults often enter a new learning experience with trepidation. Are there any barriers that may keep you from acquiring the knowledge and skills you want? Are you afraid that you don't have the ability, the time, or the resources to learn what you have decided to learn? Do you worry about being perceived as incompetent or feeling uncomfortable as you learn something new? Simply voicing these feelings or talking them through with someone else can help to dispel them.

3. *Determine your motivation for learning something new.* Your motivation for learning influences your persistence and ultimately your success. Is there external pressure? Are you motivated by an internal desire? Perhaps both? Together, an internal desire and an external demand provide the strongest motivation.

4. *Make a conscious choice to learn what it is that you want.* You need to say to yourself or out loud, "Within the next six months, I choose to learn . . . " Making a conscious choice is much more powerful than simply saying, "Gee, I'd really like to learn . . . someday."

5. *To move forward, be prepared to give up your attachment to the old way of doing things.* We often are attached to the past. Giving up that attachment may be necessary before we can move on to learn something new. It may even be necessary to grieve the loss of the old before we can move on to the new.

6. *Back up your choice with a plan.* How do you learn best? How much time do you have to acquire new knowledge or skills? What resources do you need? Do you have them, or where can you get them? Your answers to these questions are the core of an action plan to guide your learning.

7. *Establish some success criteria for yourself.* How will you know whether you are making progress or when you have reached your goal? Establishing one or two benchmarks can help you gauge your progress.

8. *Build in rewards for yourself.* Rewards are highly individualized, so pick your own. Maybe it is intrinsic—for example, simply completing your plan. Maybe it is extrinsic—for example, giving yourself a treat, such as a weekend away.

9. *Recognize that how you go about learning is an act of symbolic leadership that will not go unnoticed.* Others will observe how you approach learning and will learn from your behavior. You are a role model even though you may not be aware of it.

10. *Keep learning.* There is no end to learning, and the pace is likely to quicken rather than slow down.

> **Reflection**
>
> Book Three presents important ideas about how to establish a productive and effective learning culture in your organization and asks you to reflect on each idea. In addition, Day 30 lists actions that you, as a leader, can take to model learning within a community. Review all of the contemplations and select something that you want to understand or do better. Develop a plan for learning using the actions listed here in Day 31. To work on flattening your learning curve, consider a time frame that is shorter than what you would normally lay out for yourself.

REFERENCES

Achieve, Inc. (2013). *Next generation science standards, final draft.* Washington, DC: Author.

Ball, D. L. (1996). Teacher learning and the mathematics reforms: What we think we know and what we need to learn. *Phi Delta Kappan, 77*(7), 500–508.

Banilower, E., Cohen, K., Paisley, J., & Weiss, I. (2010). *Effective science education: What does research tell us?* (2nd ed.). Portsmouth, NH: RMC Research Corporation, Center on Instruction.

Bourexis, P., Kaser, J., & Raizen, S. (2004). *Evaluation framework for the center at IMSA.* Kill Devil Hills, NC: The Study Group.

Bransford, J. D., Brown, A. L., & Cocking, R. R. (Eds.). (1999). *How people learn: Brain, mind, experience, and school.* Washington, DC: National Academies Press.

Bransford, J. D., Brown, A. L., & Cocking, R. R. (Eds.). (2000). *How people learn: Brain, mind, experience, and school: Expanded Edition.* Washington, DC: National Academies Press.

Council of Chief State School Officers. (2010). *Common core state standards.* Washington, DC: Author.

Darling-Hammond, L., Chung Wei, R., Andree, A., Richardson, N., & Orphanos, R. (2009, February). *Professional learning in the learning profession: A status report on teacher development in the United States and abroad.* Oxford, OH and Stanford, CA: National Staff Development Council and The School Redesign Network at Stanford University.

Donovan, M. S., & Bransford, J. D. (Eds.). (2005). *How students learn science in the classroom.* Washington, DC: National Academies Press.

DuFour, R., DuFour, R., Eaker, R., & Karhanek, G. (2004). *Whatever it takes: How professional learning communities respond when kids don't learn.* Bloomington, IN: National Educational Service.

Fullan, M. (2001). *Leading in a culture of change.* San Francisco: Jossey-Bass.

Garmston, R. J., & Wellman, B. M. (2009). *The adaptive school: A sourcebook for developing collaborative groups.* Norwood, MA: Christopher-Gordon.

Hall, G., & Hord, S. (2011). *Implementing change: Patterns, principles, and potholes* (3rd ed.). Boston: Pearson.

Kaser, J. S., & Bourexis, P. S. (with Loucks-Horsley, S., & Raizen, S. A.). (1999). *Enhancing program quality in science and mathematics.* Thousand Oaks, CA: Corwin.

Learning Forward. (2011). *Standards for professional learning.* Oxford, OH: Learning Forward.

Lindsey, R. B., Roberts, L. M., & CampbellJones, F. (2005). *The culturally proficient school: An implementation guide for school leaders.* Thousand Oaks, CA: Corwin.

Lindsey, R. B., Robins, K. N., & Terrell, R. D. (2003). *Cultural proficiency: A manual for school leaders* (2nd ed.). Thousand Oaks, CA: Corwin.

Loucks-Horsley, S., Stiles, K. E., Mundry, S., Love, N., & Hewson, P. W. (2010). *Designing professional development for teachers of science and mathematics* (3rd ed.). Thousand Oaks, CA: Corwin.

Mundry, S., & Loucks-Horsley, S. (1999). Designing professional development for science and mathematics teachers: Decision points and dilemmas. *NISE Brief, 3.* Retrieved from http://wcer.wisc.edu/NISE/publications/briefs

National Research Council. (2012). *A framework for K-12 science education.* Washington, DC: National Academies Press.

Owen, J. M., Cox, P. L., & Watkins, J. (1994). *Genuine reward: Community inquiry into connecting learning, teaching, and assessing.* Andover, MA: Regional Laboratory for Educational Improvement of the Northeast and Islands.

Reynolds, L. (2000). Continuous learning skills critical to career success in new economy. Retrieved from http://www.kaplancollege.com

Senge, P. M., Kleiner, A., Roberts, C., Ross, R. B., & Smith, B. J. (1994). *The fifth discipline fieldbook: Strategies and tools for building a learning organization.* New York: Doubleday.

Stiles, K. E., & Mundry, S. (2002). Professional development and how teachers learn: Developing expert science teachers. In R. W. Bybee (Ed.), *Learning science and the science of learning* (pp. 137–151). Arlington, VA: National Science Teachers Association Press.

Thompson, C., & Zeuli, J. (1999). The frame and tapestry: Standards-based reform and professional development. In L. Darling-Hammond & G. Sykes (Eds.),

Heart of the matter: Teaching as the learning profession (pp. 341–375). San Francisco: Jossey-Bass.

W. K. Kellogg Foundation. (2001). *Logic model development guide: Using logic models to bring together planning, evaluation, and action.* Battle Creek, MI: W. K. Kellogg Foundation.

Yoon, K. S., Duncan, T., Lee, S. W. Y., Scarloss, B., & Shapley, K. (2007). *Reviewing the evidence on how teacher professional development affects student achievement* (Issues and Answers Report, REL 2007-No. 033). Washington, DC: US Department of Education, Institute of Education Sciences, National Center for Education Evaluation and Regional Assistance, Regional Educational Laboratory Southwest. Retrieved from http://ies.ed.gov/ncee/edlabs

Book 4

Leading Effective Groups

Building collaborative groups has become a core competency for all leaders. The need for people to come together and work efficiently and effectively is a key element of a continuously improving culture. Ongoing work groups examine data and results, plan interventions, or learn new content. Whatever a group's purpose, the group is usually more effective when everyone develops basic facilitation skills. As organizations increasingly use teams to carry out work, leaders need to be skilled in facilitating effective team learning and performance.

In Book Four we provide strategies and suggestions for leaders who work with groups over time. Such groups have something to learn, issues to address, studies to conduct, tasks to complete, or problems to solve. Although much of what we say also applies to groups that meet less frequently, our major focus is on leaders and their facilitation of ongoing groups.

A goal of all groups, if they are to carry out their work collaboratively, is to develop community. One component of community flows from the way group members talk among themselves and to others outside their group. "Good talk" does not just happen. It is the result of individuals developing skills and agreeing that they want to interact with each other in very specific ways. The leader's role is to build an efficacious environment so that teams can do their work in a culture of respect and continuous improvement.

Material in this book was adapted from Garmston, R. J., & Wellman, B. M. (2009). *The Adaptive School: A Sourcebook for Developing Collaborative Groups.* Norwood, MA: Christopher-Gordon Publishers, Inc., and from Garmston, R., & Wellman, B. (2012). *Adaptive Schools Foundation Seminar Learning Guide.* Highlands Ranch, CO: Center for Adaptive Schools, with permission of the authors.

We raise important questions for a leader to consider: What does it mean to be a leader of a group? What are different roles for leaders in groups? How do leaders behave in these different roles? How do people in groups talk to one another to ensure effective outcomes? For example, what is the difference between dialogue and discussion, and when should each be used?

We ask leaders to consider even more questions: How does one plan and conduct successful meetings? What are the key components of successful meetings? How does a group handle decision making, when is consensus necessary, and when will a simple majority suffice? How does a group handle conflict effectively? Monitor participation? Give and receive feedback? And finally, how should a group evolve over time?

The questions in Book Four are grouped around four themes that are interwoven throughout the 31 contemplations:

1. What does it mean to be a leader of a group? What are different roles for leaders? How do leaders involve everyone and establish clear roles and functions for all group members?

2. How do people in groups talk with each other, engage in productive interactions, and build community? What are the "norms of collaboration" that contribute to groups' effectiveness?

3. How do groups make decisions? What are the different processes for decision making?

4. How do groups address conflict and problems? What is the leader's role, and what roles and responsibilities do group members have for addressing conflict?

DAY 1: LEADING GROUPS

When clear goals have been established and members of the team are committed to them, when roles have been assigned on the basis of strengths and everyone is clear about their responsibilities and the job they are to do, when surprising events are expected and responded to, when conflict is addressed, and when members work together, team formation and improved performance is underway.

Roland Barth

What does it take to lead a group or team? Preparing an agenda? Facilitating a meeting? Creating environments conducive to sharing and learning? The answer, in each case, is a resounding, "Yes, and . . ."

Leading groups is not just about dissemination of information; it is also about creating "settings conducive to learning and sharing that learning" (Fullan, 2001, p. 79). Leaders have a responsibility to develop and practice skillful facilitation, arrange for the logistical needs of groups, and understand how to address and resolve conflict within a group.

Margaret Wheatley (2002) proposes six behaviors that characterize effective group conversations:

1. Acknowledging one another as equals
2. Staying curious about each other
3. Recognizing that we need each other's help to become better listeners
4. Slowing down so we have time to think and reflect
5. Remembering that conversation is the natural way humans think together
6. Expecting it to be messy at times (pp. 28–33)

A commitment to these behaviors can serve as the foundation upon which the skills and processes of effective facilitation of groups can be built.

Reflection

Think back over your career and recall groups that you have worked with that were effective. What made those groups effective for you? What were the characteristics of the leaders and the members of the group that resulted in effectiveness? What did you do that contributed to the group's effectiveness? What did others do? What norms or ground rules guided the group's interactions? What can you do to ensure that these effective elements are built into groups you work with in the future?

DAY 2: FOUR ROLES OF GROUP LEADERS

Good leaders make people feel that they're at the very heart of things, not at the periphery. Everyone feels that he or she makes a difference to the success of the organization. When that happens, people feel centered and that gives their work meaning.

Warren G. Bennis

What exactly is a group leader? Does this person actually direct the group's work? Help the group with its process? Intervene only when the group has problems?

The answer is, "That depends." Leaders have different roles in groups. Effective leaders know how to select and execute the right role for the right group and when and how to switch roles within a group.

The following are brief descriptions of each of the four most common roles for group leaders:

1. *Facilitator:* Being a facilitator is an appropriate role when the group's purpose is dialogue, shared decision making, solving a problem, or planning. The facilitator's role is to manage the process. He or she keeps the group on task, making sure that it does what it is supposed to do. This person is not the authority or expert and stays out of the content of the task, usually focusing only on the process.

2. *Presenter:* The role of presenters is to teach. A person in this role works with a group to broaden its knowledge, skills, or attitudes. A presenter can—and should—use a variety of instructional techniques and actively involve group members in their own learning.

3. *Coach:* Coaches help others achieve their own goals. At the same time, the coach helps colleagues strengthen their knowledge and skills in areas where they need guidance. Like the facilitator, the coach has a role that is nonjudgmental.

4. *Consultant:* The role of consultants is to provide their expertise to a group. Consultants target the content, process, or both, to help the group achieve its goals. To be effective in this role, the consultant must be trusted by the group and keep the desired outcomes foremost in mind (Garmston & Wellman, 2009, pp. 23–24).

> **Reflection**
>
> Think of the groups that you work with. For each group, which of these roles do you play? Does your role match the needs and purposes of the group? Is this role the most appropriate one for you? Are group members clear about your role? How do you know?
>
> Which of the four roles are you most comfortable with? Least comfortable with? If you need to strengthen your skills in one of the roles, which one would that be? How can you increase your effectiveness?

DAY 3: GROUP NORMS OF COLLABORATION

Without norms, groups can have great difficulty in staying true to the processes that help them be more productive as a team.

John Eller

Effective groups establish and follow certain ways of functioning, which we call *norms*. Different groups have different norms. Some may focus on how the group uses time, the roles members may play, or the conditions under which the group meets.

To have the kind of productive and collaborative groups we address in Book Four, group members must adopt productive norms. Garmston and Wellman (2012) have identified seven norms essential for collaborative work. They call them "norms" rather than "skills" because they see the actions as behaviors that *all* group members use and they become a part of the culture of the group. Thus, the behavior becomes normative, or basic, to group functioning. When these norms become second nature to groups, "cohesion, energy, and commitment to shared work and to the group increase dramatically" (Garmston & Wellman, 2009, p. 31), and a community exists.

The norms of collaboration are:

1. Pausing.
2. Paraphrasing.
3. Posing questions.
4. Putting ideas on the table.
5. Providing data.
6. Paying attention to self and others.
7. Presuming positive intentions (Garmston & Wellman, 2012).

Underlying these norms is an explicit intention to support the work that needs to be done and to develop the group and the communication skills of group members.

Garmston and Wellman (2009) suggest that regardless of the role a leader has in a group (facilitator, presenter, coach, or consultant), it is important that he or she model these seven norms of collaboration. If the leader is skillful in adhering to the norms, other group members are likely to do the same. And if current group members model the desired behavior, new group members will follow suit.

> **Reflection**
>
> Think about groups that you have been part of. Did any of these groups have a set of agreed-upon norms that supported their work? What were these norms? Were any of them similar to the ones listed?

> What differences did you see between groups that had agreed on a common set of norms and those that didn't? How would you describe the differences?
>
> Are there groups that you are part of now that could benefit from establishing shared norms? If so, how can you help this group? What norms would be most helpful to them in meeting their group goals?

DAY 4: GROUP NORM #1—PAUSING

Listen or thy tongue will keep thee deaf.

American Indian proverb

Group members, including leaders, are often so intent on what they are going to say next that they either aren't listening or fail to give themselves and others adequate processing time.

Garmston and Wellman (2012) point out that a speaker's pausing, or providing wait time, is essential so that others can process and respond to what has been said. It also gives you as the group leader the opportunity to reword in your own mind what others say to further understand their perspective.

People who are introverted normally require more quiet processing time. They internally process what has been said. Those who are more extraverted tend to process externally. They are the people who say, "I really don't know what I think until the words start coming out of my mouth." The introvert is more inclined to comment, "I need some time to think about that." Keeping a balance, so that introverts have sufficient processing time and extraverts do not get impatient or bored, is a challenge for a group and its leader.

Garmston and Wellman (2012) state that there are four types of pauses that contribute to the effectiveness of groups:

1. After a question has been asked, allowing time for everyone to process and understand what is being asked.

2. After someone speaks, allowing time to organize thoughts and reflect on what has been said.

3. When asked to respond to a question, allowing the person time to compose his or her thoughts and responses.

4. When a "collective pause" is needed, allowing time for the entire group to take notes, reflect, or consider various options. (p. 46)

Reflection

Here is a brief segment of a group interaction. Read the exchanges and answer the questions at the end.

Group Leader: One of the criteria that we have to decide in setting up this scholarship program is, given our pool of money, how many scholarships do we want to award? Do we want to give several deserving students smaller amounts of money, or would we rather give larger amounts to just two or three students? In making this decision, we need to keep in mind other possible sources of scholarships, grants, or loans that our applicants may have available to them. Along with that, we need to consider our purpose—that is, to support students of color and diverse backgrounds who want to become mathematics or science teachers.

Group Member A: I think that we need to—

Group Leader: Excuse me, Group Member A, can we all take a few moments to jot down our thoughts about this before starting to interact? This is a very important decision we're about to make, and we want everyone's best thinking.

Group Leader (after a couple of minutes): Okay, Group Member A, what are your thoughts?

Group Member A: I think that we need to give smaller amounts to up to 10 students. Investing all our money in just two or three students is too risky. We have no guarantees that they will actually continue with mathematics or science or go into teaching.

Group Member B: I think you're absolutely right. It's better to spread the money around.

Group Member C: I disagree. Our applicants deserve more support.

Group Member D: Yeah, you're absolutely right. The more support we give them, the more likely they'll stay the course and become mathematics or science teachers. Diluting our effort may deter them. There are no guarantees. Let's pick the best students and give them more support.

Group Member E: What kind of application do you think they should fill out?

Group Member A: I have a sample in my office. Would you like me to get it so we all can look at it?

Group Leader: Can we hold off on that topic for a bit and go back to our original topic of how many scholarships we want to give at what level? Group Members A and D seem to have captured the two perspectives. Can each of you be more specific by suggesting how many scholarships at what level you think would be appropriate?

Consider the following questions:

- Where do you see the group leader honoring the norm of pausing to facilitate group interaction?
- What are examples in which the group leader does not use the norm of pausing?
- If you were the leader of this group, what would you have done differently and why?

DAY 5: GROUP NORM #2—PARAPHRASING

What we've got here is failure to communicate.

Paul Newman, Cool Hand Luke

Paraphrasing is a norm that Garmston and Wellman (2012) see as essential for group understanding. It is a restatement of something that has been said. The technique is important for the following reasons:

- It enables a speaker to know whether he or she was heard correctly.
- It honors the worth of group members by recognizing the content and emotion of their contributions.
- It moves the interaction forward through synthesizing or summarizing.
- It allows for correction of any vagueness, lack of clarity, or imprecision.
- It sets the stage for probing for details and elaboration.

Paraphrasing says to the speaker that you are listening, that you are attempting to understand, and that you care.

There is a logical flow to paraphrasing. First, signal your intent to paraphrase. Paraphrases should begin with "You" rather than "I" to keep the focus on the speaker. For example: "You're suggesting that the group . . . " rather than "I hear you say that the group . . . " Other possible stems include, "You're thinking . . . ," "You're wanting . . . ," or "Am I understanding you to be saying . . . ?"

Next, choose a logical level with which to respond. There are three such levels (Garmston & Wellman, 2012):

1. Acknowledging and clarifying the speaker's content and emotion.

2. Summarizing by organizing and synthesizing discussion or by identifying themes.

3. Shifting focus to a higher or lower logical level. Going to a higher level happens when the listener connects what he or she has heard with conceptual ideas, such as goals, assumptions, or values. For example, "One assumption you are making is . . . " Going to a lower level happens when the listener anchors abstractions in the concrete by providing specific details he or she has heard. For example, "An example of what you are saying would be . . . " (p. 47).

Paraphrasing that summarizes or shifts the logical level of discourse can both support and challenge group members.

Reflection

Here are five statements made by members in a group. How would you paraphrase each one to honor the group member's content and emotion, summarize discussion or identify themes, or raise or lower the logical level of the discourse?

To help you get started, here is an example that paraphrases the speaker's content and emotion:

> *The comment:* "I'm frustrated and angry. I spent two days preparing this report for our meeting, and no one has even read it. What kind of support is that? When last we met, you all were adamant about my having this report to you ASAP. What happened?"
>
> *The paraphrase:* "You're obviously upset and rightly so. You've rearranged your schedule to get this report to us, as per our request, and none of us has read it. Your concerns are legitimate. Can we take a few minutes to figure out what happened?"

> How would you paraphrase the following statements? Remember to start with *You* rather than *I*:
>
> *Statement 1:* "I don't think this group is following its own norms."
>
> *Statement 2:* "They won't like it if we decide to hold the professional development the third week of August."
>
> *Statement 3:* "I think this curriculum is so much better than the one we're currently using."
>
> *Statement 4:* "Implementing this new curriculum will be a breeze. Nobody will have any problems with it."
>
> *Statement 5:* "I disagree."

DAY 6: GROUP NORM #3—POSING QUESTIONS

The power to question is the basis of all human progress.

Indira Gandhi

As human beings, our utterances are not always complete and clear. In our interactions, we often need to probe and ask questions, for a number of different reasons. We may seek data, information, or knowledge; or opinions, feelings, or commitments. We may also be looking for clarity, details, personal connections, past experiences, values, beliefs, or any number of other things.

The danger with posing questions is that it can often be seen as interrogation. Think back to when you were a teen and a parent found evidence that you had done something wrong. Recall the string of questions hurled at you: "What time did you get home? Where were you? Who were you with? Why didn't you call?" Our questioning of others can have a similar tone.

At the same time, our questions are legitimate, move interaction forward, and contribute to a group's ability to engage in understanding each other's perceptions, assumptions, and interpretations. It requires asking questions in a nonthreatening manner and creating an environment that is supportive of all team members to participate in open communication. Garmston and Wellman (2012) write that there are six important features in open communication, including:

1. *Full attention*: Keeping your attention on group members in contrast to reading and responding to your e-mail or otherwise being diverted.

2. *Approachable voice:* Using a well-modulated tone to indicate inquiry and exploration, rather than interrogation or challenge.

3. *Plural forms*: Speaking in plurals rather than singulars, such as focusing on varied ideas rather than one specific idea.

4. *Exploratory language*: Using words such as *some*, *might*, or *possible* to extend the conversation and invite a variety of responses.

5. *Non-dichotomous questions*: Asking open-ended questions rather than those that can be answered *yes* or *no*.

6. *Positive presuppositions*: Asking questions using phrasing that conveys positive intentions (p. 48).

Using these six elements, team members focus on two intentions of posing questions: 1) exploring thinking and 2) specifying thinking. The intention of exploring thinking is to inquire into the assumptions, perceptions, and ideas of others before advocating one's own position. It's being curious and genuinely wanting to know what others think and feel. It's also helping a group learn how to ask questions to help them move beyond just data or information. This sounds simple, but in reality it can be very difficult since it goes against our cultural norm of argumentation.

In addition to inquiring into other's thinking, posing questions allows groups to specify their thinking and entails asking "questions to construct shared understanding and to increase the meaning of what others are saying" (Garmston & Wellman, 2012, p. 50). Often, people use vague or generalized phrases that may contribute to a distorted perception of a situation. Asking questions to specify thinking and clarify the meaning of certain phrases helps groups avoid misinterpretations and vagueness.

For example, the italicized words in the following statements contribute to vagueness, and the questions that accompany each statement are ways to specify thinking.

- *Those students* are not performing. Which students specifically?
- We need to *improve* our teaching practices. Which teaching practices? What would improvement look like? What exactly would we observe?
- It seems *less important* to focus on the mathematics curriculum. How is it less important? Less important than what?
- We *have to* include the school board in this decision. Why? Who decided they have to be included? What would happen if we didn't?
- *No one ever* follows through on our decisions. Is it true that no one follows through, or just some people? Is it true that this group of

people never follows through, or only under certain circumstances? What is the evidence or data to support this statement?

> **Reflection**
>
> Think back to a recent meeting and reflect on the overall environment of the group. Was the environment conducive to open communication? If not, what might you and others have done to support more open communication? Now, anticipate an upcoming meeting and write down some ideas for how you will indicate your full attention, phrasing you might use that reflects an approachable voice, instances where you might rely on plural forms rather than singular forms of words, how you might take advantage of using exploratory language and asking non-dichotomous questions, and phrases you might use to indicate your own positive presuppositions.
>
> Here are some examples of lack of clarity in language. Can you identify the instances of vagueness? How would you phrase a question to gain greater specificity?
>
> - "What we need is more professional development."
> - "We're working to improve our faculty/staff morale."
> - "All children can learn."
> - "Those people in the front office just don't get it."
> - "They keep telling us that we have to meet accountability measures."

DAY 7: GROUP NORM #4—PUTTING IDEAS ON THE TABLE

Good ideas come from everywhere. It's more important to recognize a good idea than to author it.

Jeanne Gang

The ideas that we contribute to group interaction are what move a group forward or backward (Garmston & Wellman, 2012).

Whenever we put out an idea, we want it considered because of its own merits, not because we ourselves are advocating the idea. This is important because group members tend to react to ideas on the basis of their relationships with and opinion of the speaker, rather than on the merits of the idea itself. To separate ourselves from our ideas, we label them as *thoughts* and *suggestions*—for group consideration, not for personal advocacy.

Here is an example of how to introduce an idea. Declare your intention of presenting a suggestion to simply move the group thinking forward: "Here is one way that we might approach resolving the conflict we're facing." Another approach: "Here is a thought. How about postponing the conference until after the holiday so that . . . ?" Notice that this approach puts some distance between you and your suggestion so that it can be considered on its own value, independent of your status or position within the group.

Before putting an idea on the table, it is a good idea to ask yourself whether your contribution is relevant to the topic under discussion and if it will move your group forward.

The flip side of putting an idea on the table is taking it off. We do that when we have put forth a suggestion that no longer seems feasible or is blocking the group in some way. By removing your contribution, you take responsibility for your role in carrying out the group's work. And taking items off is easy—as long as you are not attached to your suggestion: "This clearly isn't a workable idea. Let's scrap it and move on to something else."

Reflection

A Possible Scenario

The group you are leading is exploring ways to get 95 percent of the elementary teachers to participate in a series of professional development workshops on assessment. As the discussion moves along, you find you have the following to contribute:

- Prior experience in getting almost all teachers to participate in a professional development program
- An idea on how to motivate teachers to participate under this set of circumstances

Write down the way you might state your contributions so that the group is likely to consider them on their own merit rather than because you as the leader suggested them.

A Second Scenario

In a faculty meeting, one member contributes two or three ideas and starts advocating for one of them. However, the group is still generating ideas and has not yet begun to evaluate them or make decisions. What would you do to keep the group focused on brainstorming ideas before moving on to considering the ideas' pros and cons?

DAY 8: GROUP NORM #5—PROVIDING DATA

Providing data, both qualitative and quantitative, in a variety of forms supports group members in constructing shared understanding from their work.

Robert Garmston and Bruce Wellman

A common adage about data is that "data have no meaning" in and of themselves until we interpret and make meaning of them. As a norm of collaboration, providing data ensures that groups have access to the information they need to collaboratively explore and act. It grounds conversations in reality and provides a basis for dialoguing about topics that are important and relevant for the group. As Garmston and Wellman (2012) note, effective groups "develop the capacity to discern what data are worth paying attention to and what collaborative practices help people to engage with data in ways that increase their ownership and willingness to act on conclusions" (p. 51).

Using data to structure group conversations can be supported when team members include "specific, measurable, and observable information" in their reasoning and comments; present that information or data "without judgments, opinions, or inferences"; and strive to provide a variety of types of data to "broaden understanding" (Garmston & Wellman, 2012, p. 41). They also encourage groups to develop processes to guide their use of data, such as collaborative inquiry into data (Book Five, Day 10), data-driven dialogue (Book Five, Day 12), and using third point communication (Book Four, Day 28).

Reflection

In what ways do groups that you lead rely on and share data? How often are data, evidence, and other sources of information the foundation for your conversations? Do you often consider a variety of types of data or rely more often on only one source? Do you and your teams have routine, structured processes to engage with and dialogue about data? What might you do to strengthen this norm of collaboration within groups that you lead?

DAY 9: GROUP NORM #6—PAYING ATTENTION TO SELF AND OTHERS, VERBAL COMMUNICATION

Many attempts to communicate are nullified by saying too much.

Robert Greenleaf

Skillful group members pay attention to what they are communicating, how they are communicating, and how others are responding to what they are saying. Being attentive to both verbal and nonverbal communication from oneself and other group members is another quality of effective group interaction (Garmston & Wellman, 2012).

By paying attention to the physical and verbal cues in ourselves and others, we are able to do the following:

- Spot differences in people's beliefs, values, and communication styles
- See things from a variety of perspectives
- Use the nonverbal behavior of others to modify our own behavior

Attending to your own verbal and nonverbal behavior and that of others underlies all the norms. All seven norms are interactive and synergistic rather than existing in isolation. For example, when you paraphrase, you are paying attention to others and checking your own understanding. When you remove one of your ideas from the table, you are paying attention to others. When you recast something you have said to make it more precise, you are listening to yourself and making improvements in your communication with others.

In terms of verbal behavior, noticing others' words and matching your language to them is a way of responding to important data (Garmston & Wellman, 2009). If a group member uses a metaphor, picking up that metaphor in your own speech validates the other person and builds group rapport. Consider this example: A group member describes a project as a "wild roller-coaster ride." You continue this metaphor in the group discussion with references to "peaks and valleys," "breakneck speed," "gasping for breath," and other related references, as appropriate. (Exercise some restraint so that the metaphor doesn't lose its power.)

A more subtle approach is to match auditory words with other auditory words, visual with visual, and kinesthetic with kinesthetic. For example, a group member talks about hearing a number of "discordant" ideas being expressed. You respond by saying that you will try to "orchestrate" the discussion by identifying underlying themes you think you have heard. Your auditory word matches the other person's auditory word.

Reflection

Here are some statements that contain metaphors. Read each one and decide how you might respond to the person making the statement by using or building on the metaphor used:

- "I feel that all we're doing is running around putting out fires."
- "That old building is sucking the life right out of us."
- "Managing information systems is like going over Niagara Falls in a barrel."

In this next set of examples, determine whether each statement has an auditory, visual, or kinesthetic image, and match your response to the same type of image.

- "How would you like to orchestrate our presentation?"
- "This project requires more assembly than I think we can handle."
- "Can you sketch out for me what the new plan will cover?"

DAY 10: GROUP NORM #6—PAYING ATTENTION TO SELF AND OTHERS, NONVERBAL COMMUNICATION

It's not differences that divide us. It's our judgments about each other that do.

Margaret Wheatley

Because nonverbal communication—as exhibited in posture, gestures, voice tone and inflection, facial expression, proximity, and posture, for example—often carries more of the message than the words, being able to decode it is extremely important (Garmston & Wellman, 2009). That includes knowing what messages your own nonverbal behavior communicates and being able to read the nonverbal behavior of others. Remember that in instances of a mixed message—the words say one thing, but the nonverbal behavior says something else—the nonverbal is usually the stronger message and the one that is most clearly received by others.

So, how might you get more in touch with your own and others' nonverbal messages? Let's say that you notice that when Group Member A introduced an idea, Group Member B stopped participating. She moved her chair back from the table, got her calendar out, flipped through pages, and made notes. She seemed to have disengaged from the discussion. You know her behavior changed, but you don't know why. Because total group involvement is central to your task, you want to find out what is happening and pull her back in if she has indeed left. That is an example of paying attention to nonverbal cues.

Note that in the situation described, you have not made any conclusions about Group Member B's behavior. You have just observed a change. You have avoided what Chris Argyris (1986) calls *the ladder of inference.* In the ladder of inference, a common human pathway, we select data, add meanings, make assumptions, and draw conclusions that often lead to incorrect beliefs and actions.

Assume that you had started up the ladder. Here is what might have happened. You thought you saw Group Member B look at Group Member A when he spoke. You thought the look was strange and concluded that there was something going on between them. Then, you speculated about what that could be. You ended up concluding that Group Member B had found Group Member A's suggestion offensive and was upset with him. Note that you made all of this up. Your conclusion was not based on actual data that you had verified. All of this took place in your own head so quickly that you were probably not aware of the rapid ascension. And no one observed this mental manipulation except you.

Climbing the ladder of inference too quickly is a very common human activity and one to guard against in observing group behavior. Notice behavior, but don't draw conclusions before checking in with the person to see what he or she is thinking or feeling to confirm, or not confirm, your initial impression with verified information.

Reflection

Observe nonverbal behavior. In the next meeting you attend, pay close attention to your nonverbal behavior. Are you sitting or standing? Where have you positioned yourself within the group? What is your facial expression? What is your posture? Do you have any particular mannerisms (propping up your head with your hand, playing with your hair or a piece of jewelry, twirling a pencil or pen)? If someone were to walk by, what message would your nonverbal behavior convey? Is it the message you want to send?

If you are comfortable doing so, ask a trusted colleague who is also in the meeting to give you some feedback. See whether his or her perceptions are similar to yours or whether they are different. After comparing data, is there anything you would like to change about how you communicate nonverbally?

Avoid climbing the ladder of inference. Here are some instances that can easily trigger an ascent up the ladder of inference. What alternative explanations might account for the following behaviors? How could you find out what is really going on?

- A group member yawns a lot and occasionally closes his eyes.
- One group member rarely makes a contribution unless asked. Her ideas are usually excellent.
- One group member consistently arrives 10 minutes after you start the meeting.

DAY 11: GROUP NORM #7—PRESUMING POSITIVE INTENTIONS

Change your thoughts and you change your world.

Norman Vincent Peale

We serve ourselves and our group by assuming that others have the best of intentions and are speaking and acting out of positive motives (Garmston & Wellman, 2009). If that is the case, then framing paraphrases and probes with this assumption in mind is likely to keep the group on a positive note and move the interaction forward.

By assuming positive intentions, we reduce threats, challenges, and defensiveness. We also keep emotions on an even keel by not responding immediately when something bothers us. When we hear something that could be taken in a negative way, it is best to take a deep breath, pause, and assume positive intentions. In presuming positive intentions, we ask questions in the spirit of inquiry rather than the spirit of interrogation. We also actively solicit different views and interpretations. For example, rather than saying, "I think you see my work as your lowest priority and rarely respond to my e-mails," say, "I know how busy we all are and how many priorities you are addressing, when do you think you might be able to send a response to my request?"

Reflection

Activity 1

Here are the same situations given for Norm #6 in Day 10, with different instructions this time. Assume that each person is a professional who is committed to the welfare and success of your group. Using the alternative realities you generated for the reflection in Norm #6, pose a question to each person about his or her behavior that is not threatening, less likely to produce defensive behavior, and helps you clarify intentions. We use the first instance as an example:

- A group member yawns a lot and occasionally closes his eyes. A presuming-positive-intentions response is this: "You seem tired. Have you recovered from that hectic schedule we kept last week?" A presuming-negative-intentions response: "Is this too boring for you? Don't let us keep you up."
- One group member rarely makes a contribution unless asked. Her ideas are usually excellent.
- Another group member consistently arrives 10 minutes late.

Activity 2

Here are some statements that contain presuppositions. Identify each one:

- "If the other team had done what it was supposed to, they wouldn't be having this problem right now."

162 • Leading Every Day

- "We're done with brainstorming. Now, let's go back and identify the good ideas."
- "Our previous leader should have cleared that for us before leaving."
- "If the agenda had been set up properly, we wouldn't be running over."
- "The books didn't arrive. Someone needs to call and let those people know what we think of them. They promised they would be here in 10 days."

DAY 12: DIALOGUE VERSUS DISCUSSION

The first and most difficult task of dialogue involves parking the ego and listening with an open spirit. From this receptivity can come questions, which lead to understanding.

Sources of Insight

Not only are there more effective patterns of talk (as exemplified by the seven norms of collaboration), there are also different types of talking, often with different purposes. These different ways are presented in Figure 4.1.

Figure 4.1 Ways of Talking

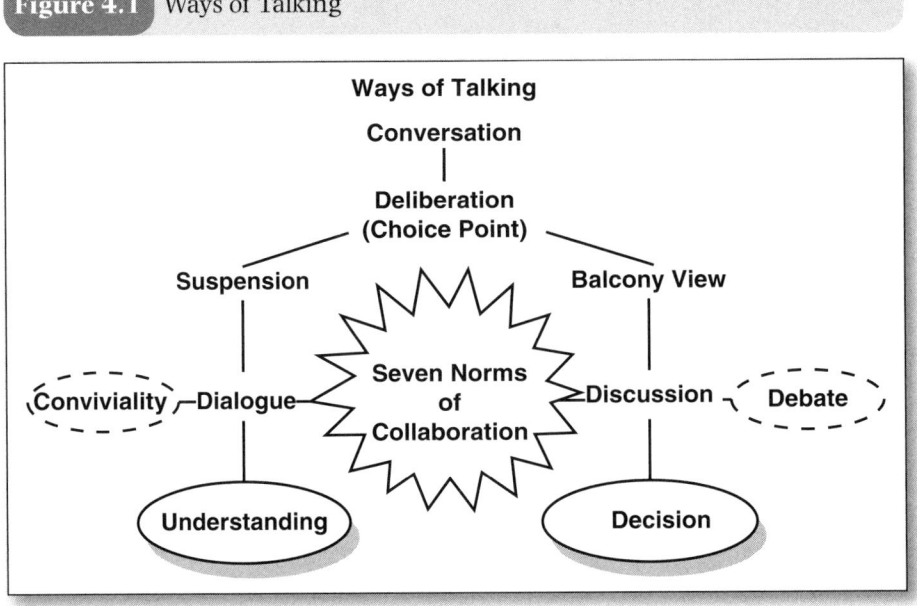

SOURCE: Garmston, R. J., & Wellman, B. M. Copyright © 2009. *The Adaptive School: A Sourcebook for Developing Collaborative Groups, second edition* (p. 46). Norwood, MA: Christopher-Gordon. Reprinted with permission of the authors.

In this schema, conversation is informal talking in which group members simply exchange information, ideas, thoughts, or feelings with each other, often with no purpose other than to enjoy the experience. At some juncture, the nature of the conversation may begin to change. If it starts to take on a more conscious, deeper purpose, it has reached a choice point. Group members decide consciously or unconsciously whether the talk goes into either dialogue or discussion.

Dialogue and discussion are two very different ways of talking, each with its own specific purpose and rules.

Dialogue is reflective learning in which group members seek to understand each other's viewpoints and assumptions by talking together to deepen their collective understanding. Dialogue often opens up the possibility of a better solution. The goal is finding common ground.

With dialogue, there is inquiry to learn and a desire to discover and unfold shared meaning, to integrate multiple perspectives, and to uncover and examine underlying assumptions. An appropriate topic for dialogue might be the purpose and role of professional development in an organization.

The purpose of *discussion*, on the other hand, is to decide something. Discussion eliminates some suggestions from a wider field, with the stronger ideas taking precedence. In discussion, there is normally an action outcome. Most organizational meetings involve some form of structured discussion. There is a purpose and an anticipated outcome that moves the organization forward. In discussion, there is telling, selling, persuading, gaining agreement on one meaning or course of action, evaluating choices and selecting the best, and justifying and defending assumptions.

How one engages in dialogue and discussion has an effect on the group's productivity. In the schema presented, conviviality is dialogue that focuses on comfort rather than real learning. Debate is discussion that relies on intimidation and intonation more than logic and reason. Neither fosters group growth and development or productivity.

According to Garmston and Wellman (2012),

> In its most ineffective form, discussion consists of serial sharing and serial advocacy without much group-member inquiry into the thinking and proposals of others. Participants attempt to reach decisions through a variety of voting and consensus techniques. When discussion is unskilled and dialogue is absent, decisions are often low quality, represent the opinions of the most vocal members or leader, lack group commitment and do not stay made. Three

elements shape skilled discussions: clarity about decision-making processes and authority; knowledge of the boundaries surrounding the topics open to the group's decision-making authority; and standards for orderly decision-making meetings. (p. 28)

Reflection

Think about meetings you've been involved in or led recently. Which type of talk happened? Was the talk largely structured discussions? Were the three elements of skilled discussion (clarity, boundaries, and order) in place? If not, how could you facilitate the development and use of them?

Did the meetings at any time degenerate into debate? Did they incorporate dialogue? Did dialogue ever slip into conviviality?

Was the type of talk appropriate for the purpose of each meeting? If not, why not? What could you have done to promote the type of interaction that best suited the purpose and desired outcome of the meetings?

DAY 13: DIALOGUE AS REFLECTIVE LEARNING PROCESS

He who differs from us, does not always contradict us; he has one view of an object, and we have another, each describes what he sees with equal fidelity, and each regulates his steps by his own eyes.

Samuel Johnson

Dialogue—what makes it different?

Recall what dialogue is: a reflective learning process in which people seek to understand each other's viewpoints and deeply held assumptions by talking together to deepen their collective understanding. The goal is increased understanding—not a decision, not a next step, just greater understanding on every person's part.

The basic internal skill in dialogue is suspending judgment (see Figure 4.1). It means being open to what is happening in the moment and to what others are thinking and feeling. Suspending judgment also involves surfacing assumptions and beliefs, which influence our perceptions of reality.

According to Garmston and Wellman (2012),

Dialogue creates an emotional and cognitive safety zone in which ideas flow for examination without judgment. Although many of the capabilities and tools of dialogue and skilled discussion are the same, their core intentions are quite different and require different personal and collective monitoring processes. (p. 26)

The value of greater understanding is that it is the basis for conflict resolution, consensus, and community building. If certain group members feel they have not been heard, they can sabotage a decision. Dialogue ensures that every person is heard and, ideally, understood. "Working from a foundation of shared understanding, group members can more easily and rationally resolve differences, generate options, and make wise choices when they move to the discussion side of the journey" (Garmston & Wellman, 2009, p. 49). The seven norms of collaboration are extremely important for establishing effective dialogue.

Reflection

The reason this contemplation focuses on dialogue rather than structured discussion is that most of us are more experienced in the latter. It may be our primary style. We are skilled and comfortable. And that is important because effective discussion is a critical skill for group members. However, so is dialogue, but most of us are not as skilled and comfortable with this form of talking. Consider the following questions:

- How readily do members of your group engage in dialogue?
- How do you encourage people to share assumptions and their thinking on issues with the purpose of shared understanding?

Think of a problem or issue you are facing that you would like to ask your group to dialogue about.

- What opportunity do you see to use dialogue with your staff and colleagues?
- How will you teach them to dialogue?
- How will you structure the opportunities for people to practice dialoguing?

How can you establish a culture in which your colleagues are skilled and willing to use dialogue to develop more shared meaning?

DAY 14: ELICITING PARTICIPATION FROM EVERYONE

An atmosphere of free exchange can be created only when participants see that a mutual sharing of opinions and ideas is welcome.

Marion E. Haynes

In virtually every group, there are those who want to talk a great deal and those who say little. Ideally, you want to hear from everyone. As a leader, you may need to rein in those people who tend to talk too much and set up structures to encourage those who are more reticent to express themselves.

One of the basic tenets of communication is that silence doesn't mean agreement or consent. Unless people talk, it is hard for you to know what they are thinking and feeling. There are numerous ways to draw out people who say little in a group. Here are a few suggestions:

- Provide opportunities for group members to write their ideas and pair with another to share their responses, as well as speak in the large group. Some may be more willing to share a response after they have had the opportunity to write it down and say it aloud to one person.
- In brainstorming, have participants first write down one or more idea or suggestion. Go around the room, asking each person to contribute one item aloud. After all contributions have been written down, have another period of writing. Keep this up until you have a sufficient number of responses for your task.
- Set up smaller groups of two to four people in which conversation may come easier for those who dislike speaking in a larger group.
- Extend your wait time so those who need time to think can do so before speaking.

You may also need to be proactive to make sure that some people do not dominate the conversation. For example:

- Establish a group norm about each member having his or her fair share of airtime. For example, the "rule of three" asks each participant to allow three other people to speak before sharing another comment. (This tends to keep the talkers under control more than it gets the reticent ones to speak up.)
- Say, "Let's hear from someone who hasn't had a chance to speak yet" before giving a frequent speaker the floor.
- If all else fails, take the person aside at a break and discuss the importance of hearing from each person and not having one or two dominate the discussion. In extreme cases, you may have to set a rule such as only one comment per 15-minute period.

Following these suggestions will earn you the respect of the group and, only occasionally, the hostility of one or two people who seem unable to control the urge to talk at every opportunity. It will contribute to group bonding—you with the group and group members with one another—and will help establish your group as a safe place to work. You will also be helping people monitor their own participation.

Reflection

Think about this scenario: By the end of the first session of your 6-week professional development series for elementary and middle school teachers, you see that you have a number of very extraverted people. Six people speak frequently, and about the same number haven't said a word beyond their introductions. Two of the outspoken teachers are from the same school, one whose test scores are the highest of any elementary school in the district.

One of your activities was a brainstorming session in which the teachers were asked to generate a list of all the algebraic concepts they thought were appropriate for students to learn at the primary, intermediate, and middle school levels. During this activity, you noticed that some teachers participated very little.

At the end, you asked for a voice vote on moving the time of the next session up half an hour. A majority said yes, so you adjusted the time.

In this scenario, what participation problems do you see? What steps could you take to balance participation? How could you make sure that you know what your more reticent members are thinking and feeling? How could you avoid making "majority rule" decisions that affect each member of the group?

DAY 15: CULTURAL PROFICIENCY

A culturally proficient leader influences others to make changes in their values, beliefs, and attitudes.

Randall Lindsey, Laraine Roberts, and Franklin CampbellJones

One of the responsibilities of a leader is to manage the culture of the group. Every group embodies a culture that can have both positive and negative aspects (Lindsey, Roberts, & CampbellJones, 2005). To the extent that a group leader is aware of the prevalent culture, he or she can use that knowledge to promote inclusiveness.

One aspect of culture that a leader needs to monitor is the emergence of any bias and stereotyping that can affect group efficacy. Bias and stereotyping are violations of the norm of paying attention to self and others and can be communicated through the language we use and how we behave. As a group leader, it is imperative for you to engage your group in recognizing, addressing, and "having the hard conversations" about any instances of bias or stereotyping that occur.

Here are seven conditions that you will want to establish to promote inclusiveness and avoid bias and stereotyping. Each one and its impact are discussed briefly:

1. *Make sure your group membership reflects your stakeholders or constituency.* A non-representative group can raise questions among the larger community that can hinder the group's efficacy. For example, a question might be, "Why is that group making decisions about educational programs for *all* students when the group membership is not representative of *all* students?" Similar issues that surface within the group ("Why are there no women here?") can also negatively affect efficacy.

2. *Each person speaks for himself or herself.* Often when individuals are a minority within a majority group, other group members will expect them to know and expound on, for example, the Native American point of view, the female perspective, or what Hispanics are likely to believe. There are two fallacies here: one is that a racial, ethnic, or cultural group has a unified perspective, which is rarely the case. There will almost always be a diversity of opinion. Second, even if there were a unified perspective, it would be inappropriate to expect an individual to know and espouse that view. It is fine to ask, "What would our various stakeholders think of this idea?" It is not appropriate to ask an individual for the opinion of what the larger group may or may not believe, perceive, or expect, unless someone is an official representative of a stakeholder or constituency group.

3. *Avoid making assumptions about group members, especially assumptions based on race, ethnicity, gender, or cultural background.* Assumptions can be either positive or negative. For example, someone might say, "I bet you don't know the way to the Eastside recreation area. You live on the Westside, right?" Or "This is a good role for Jack. He can stack the chairs and move the tables before we leave. He's a big guy; he can handle it."

In such cases, you are, in essence, speaking for the person without the person validating what is correct and appropriate for himself or herself. Making assumptions about others can decrease the sense of inclusiveness that exists in a group.

4. *Accurately acknowledge individuals' contributions.* A common occurrence in groups is discounting or ignoring someone's contribution only to affirm it when another person picks it up. Then, the idea is likely to be attributed to the second source rather than the first. There also is a good

chance that the first contributor is perceived as a lower-status person and the second as a higher-status individual. If this occurs, you can say something like, "I think that's what Julia just suggested. What a great idea."

5. *Avoid jokes, puns, or other expressions of humor that reflect negatively on a particular group.* With the heightened awareness of diversity issues in recent years, this behavior appears to have lessened. However, it does still exist. Attempts to be funny using racial, ethnic, cultural, or sexual humor are more likely to be sources of embarrassment than sources of humor and obviously reduce the levels of inclusiveness and safety within the group.

6. *Avoiding derogatory language or offensive terms.* Referring to any group member using a derogatory or offensive term—publicly or privately—is simply crude and degrading. Moreover, it is likely to backfire. The news media have reported numerous stories about people who have lost their positions by making racial and sexual slurs. Offensive terms also include name calling. Referring to another group as "nutcases" is not in the spirit of inquiry.

7. *Always consider the cultural aspect in decisions made.* Unless universal in their design, policies, programs, and procedures will have a cultural orientation. If the orientation is not recognized and accounted for, the likelihood of bias exists. For example, if a group planning an after-school recreational program for middle school students does not consider the interests and prior experiences of the young people, the program may not attract the students targeted for the activities.

The presence of any bias or stereotyping in a group usually indicates that the norm of paying attention to oneself and others is not being followed. Group members who don't realize the impact of their behavior on others can affect the group's efficacy and perhaps even the outcome of its work. It is the group leader's responsibility to challenge any instance of bias or stereotyping and engage the group in discussing the "undiscussables."

Reflection

Here is an opportunity to practice. What follows are several statements reflecting bias and stereotyping. Imagine yourself leading the group. How would you handle the situation?

- "I'm sure that Destiny won't be able to meet on Saturday. I bet she has to take care of her kids."

- "I heard the best dumb blonde joke the other day. These two blondes were walking down the street . . . "
- "Lester speaks Spanish, too. The two of you should talk."
- "What is the Puerto Rican take on this situation?"

How can you, as leader, heighten group members' awareness of the negative effects of bias and stereotyping?

DAY 16: ESTABLISHING CLEAR ROLES AND FUNCTIONS

Nothing strengthens the judgment and quickens the conscience like individual responsibility.

Elizabeth Cady Stanton

To operate efficiently and effectively, groups need to be clear about their roles and functions. It is the group leader's responsibility to make sure clarity exists about (1) how the group was formed, (2) which people participate and why, (3) the charge of the group, (4) how the charge relates to the organization's overall mission and vision, (5) what resources the group has at its disposal, (6) the time frame, (7) reporting responsibilities, and (8) how the group decides to go about its work.

Groups that are clear on all these factors are much more inclined to tap into one of their energy sources: efficacy. Members are more likely to believe that their group has the capacity to act and is willing and able to do so. The leader considers the parameters of the work, conveys them to the group, and answers any questions or resolves any issues that might be in the way (or works with group members to address unresolved issues).

One important step is for the leader and the group to set guidelines for how the group will go about its work. Here are some items on which the group should agree:

Logistics

- Meeting dates, times, and locations
- Structure of meetings (for example, agenda, time designations for items, distribution of written documents prior to the meeting, and so on)
- How to keep and disseminate records of the group's work
- Whether there will be refreshments and, if so, how they will be provided

How the Group Functions

- Determining roles for group members (for example, convener, recorder, facilitator, or reflector)
- Establishing processes for decision making
- Delineating guidelines for handling conflict
- Deciding how to handle issues of confidentiality and any conflict of interests
- Establishing limits of legal and/or fiduciary responsibility, if applicable
- Observing basic conversational courtesies: listening to each other, not interrupting, being respectful of each other, and carrying on one conversation at a time
- Specifying guidelines for giving and receiving feedback
- Honoring spontaneous humor and fun as the group works
- Determining how the guidelines will be adhered to or enforced

How Individuals Function

- Using "I" statements when speaking for oneself (except in paraphrasing)
- Notifying the convener (or other designated person) when unable to attend a meeting
- Being on time for meetings and staying for the entire meeting
- Responding to voice mail and e-mail messages within a reasonable length of time
- Agreeing to do what each member commits to doing or renegotiating the task with the group
- Agreeing to turn off cell phones during meetings

Although the group should decide most of these items itself, the leader sets a tone for how he or she wants the group to function by requesting that the group set ground rules and that members follow them. Again, this is an important step in building efficacy. Establishing these operational guidelines in a group is very common. What is rarely done, however, is to agree on how the guidelines will be enforced. All too often, established guidelines are ignored because there is no guideline set for enforcing the agreed-upon behavior. Members may feel uncomfortable pointing out inappropriate behavior, so that very quickly in the life of a group, the guidelines may be negated or followed only when members find it convenient or easy.

As a leader, you can make a valuable contribution to your group by establishing a process for ensuring that members follow the guidelines. This might entail giving each person explicit permission to alert his or her peers to infractions and clarifying the expectation that they do so—that is part of being an effective group member. In fact, in the early life of the group, you might want to practice intervening with members who violate the guidelines so your group will feel more comfortable enforcing them. Here is a place where the skills of giving and receiving feedback (see Days 22 and 23) become very important.

> **Reflection**
>
> Think about a group that you currently work with and serve in a leadership role. In what ways have you provided guidelines for how the group manages logistics? How the group functions? Set norms for how individuals function within the group? What specific roles or functions need improvement? How can you facilitate and lead those improvements?

DAY 17: STRUCTURING AN EFFECTIVE MEETING

> *Ask any group of managers in any country in the world to list their three most time-consuming activities. Invariably, "meetings" will appear among the three. I have asked this question of more than 200 groups, and in every case but three, more than three-quarters of each group indicated that half their time spent in meetings is wasted. The problem . . . is not being sure which half.*
>
> Alec R. MacKenzie

Ask Alec MacKenzie's question, and you will get the same answer: unnecessary meetings, meetings that accomplish nothing, or meetings that go on and on. These meetings may be face-to-face or by telephone or video conference. There is no inherent value in a meeting for the sake of a meeting. Every meeting needs to have a purpose, anticipated outcomes, and an effective process that involves all members.

Good meetings just don't happen; they are the result of careful planning and leadership. One key is building a workable agenda and following it (Mundry, Britton, Raizen, & Loucks-Horsley, 2000; Scholtes, Joiner, & Streibel, 2003).

Here are some suggestions on structuring an effective meeting:

- Have and communicate a clear purpose for the meeting.
- Build an agenda around the purpose. Gather input from group members about the agenda. Others may want to add, delete, or reorder items.

- Determine which items are information items for which discussion is appropriate; identify which are action items that should result in a clearly defined next step; and label the items as appropriate.
- Decide how much time to allot to each item and indicate that on the agenda. You can negotiate more time if necessary, but at least you have a proposed plan for staying on schedule.
- Describe the process to be used for each item, including the domain of talk and the decision-making strategy (for example, majority preference) for the action items. Each topic on the agenda needs to have a process associated with it so members know how to approach the item.
- Place controversial topics at or near the beginning of the agenda. Placing such topics at the beginning of the meeting ensures that the group will have sufficient energy to address the topic.
- Use the consent agenda to save time. In a consent agenda, routine items are grouped together and voted on as a package. Examples include previous meeting minutes, internal reports, and correspondence. If any member objects to an item being included on the consent agenda, it is pulled out and addressed separately (Board Source, 2009).
- Distribute the agenda prior to the meeting. Group members need to have sufficient time to review an agenda and prepare for the meeting. They may want to gather data, read certain articles, or prepare a presentation.
- Before starting the meeting, review the agenda with group members to see whether there are any suggestions for changes. Incorporate changes as appropriate and then begin the meeting.
- Stick to your agenda unless the group decides to renegotiate items or time. Often, issues will emerge that a group had not predicted, and an agenda will need to be modified.
- Have someone take notes. Depending on the purpose of your meeting, you may need detailed minutes. In most instances, a page of action notes is sufficient—a listing of the next steps decided on and who is responsible for what. These serve as a record of the meeting and should be distributed to group members and others who need to know about your group's work.
- Conclude by assessing the effectiveness of your meeting. Each group member could complete the following stems: "What I think we accomplished today in our meeting is . . . ," "What I wish we could have done differently is . . . ," or "What I still feel unresolved about is . . . "

Reflection

Sketch out a tentative agenda for an upcoming meeting. Distinguish between information items and action items. Assign times to each item as well as a process. Put any controversial items up front. Decide who will take notes and what type of notes you want. Send out the agenda beforehand.

At the end of your meeting, ask for feedback. What did people feel they accomplished and what suggestions do they have for future meetings?

DAY 18: PROVIDING LOGISTICAL SUPPORTS

Success is the sum of the details.

Harvey S. Firestone

Good logistics won't save a poorly designed meeting, but a well-planned event or activity can be ruined by poor logistics.

Planning meeting logistics is beyond the scope of this book. There are many excellent resources available that provide detailed guides to meeting planning. However, several aspects of logistics directly affect any group's ability to do its work and are important to review.

As a leader, you need to make sure that the following have been addressed to support your group:

- *Provide group members with complete pre-meeting information in a timely manner.* Your event can get off to a shaky start if members have not been informed about time, place, parking, agenda, and other logistical aspects of the meeting. Informing your members enables them to come prepared to do the group's work.

- *Select a room that is appropriate for the group's work.* Not any vacant room will do. The room needs to accommodate the work the group is doing. That includes the configuration of space, access to natural light, the positioning of the table(s) and chairs, electrical outlets, Internet access, and the acoustics.

- *Provide appropriate materials for the group's work.* These may include audiovisual aids; computers; charting materials; and prepared reference materials, handouts, or worksheets. Print materials need to be error free and look professional. There must be adequate space on the walls for putting up posters or flip chart sheets to help the group track its work.

- *Arrange for refreshments.* Groups can work more effectively if they have ready access to food and drink for the duration of their event. Unless you start a meeting right after a meal, it is a good idea to have food and drink available at the beginning of a meeting rather than halfway through or at the end.

- *Plan the agenda so that members can make a transition into the meeting.* People often come into a meeting with the day's events—rather than the meeting—primary in their minds. They may be thinking about a conflict they are having, the report they are working on, or getting to a meeting after this one. If you structure a transition activity at the beginning, you will help members focus on the immediate situation. One way of doing that is to pose the question, "What is foremost in your mind right now that you want to put on hold for the next two hours, and what are your expectations for this meeting?" Having each person respond can make the transition, and you can then proceed with your agenda.

> **Reflection**
>
> Think about your next meeting coming up. Have all these logistical supports been provided for? If not, what do you need to attend to? What can you do to better ensure that group members have what they need to participate fully?

DAY 19: SETTING UP THE MEETING ROOM

When facilities are proper, they go unnoticed.

Marion E. Haynes

What do you do when company comes to visit? Clean the house? Make sure the guest room is ready? Make a trip to the grocery? Ask the kids to put their toys away?

These are typical ways in which we prepare to welcome our guests and make them comfortable. But how many of us do this for our meetings? It is what David Perkins (1992) calls defining the *surround*. The surround is comprised of the features that influence thought and action in a group. These may be psychological, emotional, cognitive, or physical in nature. As a group leader, you have some influence on all of these, but you have the most control over the physical features of the meeting room.

What is important to know about the physical features? Here are some points to remember (Garmston & Wellman, 2009):

- *Everyone should be able to see and hear each other.* There are many different seating arrangements for groups of all sizes: semicircle, horseshoe shape, and so on. Depending on the acoustics, a group of 40 or more may require amplification.

- *Every participant should be able to see the group leader and the flip chart, screen, or other visual aids.* Seeing visual aids and the facilitator is essential for the group to proceed with the work. Participants should face away from the door or entryways.

- *The chairs and tables (if used) should be appropriate for the size of the group.* Extra tables and chairs that are not used disturb the energy balance in the room and should be removed. Taking out empty chairs allows for a more direct group connection.

- *The arrangement of the room should allow for individual movement and for subgroupings; participants need to see the whole room as their space rather than restrict themselves to a particular chair.* People have a tendency to select the same seats in meetings. Changing seats produces more energy in the room and gives participants a different perspective.

- *Tools for helping the group with its work (for example, flip charts, whiteboards, or other recording devices) should document the group's work.* Certain tasks such as planning, problem solving, and decision making require access to data as well as charting materials. Being able to post written materials on the wall, write on flip charts, or project text onto a screen is critical to a group's work.

- *In setting up the room, provide different areas where the facilitator can be strategically positioned to lead the group.* For example, one of the facilitator's jobs is to give instructions, and that is best done with three different communication mediums: space, voice, and language. When giving directions, the facilitator selects and stands in the same spot, uses a credible voice that elicits support, and gives the directions. Then, he or she moves to a different place and checks for understanding, using a softer, more approachable voice. The facilitator has now established a physical space in which he or she can change roles, from checking in with group members to correcting and clarifying behaviors.

Reflection

Activity 1

Think of a recent meeting that you attended. Recall the room arrangement. Did it satisfy the following criteria? Did it:

- Allow participants to see each other?
- Enable participants to see the facilitator and any visual aids?
- Seat nonparticipants separately from participants?
- Match the chairs to the number of participants?

- Have sufficient room for people to move around?
- Have adequate tools to support the meeting?

If there was something amiss, what could you do to correct it for the next meeting?

Activity 2

Recall the last time you gave directions to a group. How did you do so? Did you use your physical space effectively to reinforce communication as described above? What would you do differently in the future?

DAY 20: GROUP DECISION MAKING

The word decide means to kill choice: Out of many options, the group selects some ideas to survive and others to be set aside.

Robert Garmston and Bruce Wellman

Many groups get stuck because they are not sure how to make a decision.

There are many ways a group can go about its decision making. Actually, the way a group makes a decision may depend on the nature of the decision to be made. Not all decisions require the same amount or base of support. Some need a lot; others need much less.

Table 4.1 shows four major ways that a group may make a decision and the best use of each.

Table 4.1 Guide for Decision Making

Option for Decision Making	Best used for . . .
Full consensus	Critical issues where full support is desired (e.g., changing the vision and mission of an organization)
"Sufficient consensus" (See Day 21)	Decisions a group makes where 80 percent support is sufficient to safely move forward (e.g., next year's budget)
Majority vote	Routine decision making (e.g., changing the order of items on the agenda)
Delegating to a subgroup or individual group member	Non-controversial or highly routine matters having limited impact (e.g., deciding how to honor the out-going group facilitator)

For any of these decision-making options, the full decision may lie with the group or some part of the group, or the group may solicit input from non-group members, such as other staff members, administrators, or stakeholders. Also, a seemingly innocuous decision (e.g., adding a new member to a group) can become controversial and require a broader base of support.

Generally, the more a decision requires commitment to any kind of collective action, the more broadly based the decision needs to be.

> **Reflection**
>
> Here are some decisions that a group might be making. Using the approaches listed, how should each be made?
>
> - Set a date for the next group meeting.
> - Select a new group leader.
> - Determine the focus of the next professional development program.
> - Recommend a new curriculum.
> - Decide what type of folders to use in the next professional development activity.
>
> Think about the groups you are currently leading. Are the members in each of them clear about how they make decisions? Do they make decisions in different ways depending on the level of commitment needed? If your answer to either question is "No," what can you do to strengthen their abilities to use appropriate decision-making processes?

DAY 21: REACHING CONSENSUS

> *A genuine leader is not a searcher for consensus but a molder of consensus.*
>
> Martin Luther King Jr.

Groups often talk about wanting consensus, but consensus is very hard to achieve, and in many instances, not necessary. Some decisions don't require that broad a base of support. Some groups are not constituted in a way that makes consensus possible. In other instances, they may not have the time or resources to push for a full consensus.

For most groups, what Garmston and Wellman (2012) call *sufficient consensus* is enough. Sufficient consensus means that at least 80 percent of the group agrees and are prepared to act. The remaining 20 percent may not concur, but they have agreed not to sabotage the action. They are not in agreement, but they can live with the decision—whatever it may be.

However, if full consensus is required of a group, Garmston and Wellman (2012), referencing the Center for Conflict Resolution (1981), provide a list of conditions that need to be present before a full consensus is possible:

- There should be clarity about the group's purpose and how it operates.
- Power in the group needs to be distributed equally. Consensus doesn't work in hierarchical groups.
- The group needs to have the autonomy to choose consensus. A group may find it difficult to reach full consensus if it is getting pressured to make a decision and move on.
- Consensus requires a great deal of time and patience, which a group may not have.
- Group members must be willing to spend time examining their own functioning and their processes.
- Individual group members must be willing to reflect on their own thinking and be open to change.
- Group members and the group as a whole must continually sharpen communication, participation, and facilitation skills. (p. 65)

Reflection

With this list of the requirements for effective consensus building and the caveat of sufficient consensus in mind, think of the groups you lead.

Are any structured for consensus building? If so, which ones? How do you know? What types of decisions might they be making in which a full consensus is necessary? For what types of decisions would a sufficient consensus be more appropriate? As a group leader, how do you establish the structures and conditions within a group for consensus building?

Here is a reminder: Effective groups don't always use consensus; their decisions depend on the situation. More consensus building is not always necessary or even desirable.

DAY 22: GIVING FEEDBACK

Feedback is the breakfast of champions.

Ken Blanchard

Groups that subscribe to continuous improvement are committed to giving and receiving feedback. This is one way in which groups learn and are able to make course corrections. Feedback is absolutely essential if individuals and their groups and organizations are to be efficacious. In fact, the exchange of feedback should become part of an organization's culture. Giving and receiving feedback should be as common as getting a new assignment. It is simply part of how a group or an organization goes about its work.

What follows are some ground rules for giving feedback. See Day 23 for those on receiving feedback.

1. Start by asking the individual or group how things went from their perspective. This helps diffuse the tension that often exists before a feedback session starts. It also allows you (the one providing the feedback) insight into others' perspective.

2. Feedback (group or individual) should start with the positive. What was done well? How was it done so well? What was its impact? Knowing what they are doing well is as important for people as knowing what they need to improve on.

3. Follow the "sandwich approach" of starting with positive feedback, followed by negative feedback, ending with positive feedback again. People are more motivated to work on deficiencies if they feel positive about their overall performance (Lickerman, 2010).

4. Make sure the feedback is concrete, specific, and actionable. Compare "You're not a good writer" to "Your report did not follow our report template." Not only is the latter more specific, it is an objective statement of fact rather than the former, which is emotionally charged.

5. Allow time for the individual or group to process the feedback received and respond to it. The recipient of feedback may want to paraphrase what you have just said or ask a question.

6. Ideally, provide feedback in a face-to-face setting. Feedback by telephone, voice mail, or e-mail is less effective. The nonverbal communication channel is reduced or absent, and your message can easily be misconstrued.

7. Provide feedback on a regular basis. If feedback is provided on a regular basis, there are less likely to be surprises in the more formal performance review. This will also make feedback more routine, the way business is always done rather than occurring just once a year.

> **Reflection**
>
> Think of an individual or group to whom you need to provide feedback. Sketch the feedback you want to provide on a sheet of paper.
>
> Now, go back and review what you've written against the guidelines described above. To what degree does your feedback follow the guidelines? What changes will you make, and why?

DAY 23: RECEIVING FEEDBACK

> *Evaluation and especially self-evaluation are highly and positively related to learning. Evaluation is no less important than encouragement. Feedback, including negative feedback, is essential for human growth.*
>
> Roland Barth

The companion to giving feedback is receiving it. Receiving feedback provides groups and individuals with the knowledge of what they are doing well and motivates them to make changes. Receiving feedback well is just as important as delivering feedback well. Furthermore, it's not the feedback per se that's important but what you do with it. Here are seven guidelines for receiving and acting on feedback (McCarthy, 2008).

1. *Seek out feedback regularly.* Even if your supervisor or colleagues do not normally provide feedback, request it. By doing so you affirm your commitment to continuous improvement and help establish feedback as an organizational norm.

2. *Paraphrase what you've been told.* You may do that verbally or silently in your mind. Jot down a few notes. Take whatever time you need. Ask questions, if necessary. If the provider hasn't done so, ask for specific examples of what you have done or not done well and any suggestions of new behaviors on your part.

3. *Be aware of your emotions.* Feedback sessions, especially those that occur infrequently, are likely to be emotionally laden. Even positive feedback will trigger an emotional response. Monitor any tendency to be defensive, provide excuses, or blame others for any negative feedback you receive.

4. *Thank the person for providing the feedback.* Regardless of whether you agree or disagree with the feedback, acknowledge the provider's message. Feedback is the beginning, not the end. Now it's your turn to determine what actions to take.

5. *Take time to assess the feedback received.* Particularly, if you've received any negative feedback, take time to process it. Speak with a colleague or trusted friend. Don't do anything rash until you've seriously evaluated the feedback.

6. *Develop a plan to address negative feedback you have received that you see as valid.* If you choose to directly address some part of the feedback you received, a plan can help keep you on track. Make sure the person providing you the feedback knows of your plan. Keep him or her informed on your progress.

7. *Ask for whatever supports you need to carry out your plan.* Perhaps you need to take a course to strengthen your skills. Perhaps you need more opportunities to practice. Perhaps you need a mentor or coach. Your organization should be willing to help you address feedback you have received. Also, consider what you can do on your own to support your plan.

Reflection

Think of the last time you received a major piece of feedback. How did you respond? Were you able to listen? Were you able to admit that you acted inappropriately, if that were the case? Did you feel yourself getting defensive? Was your reaction two weeks later different from your reaction immediately afterwards? Did you develop a plan? If so, how successful has your plan been?

As a leader, how can you help your group members learn to give and receive feedback?

DAY 24: HANDLING PROBLEMS

Leadership has a harder job to do than just choose sides. It must bring sides together.

Jesse Jackson

It is inevitable. Some groups will experience problems, such as breakdowns in communication, members who do not perform adequately, and misunderstandings about the work they are responsible for completing. It will be your responsibility to give them some help. What will you do? Here are some options:

• *If possible, anticipate and prevent the problem in the first place.* Although it is not always possible, many problems can be averted if a group has been formed properly and takes time up front to prepare to function as a team. For example, a group should make sure that it has the right mix of people, is clear about its purpose, and has sufficient resources. Members should take time to get to know each other and establish a set of norms for group behavior. If a group that you are responsible for hasn't taken these first steps, you are likely to encounter problems sooner or later.

- *Let the group deal with the problem.* Think of any problem as belonging to the group rather than to individuals. When a group has difficulties functioning, the source usually lies within the system rather than with individual group members. The group as a whole is often doing something that has let the problem develop or has exacerbated the problem. Therefore, it should be the group's responsibility to resolve it. If at all possible, help the members solve it for themselves.

- *Intervene if you think it necessary to get the group back on task.* Sometimes, the group can't solve the problem itself, and you will need to intervene. That intervention may be minimal or more extensive, depending on the nature of the problem.

- *Talk to some group members privately.* Either give them feedback about their own behavior or suggestions as to what they can do in the group.

- *Meet with the group.* You might simply observe the way a group functions and provide feedback. Or you may need to play a more assertive or confrontational role to help the group deal with its problem.

- *As a strategy of last resort, restructure the team by removing some people and/or adding others.* This approach, unfortunately, can tarnish a team's image and inhibit its functioning even though the team member or members are gone (Scholtes et al., 2003, pp. 7.8–7.13).

Reflection

Think for a moment of a group you were responsible for that had a problem completing its work. Was it a problem that could have been prevented? Did the group solve the problem itself? Did you have to intervene? What was the end result? What would you do differently the next time one of your groups encounters a problem?

DAY 25: OPTIONS FOR RESOLVING CONFLICT

> *Conflict can be seen as a gift of energy in which neither side loses and a new dance is created.*
>
> Thomas Crum

Learn to love conflict! Yeah, sure. You must be kidding. Why should I learn to love conflict? Conflict is nothing but trouble.

Many of us have been conditioned to avoid conflict or become skillful in minimizing its impact. But there is a cost in doing so. Conflict that is suppressed or avoided tends to reappear. It often takes the form of passive-aggressive behavior in which a person appears to go along with a decision but then sabotages it. Avoiding conflict also lessens the chances that all alternatives will be explored and the most effective decision made.

Here are several common ways in which groups deal with conflict. All except one (possibly two) fail to resolve the issue:

- *Avoid the conflict.* Some people believe there is no value in attempting to bring conflict out in the open and resolve it. They may also be fearful of the consequences; therefore, they will attempt to avoid the conflict.

- *Smooth it over.* If the conflict can't be avoided, the next best strategy, according to the conflict avoiders, is to minimize the conflict so that relationships remain intact. There is an attempt to assuage individuals and move on. The real issues are never dealt with and are likely to resurface.

- *Force the conflict.* This strategy attempts to overpower group members to get them to accept a certain position. Personal relationships are disregarded; achieving the goal is more important. This is a competitive, win/lose approach that may backfire when the conflict reemerges.

- *Compromise.* In a compromise, the different sides each give up something for the greater good. Compromising is tricky. Sometimes it works; sometimes it doesn't. It can be either a lose/lose or a win/win strategy, depending on how much the different sides have to give up.

- *Problem solve.* Face the conflict head on and work through it. This strategy is the one that retains both personal goals and group relationships. It is most likely to produce a win/win outcome for all concerned. It does, however, require skill to be successful. Problem solving draws heavily on the norms of how people in groups talk to one another (Scholtes et al., 2003, pp. 7.4–7.7).

Your approach to group conflict is a choice you make. Selecting from a range of behaviors, whose strengths and limitations you are aware of, helps you meet your goals in each situation.

Reflection

Think of situations in which groups you have been part of have encountered conflict. Which of the above approaches did your group take? With what results?

> Which of the approaches listed is the one you naturally gravitate to? As a leader, one of your greatest gifts to your groups is your ability to face conflict directly and work through it. If you are not comfortable using problem solving in a conflict situation, what can you do to strengthen your confidence and comfort level and encourage the same in your group members?

DAY 26: CONFLICT AS OPPORTUNITY

The question is not how to eliminate conflict but how to capitalize on its constructive aspects.

Marion E. Haynes

A prerequisite to facing conflict directly and working through it is having a mind-set of conflict as an opportunity. Conflict is a chance to look at situations from a new perspective and perhaps generate an entirely new solution. That is what conflict can provide, especially when people demystify conflict.

According to Garmston and Wellman (2009), conflict is nothing more than energy moving through a system. The meaning that people bring to the energy produces the conflict. And that meaning comes from one's own background, along with the culture of the group. Just as group members perceive reality through their own lenses, they also see conflict in highly individualized ways.

A useful distinction can be made between affective conflict and cognitive conflict. *Affective conflict* is interpersonal conflict. It is Usain and Erin versus Carlos and Denita, or the primary versus the intermediate team. This type of conflict deters group functioning. It contributes to decreased commitment, less cohesiveness, decreased empathy, and decisions that do not produce the desired results.

Cognitive conflict is a disagreement over ideas and approaches. It is a difference of opinion about, for example, how teachers should address students' misconceptions in the science classroom or how much problem solving students need to do in mathematics. This type of conflict is characteristic of a high-performance group. It separates the ideas from the people and holds the ideas up for close examination. It leads to greater commitment, increased cohesion, heightened empathy, deeper understanding, and decisions that produce the desired results.

Thus, one significant goal of an effective group is to increase cognitive conflict and reduce affective conflict.

> **Reflection**
>
> Think about a group you have led that experienced conflict. Was the conflict affective or cognitive? How do you know? What happened? How was the conflict resolved—or was it?
>
> How can you help a group avoid affective conflict and stay within the realm of cognitive conflict?

DAY 27: FACILITATING CONFLICT

The doors we open and close each day decide the lives we lead.

Flora Whittemore

As a leader, you have a responsibility to model conflict resolution directly. However, although you may be skillful in doing so, you may be dealing with other people who are not as skilled.

If emotions rise to the surface and interaction becomes heated, keeping yourself under control is a basic survival skill. It takes a high level of emotional maturity and some highly developed skills to avoid getting sucked into the maelstrom of conflict. Here are some suggestions for remaining under control (Garmston & Wellman, 2012; Scholtes et al., 2003):

- *Breathe deeply.* Take a deep breath or two or three before saying a word. Under stress, our breathing becomes shallow, and oxygen is not distributed as well throughout our bodies.
- *Remember that the behavior of others is rarely malicious or evil in intent.* Most people are motivated by positive intentions.
- *Feel the energy of the conflict and move toward it rather than away.* Often in the midst of conflict, we want to retreat, to physically leave the premises, or at least to put some psychological distance between ourselves and the conflict. We are in a better position to dispel the conflict by moving toward and embracing it—physically and psychologically.
- *Know that the behavior of the people involved in the conflict is rarely planned, thought out, or calculated.* In most instances, conflict arises out of events, not deliberation.
- *Remember that conflict may stem from events, but it is not born out of the moment.* All conflicts have some history (for example, a previous conflict or negative experience).
- *Use paraphrasing.* Remember that paraphrasing shows the other person that you value his or her thoughts, feelings, and positions. It also helps you keep the focus off yourself and on the other person. (See Day 5.)

- *Try to keep the conflict cognitive rather than affective.* Separate the issues from the people who are connected to them.
- *If you feel yourself "losing it," take a break, at least for yourself and perhaps for the entire group.* Get a drink of water, make a trip to the restroom, or go outside for some fresh air.

Reflection

In reviewing this list of suggestions, which ones do you use and feel comfortable with? Which ones might you try?

As a leader of groups, how can you help other group members use these techniques for themselves?

DAY 28: RESOLVING VALUE CONFLICTS

Transformation comes more from pursuing profound questions than seeking practical answers.

Peter Block

Everyone was on edge. A faculty meeting to resolve some issues between the principal and staff was about to begin. The principal wanted to make some changes in school practices that many of the staff opposed. True collaboration had been lacking; transparency, honesty, and trust were either missing or inconsistent. At the core of the conflict was a difference in values among the staff. What could the principal and school leaders do to facilitate a positive outcome of this meeting?

Conflicts based on differences in values are especially challenging to address. Values are tightly held and may not be apparent; therefore, getting to the real issue becomes difficult. Knowing that sometimes values must shift for a real change to occur, leaders can use different tools to support a group's reflection on their values and examine the ways in which there are differences among those values. Here is one way for dealing with value differences in groups.

Part One: Start by asking everyone in the group to write what they see as the school's current values on separate sentence strips and post them on a wall for all to see (e.g., "We value having data but not using it."). Next, faculty and school leaders write their desired values as a collective staff (e.g., "We value using data to inform our teaching.") and post those on a different wall. Scanning the two sets of sentence strips shows where the school currently is and where staff and administration want it to be, bringing the inconsistencies out into the open so that the group can dissect them and move forward (Garmston and Wellman, 2009).

Part Two: The anonymous list of desired values creates a safe focus to examine how a staff truly feels about their school. It creates what Grinder (1998) and Zoller and Landry (2010) describe as a third point from which statements can be examined through dialogue and inquiry. Faculty and administrators can look at a specific statement and ask clarifying questions. The authors of the statements can answer if they wish; paraphrases are offered, and probing questions are asked. As the dialogue continues, group members combine some sentence strips while deleting others, including ones that they themselves had written. Strips are winnowed until the core values are identified, collectively understood, and agreed upon.

Some benefits from this process include the following:

- Group members dialogue and engage in inquiry; they speak to each other to understand one another, not to assert a particular position or belief.
- Group norms are followed, such as putting ideas on the table for consideration and later taking some ideas off.
- Assumptions are overtly suspended, and group members presume positive intentions.
- Group members talk with—not at—each other.

As this deeper level of interaction takes place, values begin to shift and a sense of urgency emerges. One caution: This process is intense. There will most likely be expressions of emotion as group members address their deeply held values and concerns. This is necessary to get the agreement on values that the process is designed to produce.

> **Reflection**
>
> If you have used this process previously, what has been your experience? Is there anything you might do differently next time?
>   If you have never used this process, what do you need to feel comfortable doing so? What sources of support do you have available?

DAY 29: DEALING WITH DISRUPTIVE PEOPLE

> *Unprofessional behaviors noted during professional development sessions: Brings a laptop computer, not to take notes, but to play*

solitaire or other computer games; brings a pillow to the session, not to provide a softer seat, but as a headrest; and brings a Game Boy and plays continuously, occasionally cheering for himself.

Thomas Guskey

As long as there are groups, there will be people in them who exhibit difficult behavior. Often, these individuals don't want to be in the group in the first place.

As a leader, you cannot allow the inappropriate behavior of a few people to control the group. There are constructive techniques for dealing with a person who is disruptive because he or she doesn't want to be part of the group:

• *If people don't want to be in your group, confirm their sentiments rather than trying to convince them of the advantages of their participation.* There may be individuals who prefer to be some place other than in your group, especially when participation is required. The best way to diffuse these people is to simply accept their feelings: "You're saying that you don't want to be here and that attendance creates a hardship for you. I'm not in a position, however, to do anything about that. Perhaps you should speak with . . . " Another possible response might go something like, "Yes, I know you resent the compulsory attendance policy. I hope you'll find something today that will be useful. If you have any specific questions or concerns, please see me at break." People will often drop their hostility once they have expressed their negative feelings, especially if you respond with a paraphrase.

• *Deal directly with the person privately.* If you chose the one-on-one approach, take the person aside. Try to determine the source of the person's behavior. Does he or she not want to be part of the group? If not, why not? Is it best for this person to leave? If he or she stays, what can mitigate the inappropriate behavior? Does this person need anything from you or the group? If so, can you and/or the group provide the necessary support?

• *Instead of dealing directly with a recalcitrant person, allow group pressure to emerge.* Sometimes, approaching people directly is not the best strategy. Having group members deal with difficult individuals as peers may be much more effective. Members will often do this on their own; you need not do anything. If not, at some point you may want to turn to the group to ask members how they feel about something the difficult person has said or done. If the situation is best handled privately, you may want to ask one or two group members to speak to the person at the first opportune moment.

- *Set up circumstances that allow people who should not be there to exit gracefully.* If participation in the group is voluntary, a person may realize that he or she doesn't belong and leave. This can occur naturally when the group is establishing itself: clarifying purpose, adopting norms of behavior, assigning roles, and outlining tasks to be completed. An individual may see that participation just isn't appropriate or possible and withdraw from the group.

Whatever strategy you choose for people who don't want to be there, use it promptly. By doing so, you establish the group as a safe place to work. Your actions show that you will not allow one or two people to disrupt the group's progress.

Reflection

Consider this situation: You are co-instructor of a 6-week professional development series for elementary and middle school teachers. The focus is on incorporating algebraic concepts in grades K–7. The goal is to better prepare students for taking algebra in grade 8, which is now a required class unless students are specifically exempted.

There are 30 teachers signed up for the program, two from each elementary and middle school in your district. Most teachers volunteered to participate in the series; a few were appointed by their principals.

At the first meeting, you notice two people whose behavior is atypical for a professional development group. One is an elementary teacher; the other, a middle school teacher. They sit slightly apart from the group, fidget in their seats, read the newspaper, check their cell phones, and occasionally just get up and leave for a short period. You notice that others in the group are reacting to their behavior and making side comments.

As the morning progresses, they continue their behavior. You find yourself getting irritated. What do you do at this point? What might you have done at the first indication of their unusual behavior?

DAY 30: BEGINNINGS AND ENDINGS

Begin at the beginning and go on till you come to the end; then stop.

Lewis Carroll

The success of a meeting often depends on how it begins and how it ends. At the beginning, the facilitator sets the tone, connects people, establishes expectations, and invites people to work. At the end, facilitators honor and acknowledge the contributions and clarify important next steps. As group leader, what you do and say directly influences the outcomes of your group's deliberations. You want to begin with something that will grab people's attention and motivate them to actively participate in the meeting. You want to end with something that captures the work of the group and takes you forward to your next steps. Here's an opportunity for you to assess some typical beginnings and endings.

Beginnings

Think about the talks or speeches people have given at the various meetings you have attended over the years—especially their beginnings. How many do you recall? How do most people start? Here are some examples of opening statements. Which do you see as strong? Weak? Why?

- "Albert Einstein said, 'I never teach my pupils. I only attempt to provide the conditions in which they can learn.'"
- "I really appreciate you giving up your Saturday morning to be with us."
- "You won't believe what has happened as a result of our last meeting!"
- "We want to start by introducing and thanking the people who made today possible."
- "I start by offering you a guarantee! By the time this session is over, you'll be able to . . . And if you can't, I'll . . . "
- "We're still missing a couple of people. Let's wait for just a few minutes before starting."

Endings

Think about the various meetings you have attended over the years—formal addresses people have made or informal comments at the conclusion of an event. Are there any that stand out in your mind? How do most people end? Here are some examples of closing words. Which do you label as strong? Weak? Why?

- "Thanks so much for coming. This was a good session. We'll meet again in two weeks. Don't forget to send me an e-mail if you have any questions."
- "I want to thank each of you today for your hard work. Roger, your intervention got us unstuck. Travis, Anya, and Carlos, each of you moved our group forward . . ."

- "I want to close with a short poem that I wrote last night about this group's work."
- "With that decision, we've gone about as far as we can go. Let's call it quits for today."
- "Here are three cartoons that capture the essence of our work. What do you see in the first one . . . ?"
- "Our time has expired. Someone else has reserved this room. Let's stop and pick up tomorrow at 8:30."

> **Reflection**
>
> Think of a meeting you've recently led. How did you begin? How did you end? Can you assess the impact of your beginning and ending on the group? What might you have done differently?

DAY 31: SIX DOMAINS OF GROUP DEVELOPMENT

When you start out in a team, you have to get the teamwork going and then you get something back.

Michael Schumacher

So, once a group, always a group? Is this right?

Although the configuration may remain the same, group dynamics evolve. All groups attempt to balance getting the work done with attending to process, which creates ongoing tension.

Six domains influence how effectively a group functions (Garmston & Wellman, 2009). For success in each domain, group members need to have domain-specific knowledge, skills, and structures. What follows is a brief explanation of each domain, its underlying assumptions, and what is necessary for the group to function effectively in that domain.

1. *Getting work done:* Group members understand that tension between task and process is ongoing and believe that it and the group's work are manageable. Key knowledge includes being able to function in modes of both dialogue and discussion, knowing how to conduct successful meetings, being able to facilitate groups, and skill in designing efficient and effective meetings.

2. *Doing the right work:* The underlying assumption here is that vision, mission, and values focus group energy and help ensure that the group is doing the right work. Members need to know how to live with conflict,

work with problems that seem unmanageable, increase their adaptability, and create a sense of community.

3. *Working interdependently:* The key underlying assumption for this domain is that diversity is an asset and subgroups must work together and see each other as valuable resources. They must adhere to the seven norms of collaboration. They must also be proficient in discussion and dialogue, meeting management, facilitating groups, and living with conflict.

4. *Managing systems:* Knowing when to reject linearity and think more systemically and systematically as the tasks become more complex is the underlying assumption. Key knowledge includes living with conflict, handling unmanageable problems, being adaptive, and creating community.

5. *Developing groups:* Regardless of its current productivity, a group can always be more efficient and/or more effective. Adapting to change is a task for both individuals and groups. The underlying assumption is that both individual and group orientations are required to plan and implement significant change. The requisite knowledge includes information on these six domains, living with conflict, valuing community, and the principles for creating community.

6. *Adapting to change:* The underlying assumption here is that if groups are to be effective, they must constantly adapt to external environments. The more unstable the environment, the more the group must maintain an outward orientation. Required knowledge includes working with conflict, adapting to change, and creating community.

It is easy to see how interrelated these six domains are. For example, skill in dialogue and discussion are essential for two of the six. Being effective at dialogue requires internalization of the norms of collaboration.

Reflection

It is helpful to assess a group's stages of development in these six domains. Garmston and Wellman (2009) suggest a five-point rating scale set up on a continuum (see Table 4.2). Table 4.3 shows the ratings along the continuum, from "1: Beginning" to "5: Innovating." Both can be used to help you and your groups assess their development.

Think of a group that you are part of. What do you see your group doing well? Where could your group function better? What knowledge and skills do you and your group members need that you don't have? What can you do to move your group forward?

Table 4.2 Assessing the Six Domains of Development

Domain	1 Beginning	2 Emerging	3 Developing	4 Integrating	5 Innovating
Getting work done					
Doing the right work					
Working interdependently					
Managing systems					
Developing your group					
Adapting to change					

SOURCE: Garmston, R. J., & Wellman, B. M. Copyright © 2009. *The Adaptive School: A Sourcebook for Developing Collaborative Groups* (p. 120). Norwood, MA: Christopher-Gordon. Reprinted with permission of the authors.

Table 4.3 Stages of Development

Stage of Development	Descriptor
1. Beginning	Unconscious incompetence (don't know what they don't know)
2. Emerging	Unconscious incompetence and conscious competence
3. Developing	Conscious competence
4. Integrating	Conscious competence and unconscious competence
5. Innovating	Unconscious competence

SOURCE: Garmston, R. J., & Wellman, B. M. Copyright © 2009. *The Adaptive School: A Sourcebook for Developing Collaborative Groups* (p. 119). Norwood, MA: Christopher-Gordon. Reprinted with permission of the authors.

REFERENCES

Argyris, C. (1986). Skill incompetence. *Harvard Business Review, 64*(5). (*Harvard Business Review* Reprint #86501)

Avery, M., Aurine, B., Streibel, B., & Weiss, L. (1981). *Building united judgment: A handbook for consensus decision making.* Madison, WI: The Center for Conflict Resolution.

Board Source. (2009). *Q & As: What is a consent agenda or consent calendar?* Retrieved August 13, 2012, from https://www.boardsource.org/Knowledge.asp?ID=3.70

Fullan, M. (2001). *Leading in a culture of change.* San Francisco: Jossey-Bass.

Garmston, R. J., & Wellman, B. (2012). *Adaptive schools foundation seminar learning guide.* Highlands Ranch, CO: Center for Adaptive Schools.

Garmston, R. J., & Wellman, B. M. (2009). *The adaptive school: A sourcebook for developing collaborative groups* (Vol.1, 2nd Ed.). Norwood, MA: Christopher-Gordon.

Grinder, M. (1998). *Patterns of permission: The science of group dynamics.* Battleground, WA: Michael Grinder & Associates.

Lickerman, A. (2010). *How to give and receive feedback.* Retrieved December 23, 2012 from http://www.psychologytoday.com/blog/happiness-in-world/201002/how-give-and-receive-feedback

Lindsey, R., Roberts, L., & CampbellJones, F. (2005). *The culturally proficient school.* Thousand Oaks, CA: Corwin.

McCarthy, D. (2008, January 13). *18 tips for receiving feedback.* Retrieved December 23, 2012 from http://www.greatleadershipbydan.com/2008/01/18-tips-for-receiving-feedback.html

Mundry, S., Britton, E., Raizen, S., & Loucks-Horsley, S. (2000). *Professional meetings and conferences in education: Designing, planning, and evaluating.* Thousand Oaks, CA: Corwin.

Perkins, D. (1992). *Smart schools.* New York: Free Press.

Scholtes, P. R., Joiner, B. L., & Streibel, B. J. (2003). *The team handbook.* Madison, WI: Oriel.

Wheatley, M. (2002). *Turning to one another: Simple conversations to restore hope to the future.* San Francisco: Berrett-Koehler.

Zoller, K., & Landry, C. (2010). *Choreography of presenting: 7 essential abilities of effective presenters.* Thousand Oaks, CA: Corwin.

Book 5

Leadership for Results

The stakes are high and getting higher all the time. Every type of business and organization is being asked to demonstrate its value and results. It is no longer sufficient to simply provide a service or sell a product; one must also be able to show the value produced from the service or product. Job performance evaluation systems are also increasingly using rigorous measures to assess employees' impact and contributions. For example, if you are a professional learning consultant, it is essential to show that your clients learn and improve their practice. If you are a teacher or principal, your performance is now measured in part on how much growth your students achieve. At no other time have organizations been more accountable for demonstrating results. But accountability systems alone are insufficient to produce meaningful results. Leaders must engage and inspire staff to go after results with creativity and invention and be empowered to achieve desired outcomes. Actions must be specific and realistic for addressing problems, and staff may need new knowledge and skills.

The focus on getting results led us to add this fifth book—Leadership for Results—in this edition of *Leading Every Day*. As we have worked with educational organizations over many years, we often see that a focus on results is missing from the education improvement equation. One of the first questions we ask when we begin work with an improving school or district is: "What are your goals and your criteria for success?" Too often these are vaguely defined and only understood by few. We have seen the opposite as well, when schools set and focus on the narrowest of goals—e.g., raising test scores—without considering if this is the best goal nor what it will take to reach it. We've come to believe that an essential role of leaders is to engage and involve everyone in setting worthwhile goals, defining what success will look like, and supporting them to take specific and realistic actions that will lead to desired results.

As presented in Day 1 in this book, results-based leadership is a way of working and thinking that focuses on achieving the most important outcomes. For schools, the most important outcome is student success, including learning and socio-emotional well being. Other outcomes that support student success include creating a positive school climate and safety, providing a guaranteed and quality curriculum, engaging students and families, and providing excellent instruction and appropriate interventions. Reaching such goals requires leaders to guide staff through a complex process of ongoing planning, action, data analysis, revising, more planning, and more action.

The contemplations in Book Five support leaders to take a results-based approach to leadership. It contains a collection of messages about leaders' roles in bringing about results and outcomes. We ask leaders to explore questions, such as: In what ways do you pay attention to the bottom line of results? How do you support mutual accountability? Do you have processes for engaging in analysis of data, such as collaborative inquiry? In what ways do you monitor and measure progress? How do you support staff to generate and test new ideas? Do you routinely anticipate barriers to achieve results? How do you engage others in problem-solving? In what ways do you focus on building a culture of trust?

The questions in Book Five are grouped around four themes that are interwoven throughout the 31 contemplations:

1. What do results-based leaders do? How do leaders ensure that their organizations and the people in them accomplish what they intend? How do leaders promote a culture of continuous improvement?

2. How do organizations use data and evidence? What role do leaders play in supporting others to engage in collaborative inquiry?

3. What are the processes for identifying problems? How do you select outcomes? How can leaders ensure that interventions are aligned with the intended outcomes and results? In what ways do leaders support others to generate innovative solutions to problems?

4. How do leaders monitor progress and reflect on their results?

DAY 1: RESULTS-BASED LEADERSHIP

In an effective results-oriented management system, those who are held accountable for results believe that the results are important and that they themselves can do something about them.

Phillip C. Schlechty

As the field of education has increased its focus on results and meeting higher standards, leaders at all levels in educational organizations are changing the way they think about meeting and demonstrating outcomes. Ideally, clear performance indicators are established and measured, and results are used to inform ongoing improvements. Everyone, not just a few people, takes responsibility to define specific, realistic, and measureable goals; set clear objectives; and communicate about and monitor for results.

The way leaders enact results-based leadership varies widely, and Fullan (2011) suggests that leaders be sure to avoid blaming when results fall short. When leaders use teacher evaluations and test results to punish staff rather than to continuously improve the organization and build capacity, they do more harm than good. A better approach is to be a results-based leader. Results-based leaders clarify the goals and maintain a laser focus that persists until goals are met (Collins, 2001). They do not waver. They build systems so that everyone can carefully track results. They reward and recognize those whose actions are consistent with the goals, create a sense of accomplishment and optimism, and focus on what *was* accomplished, not only on what staff did not do. Barriers to success are anticipated and removed to increase everyone's chance for success.

For many years we have used the *Dimensions of Success* model adapted from the work of Interactions Associates to support leaders to understand the complexity of reaching results. The model teaches that a focus on the task alone is inadequate to achieve success. Rather, leaders must address three interdependent dimensions to lead organizations to success. The dimensions are task, process, and relationships. *Task* refers to the activity or goal—what you will accomplish. Being clear about this is essential. *Process* refers to the way the work will get done—how you will achieve the results—and almost always considers what people will need to learn to get the work done. *Relationships* refer to how people in your organization are engaged in and relate to the task and process and the level of trust and support among them related to the task.

Often leaders are focused only on one of these dimensions such as when a committee selects a new textbook for use (task), without considering how it will be adopted and implemented (process), or how much trust staff have in each other to implement the new program (relationships). When leaders think through all three dimensions, they are more likely to produce less confusion, better morale and higher productivity, and, most importantly, reach results.

> **Reflection**
>
> A danger in the accountability movement is that results will be used to blame instead of to build capacity and improve. How does your organization use results to make improvements and plan next steps? How can you avoid blaming and adopt a problem-solving and improvement stance?
>
> How do you use results to communicate and create a sense of accomplishment and optimism? When you see someone who is acting in ways that are consistent with goals, how do you recognize and reward their behavior?
>
> When you are launching new initiatives, where do you tend to focus—on the task itself? The process? The people and how they will engage with the task? What might you do next time to focus equally on all three *Dimensions of Success*—task, process, and relationships?

DAY 2: ROLE OF LEADERS TO ACHIEVE RESULTS

> *Leadership is second only to classroom instruction among school-related factors that affect student learning in school.*
>
> The Wallace Foundation

The Wallace Foundation sponsored a decade of research to uncover roles and practices of school leaders that lead to results. In Book One, Day 1, we share the five key practices of effective leaders suggested by this research, which include:

1. Having a vision of and high expectations for academic success for all students

2. Making sure your climate is hospitable to education, which includes creating the optimism and no-blame environment discussed in Book Five, Day 1 and building a sense of community

3. Cultivating leadership in others because successful schools have many people who lead

4. Improving instruction, including that principals and other leaders are observing in classrooms all the time and providing feedback into what is working and what needs improvement

5. Managing people, data, and processes to support growth and improvement, which involves engaging staff in collaborative inquiry, interpreting data, dismissing people who do not have the capacity to learn and improve, and carefully managing a set of six processes (The Wallace Foundation, 2013)

Researchers at Vanderbilt University identified six key processes that effective principals manage to address their "most important leadership responsibilities" (Wallace Foundation, 2013, p. 15). These include: planning, implementing, supporting, advocating, communicating, and monitoring. As The Wallace Foundation writes:

> The school leader pressing for high academic standards would, for example, map out rigorous targets for improvements in learning (planning), get the faculty on board to do what's necessary to meet those targets (implementing), encourage students and teachers in meeting the goals (supporting), challenge low expectations and low district funding for students with special needs (advocating), make sure families are aware of the learning goals (communicating), and keep on top of test results (monitoring). (p. 15)

Successful school leaders combine their use of the five practices and these six processes to get results. Ongoing communication and active outreach is essential. As Shoemaker, Krupp, and Howland (2013) point out, it is important for leaders to share stories of successes and failures in the organization to build institutional wisdom and support everyone to learn what's working and why. They recommend instituting after-action reviews, documenting lessons learned, communicating about new insights, and continuing to model a culture of inquiry and learning.

Reflection

Managing people, data, and processes is one key role of leaders. Consider how you manage the following key processes: planning, implementing, supporting, advocating, communicating, and monitoring. On a scale of 1 (low) to 5 (high), how would you rate your effectiveness on each process? Set goals for improving processes you rated a 3 or below.

Ask yourself:

- How carefully do I plan and how do I use data in the planning process? What else is needed?
- What am I doing to ensure that staff understand their role and are implementing activities to get results?
- What help and support do teachers and students need and how do I know? Am I providing adequate support? What else is needed?
- What policies and actions do I need to challenge in the organization? What will I advocate for or against?

- How proactive, consistent, and frequent is my communication about goals and results? What more is needed?
- How well do I know what is going on in my organization and the results we are getting? What additional monitoring do I need to do?

DAY 3: USING RIGOROUS EVIDENCE

Education is a field where there are many good intentions and many good innovative ideas, but where ideas and interventions often go in and out of practice with little regard to rigorous evidence.

Jon Barron

The use of evidence goes hand in hand with measuring results. Here are several situations in which leaders need to use the most rigorous evidence they can to make sure that their conclusions are valid:

- When choosing new programs or interventions (see Book Five, Day 18)
- When evaluating staff performance
- When evaluating programs (see Book Three, Day 27)
- When assessing student learning

In all of these situations, the rigor of the evidence is improved by using multiple sources of data (e.g., standardized tests, locally developed assessments, and classroom observations conducted and scored by multiple observers, on multiple days).

Getting results often rests on whether a leader chooses the best programs to implement. Making such a choice is clouded by the many claims in the marketplace about a program's effectiveness. Leaders must be disciplined to ask, "What is the quality of the evidence I have? Is it the best available evidence? What else do I need to know?" Make it a habit to ask staff, students, and families for evidence to back up claims that a practice is (or is not) working.

Another important facet to using rigorous evidence is to become a good consumer of educational research. Author Douglas Reeves (2012) suggests that educators review research with the following points in mind:

- *Independence of the research:* There should be five levels of independence: (1) conclusions come from different, independent, and even competing researchers; (2) conclusions come from different samples, such as samples chosen at random, not only "samples of convenience"; (3) conclusions are tested through different, multiple methods by different researchers; (4) conclusions come from different contexts geographically and demographically; and (5) data come from different student populations.

- *Precise terminology used*: When reading education research, the consumer must be aware of what is being described. Did the study examine inquiry learning or something else? All programs with the same name or label are not the same.

- *Candor of researchers*: Reeves suggests that credible researchers openly acknowledge research limitations.

- *Replication of research findings*: Research is more credible when the same findings have been replicated in more than one setting. Leaders need to avoid relying on one study that suggests something works. Dig deeper—any good researcher will include a discussion of results from similar research. Use these summaries to fully understand what is known before taking action.

Reflection

For leaders to be credible, they must be able to point to rigorous evidence that the practices they support are having desired results. How often do you ask everyone to reflect on the effectiveness of the practices they use? Over the next few days and months, look for opportunities to ask: "Is this practice working? What evidence do we have to back up our claims? If we don't know if something is working, how can we find out?"

Likewise, effective leaders are good consumers of educational research. How critical are you about research-based claims? How can you model being a critical consumer of research using the points suggested by Douglas Reeves?

DAY 4: BEING AN ACCOUNTABLE LEADER

The real value and benefit of accountability stems from the ability to influence events and outcomes before they happen.

Roger Connors and Tom Smith

What does being accountable mean? Bandied about in education and in other fields, accountability is often seen as a consequence of poor performance. Because of its history, being accountable was something to be feared.

Consider a new definition of accountability: "A personal choice to rise above one's circumstances and demonstrate the ownership necessary for achieving desired results—to See It, Own It, Solve It, and Do It" (Connors, Smith, & Hickman, 2010). Such a definition is much more empowering and positive. What can you do, regardless of your circumstances, to achieve the results you desire? Once you "Own It," you are much more inclined to take actions to "Fix It" (Hyatt, 2012). Adopting this definition can help you and others in your organization to do everything possible to achieve the results you desire.

So what are the characteristics of accountability for leaders? For our purposes, here are four:

1. *Focusing on results.* Emphasis is not only on you getting your job done or carrying out the responsibilities of your position description, but also on getting the results that you and your organization have agreed to achieve (National School Boards Association, 2012; Connors, Smith, & Hickman, 2010).

2. *Being willing to delegate.* You can't achieve the results you desire without the help of others in your school or organization. They, too, have to "Own It" in order to "Fix It" (National School Boards Association, 2012).

3. *Keeping promises and honoring commitments.* You build trust and good will in your work and the work of others by keeping your promises and honoring commitments that you have made (National School Boards Association, 2012).

4. *Taking full responsibility.* When something goes awry, you take full responsibility. You are forthcoming about your role and what corrective actions you are going to take. There's no blaming of others and no defensiveness or excuses on your part (Hyatt, 2012).

Establishing a culture of accountability in an organization requires defining clear outcomes and communicating them to all staff (Connors, Smith, & Hickman, 2010). One basic principle of accountability is that people cannot be held accountable for what they have not been informed of (Gilbert-Jamison, 2012). By establishing and communicating clear, realistic, and credible outcomes, leaders help staff to align their work with the desired outcomes. Finally, the administration or management must also subscribe to accountability of results if they expect others in the organization to be accountable (Connors, Smith, & Hickman, 2010).

> **Reflection**
>
> What are you accountable for? Are the four characteristics above present in your approach to leadership?
>
> Does your organization have a culture of accountability? If not, how can you help establish such a culture by modeling the behaviors discussed here?
>
> Write down five actions you can take to strengthen your accountability and the culture of accountability in your organization.

DAY 5: ROLE OF POLICY IN ACHIEVING RESULTS

Surround yourself with the best people you can find, delegate authority, and don't interfere as long as the policy you've decided upon is being carried out.

Ronald Reagan

"So what's policy got to do with it?" you ask. Actually, as it turns out, quite a bit.

Policies are the foundation that supports an organization's programs and practices. Without solid policies, an organization lacks direction in fulfilling its vision and mission. Staff may be hindered in doing their work by not having proper and clear guidance.

Lack of a policy or poorly written policies can contribute to a number of problems that keep you from achieving the results you want. Organizations often do not keep their policies current, which leads to confusion as to what is and isn't the current policy. Staff may find themselves with a policy that mandates one thing and a new reform effort that is in direct conflict. A policy that benefits one part of an organization may have a negative effect on another. An organization that makes major changes to its work or mission without a policy statement explaining its new position causes confusion and resistance in the community.

As leader, how can you keep your organizational policies current? You can begin by conducting a policy audit. A policy audit involves reviewing all of the federal and state legislation, board policies, regulations, memos of understanding, contract language, and similar documents that set forth expectations. Usually a policy audit is conducted by topic, such as professional development, recruiting and hiring, health and safety, or graduation requirements. Having all policies together on one topic can reveal duplication or omissions and possibly strengthen linkages.

An effective policy should do the following: (1) follow all relevant laws; (2) incorporate provisions that reflect research and/or best practice;

(3) specify outcomes that are clearly stated and measureable; (4) be equitable; (5) have sufficient funding; (6) specify accountability; and (7) state the purpose of the policy and what is to be achieved (Desimone, Smith, & Phillips. 2007; Bevis & Chudgar, 2007; Leonard, 2013).

In addition, the anticipated effects of the policy should be known (to the extent possible) and communicated along with the policy. The policy needs to have a broad base of support from both within the organization and by stakeholders external to the organization. Finally, the statement should not include details involved in carrying out the policy. These details can be in a procedural document that can be revised as needed without a policy revision.

> **Reflection**
>
> What current policies are in place to support your goals? Which ones need to be added, removed, or edited to better support your endeavors? Who do you need to talk with to raise awareness of the need to change existing policy? How can you make sure these necessary revisions take place?

DAY 6: BUILDING A CULTURE OF CONTINUOUS IMPROVEMENT

> *What is important is to keep learning, to enjoy challenge, and to tolerate ambiguity. In the end there are no certain answers.*
>
> Martin Horner

Throughout *Leading Every Day* there are messages about how leaders create a culture of success and engage in continuous improvement and professional learning to reach desired results. The habits of mind of leaders who support continuous improvement are many. They encourage open communication and support staff to innovate and learn from successes as well as failures. They expect high levels of collaboration and use of data, and promote dialogue.

Dennis Sparks (2007) suggests six essential habits that leaders use to promote continuous improvement and results. The habits paint a picture of an organization that is alive with dialogue, clear about its purpose and values, optimistic, and data driven. Leaders seeking to build a culture of continuous improvement do the following:

1. Create a sense of possibility, self-determination, and commitment.

2. Establish clear, focused goals, purpose, and values.

3. Engage the whole community in sustained, persistent interaction.

4. Promote a culture for sharing clear, succinct, data driven, and powerfully stated points of view.

5. Engage in committed listening.

6. Rely on data to support conclusions (Sparks, 2007).

Being organized for continuous improvement starts when staff are free to talk openly without fear about what is working and what isn't and are challenged to propose and commit to new ways of working together.

Reflection

How resilient is your organization? Do you encourage staff to dream about possibilities and share information on the actions they have taken to improve results? How do you recognize staff members who take initiative to make improvements?

Think about your recent communications with staff. Do the messages you send encourage innovation and continuous improvement? How often do you say, "We can't because . . . " versus saying, "We could if . . . "?

What is your organization's history of improvement? Do you have a history of sustained, persistent focus on engaging staff in discussing and making improvements? Or is your history one of too many priorities adopted and soon abandoned? What would you like to do to strengthen your focus on achieving ongoing improvements?

DAY 7: EQUITABLE ACCESS TO DATA

Revise practices, policies, and regulations to ensure privacy and information protection while enabling a model of assessment that includes ongoing gathering and sharing of data on student learning for continuous improvement.

U.S. Department of Education

Schools are inundated with data, and the wealth of data can often be overwhelming. Teachers often ask, "What do we do with all of this data? How do we make sense of all these reports? What do we do when the most helpful data from state tests are only available to the principal?"

In order for teachers to effectively analyze and use student-learning data, they first need to have access to it. In the United States, most states have developed data management systems to manage the results from the statewide standardized tests. Reports can be generated for statewide, district-wide, and school-wide learning results, as well as individual teacher's students. However, access to an individual teacher's students' data is restricted by passwords, and those are often provided only to school administrators. In order for teachers to effectively use data, they need the access to those data that are closest to their practice—test results for the students in their classrooms. Making these data accessible to all teachers is essential.

Many districts have more localized, common assessments in place to serve as benchmarks of learning before students take the state standardized tests. These data align closely with the state standards but are administered at several points during the year, with results indicating students' growth and learning over time. In most cases, the results are also entered into the district or state data management system, but teachers are often overwhelmed by the sheer variety of reports that can be generated. Ensuring that teachers know and understand the data reports, and which can be most helpful to informing instruction, is essential.

Teachers also have their own classroom assessments, including student work, science journals, mathematics problems of the week, end-of-course assessments, and other artifacts of students' learning. Clearly, individual teachers have access to all of these sources of data, and the key is to facilitate dialogue among groups of teachers to use these data to inform not only their own teaching but also that of their colleagues. For example, a group of teachers coming together to examine student work with the intent of identifying gaps in the curriculum can be even more powerful for instruction than an individual teacher reflecting on what his or her own students have learned.

It is essential for leaders to ensure that teachers have access to the data that can be most informative for improving instruction, that they understand the data reports that are available to them, and that they have time and structures in place to collaboratively engage in data analysis and use. As Boudett and Mundy (2006) note, school leaders can greatly enhance the work of teachers' analysis of data by taking on three key tasks, including:

1. *Creating a data inventory*, to know exactly which data are available

2. *Take stock of data organization*, to assess the ease of access and organization of the various results and reports that are generated

3. *Develop an inventory of the instructional initiatives currently in place*, to identify which initiatives are addressing specific content areas and raise awareness of the level of implementation of each initiative (pp. 14–20)

Reflection

What data management systems are in place in your state, district, and/or school? To what extent are you aware of the variety of data sources and reports that are available? In what ways have you helped teachers understand those sources and reports?

How often do teachers convene in collaborative teams to analyze data and student work? Have you provided the necessary guidance and facilitation tools they need to engage with those data? What more might you do to ensure that teachers have the time and structures they need to work with each other?

Have you taken any of the three steps to support teachers' use of data—data inventory, data organization, and inventory of instructional initiatives? If not, write down a few immediate next steps to ensure that you move forward gathering this information.

DAY 8: PURPOSEFUL USE OF DATA

Data are very logical—we merely need to think about what we want to know and why, and then think about the data we have, or need, to answer the questions.

Victoria Bernhardt

Day 7 discusses the critical need to provide educators with access to data in order for them to effectively use it to guide instructional decisions. But, once they have all of those data, what is next?

As the opening quote indicates, one way to approach the plethora of data available these days to schools and teachers is to ask questions and then identify the data that can best be used to help answer the question. Table 5.1 summarizes questions related to student learning and provides a suggestion for sources of data (Love, Stiles, Mundry, & DiRanna, 2008).

Table 5.1 Questions and Their Data Sources

Questions	*Possible Data Sources*
Who are the students in our school? Is our population changing over time?	Enrollment data for the last three to five years, disaggregated by student populations
How do our students perform in comparison to students at similar schools and at the district and state levels? What trends in those data are there over time?	Three or more years of aggregated state-level standardized test scores, in all content areas for all grades

Questions	Possible Data Sources
How do different student populations perform? Are there achievement gaps between different student populations? How have these gaps changed over time? Are we serving all of our students?	Three or more years of disaggregated state-level standardized test scores, in all content areas for all grades
What standards or learning outcomes are most challenging for our students within the content areas? Has this changed over time?	Three or more years of standards or learning outcomes data from the state-level standardized test, in all content areas for all grades District-level benchmark or common assessments, disaggregated by standards or learning outcomes
What specific knowledge, skills, and concepts are our students' strengths? Which pose difficulties for them? What types of questions (short answer, multiple choice, extended response, etc.) pose challenges for them?	Most recent state-level standardized test disaggregated into item-level responses, for all content areas and grade levels District-level benchmark or common assessments, disaggregated by item-level responses Classroom formative/summative assessments Student work

> **Reflection**
>
> How confident are you and your staff with finding and accessing the "right" source of data to answer specific questions? How often do you and your staff start with a question and then go to the data, rather than starting by looking at the data? How might you introduce to your staff the idea of starting with a question prior to looking at data?

DAY 9: THE POWER OF DATA

With data collection, 'the sooner the better' is always the best answer.

Marissa Mayer

All too often, people dismiss data. They may say that data are unimportant, inaccurate, or biased. Or, people may feel unprepared to effectively interpret and make meaning of data or how to best use the data.

Helping people understand the power of data is one role of leaders. A colleague introduced us to an engaging group exercise that leaders can use to illustrate the power of data.

Locate four different apples: a real apple, a wooden or ceramic apple, a picture of an apple from a magazine, and the word *apple* written in large letters on a piece of paper. You'll need one of each for every small group that you have. Introduce the activity by saying that the groups are going to do an exercise that will reveal some interesting information about data.

Distribute a real apple to each group and ask them to make a list of words or phrases that describe the apple. Members may even cut the apple open or take a bite out of it to gather more data. The result will be a fairly long list.

Remove the real apple and give them the ceramic or wooden apple. Have them cross off of their list of descriptors those that no longer apply to this apple, such as tasty, not ripe, mushy, or sweet smelling.

Remove the ceramic or wooden apple and give each group a picture of an apple. Instructions are the same; cross off the descriptors that do not apply to this apple. So, now off come descriptors like smooth texture and weight.

Finally, remove the picture and give them a sheet of paper with the word *apple* written on it. And once again, ask the group to cross off any descriptors that do not apply, for example, color and shape.

Remove the sheet of paper and put the four representations of apple in a place where everyone can see them. Ask each individual to write down what they experienced in this exercise, and then ask them to share their observations with the group.

Reflection

For debriefing this activity and helping the group members reflect on the power of data, here are some questions to ask:

- Which apple has the most descriptors? The least? Why?
- How many of our senses are used when observing the real apple? The word *apple*?
- If you were teaching the vocabulary word *apple*, which apple would give your students the fullest experience of what an apple is?
- What does this exercise have to do with data?
- What does this exercise have to do with data in teaching and learning?
- In your experience, what data do you actually have to help you make instructional decisions? Do your data resemble the real apple, the fabricated apple, the picture of an apple, or the word *apple*? What data do you wish you had? Give some examples of how having the most authentic data can help the teaching and learning process.

DAY 10: COLLABORATIVE INQUIRY

Collaborative inquiry unleashes the resourcefulness and creativity to continuously improve instruction and student learning.

Nancy Love, Katherine Stiles, Susan Mundry, and Kathryn DiRanna

What is *collaborative inquiry*?

As the individual words in the phrase indicate, it is a process for working in teams (collaborative) to ask questions (inquiry) focused on a specific purpose. It involves groups of educators working together to examine artifacts, evidence, and data generated from teaching and learning to identify areas in need of improvement, as well as areas of success to celebrate.

In one specific process—the *Using Data Process* (Love et al., 2008)—collaborative inquiry is defined as "a process where teachers construct their understanding of student-learning problems and invent and test out solutions together through rigorous and frequent use of data and reflective dialogue" (p. 5). The *Using Data Process* is a systematic improvement process that provides a framework for teams of teachers to follow as they engage in collaborative inquiry.

Figure 5.1 illustrates the structured *Using Data Process* that includes five components and 19 tasks aligned with the components. At each step in the process, data and research inform the work of the team; and once specified results are achieved, the inquiry continues with a focus on new or additional data or student learning problems (indicated by the lines and arrows in Figure 5.1).

The first component, *Building the Foundation*, includes four tasks that are designed to guide teams of teachers through the critical stage of building commitment and a culture devoted to examining data and improving teaching and learning. The tasks also help teachers examine their existing culture and cultural proficiency and focus their work together on shared values, standards, and vision.

The second component, *Identifying a Student-Learning Problem*, includes a series of tasks that provide guidance for teachers to build their own understanding of data and use data to "drill down" into different sources of data to identify a specific student-learning problem. As noted by the titles of the tasks in this component, the "drill-down" process entails moving through an analysis of data from the aggregate level to examining student work and thinking.

The third component, *Verifying Causes*, is a critical step and one that is often omitted in improvement efforts. It entails teachers looking carefully at the possible causes for the student-learning problem and examining

Figure 5.1 Handout H1.2: The Using Data Process Components and Tasks

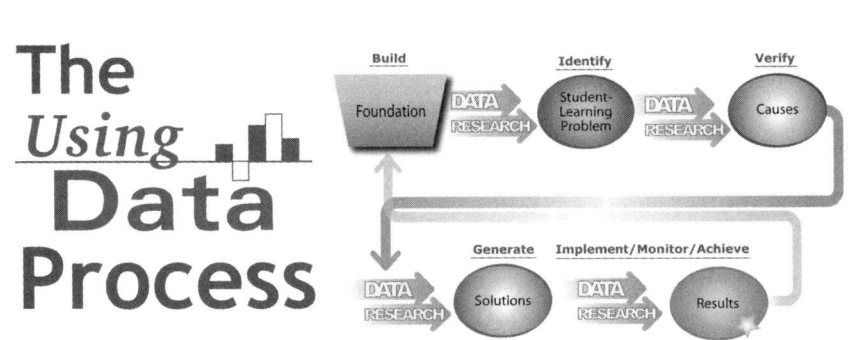

BUILDING THE FOUNDATION
- Task 1: Launch the Data Team
- Task 2: Reflect on Our School
- Task 3: Raise Awareness of Cultural Proficiency
- Task 4: Commit to Shared Values, Standards, and Vision

IDENTIFYING A STUDENT-LEARNING PROBLEM
- Task 5: Build Data Literacy
- Task 6: Drill Down Into State CRT Data: Aggregate-Level Analysis
- Task 7: Drill Down Into State CRT Data: Disaggregate-Level Analysis Data
- Task 8: Drill Down Into State CRT Data: Strand-Level Analysis
- Task 9: Drill Down Into State CRT Data: Item-Level Analysis
- Task 10: Examine Student Work
- Task 11: Drill Down Into Common Assessments and Other Local Student-Learning Data Sources
- Task 12: Identify a Student-Learning Problem and Goal

VERIFYING CAUSES
- Task 13: Conduct Cause-and-Effect Analysis
- Task 14: Verify Causes Through Research and Local Data

GENERATING SOLUTIONS
- Task 15: Build Your Logic Model
- Task 16: Refine Outcomes and Strategies
- Task 17: Develop a Monitoring Plan

IMPLEMENTING, MONITORING, AND ACHIEVING RESULTS
- Task 18: Take Action and Monitor Results
- Task 19: Celebrate Success and Renew Collaborative Inquiry

SOURCE: Love, N., Stiles, K. E., Mundry, S., & DiRanna, K. Copyright 2008. *The Data Coach's Guide to Improving Learning for All Students: Unleashing the Power of Collaborative Inquiry.* Thousand Oaks, CA: Corwin. Reprinted with permission.

research and additional data about instructional practices in order to draw conclusions.

The fourth component, *Generating Solutions*, includes three tasks that focus on using a "logic model" approach to develop a plan for interventions and outcomes to address the verified cause, as well as specific strategies for monitoring and evaluating the effectiveness of the interventions.

The final component, *Implementing, Monitoring, and Achieving Results*, includes implementing the logic model's plan, gathering the data that will be used to monitor the effectiveness of the interventions, and evaluating the overall achievement of the specified goals and outcomes.

Reflection

To what extent does your organization or school have a culture that supports collaborative inquiry? As a leader, what might you need to do in order to support a collaborative approach to problem identification and solving problems?

Do you and other staff engage in a structured process for using and examining data? If not, what might you need to do to use a process similar to the one described? For example, do you and/or other staff have the knowledge, skills, and capacities to engage in such a process? Do you have the time, schedules, and structures needed for thoughtful data use? If not, what might you need to do to create the capacity for highly effective use of data?

DAY 11: ENGAGING EVERYONE WITH DATA

The school change leadership team must be committed to initiating and maintaining communication among the entire school community and to building consensus around the change process based on meaningful data . . . and allowed adequate professional time to collect and analyze data for the school.

Ruth S. Johnson

Throughout *Leading Every Day*, we have emphasized the importance of a collective, collaborative approach to leading and facilitating continuous improvement in schools and districts. Engaging in the use of data to improve teaching and learning is no different—it is not an individual endeavor but one best conducted by the entire staff and in collaborative teams.

What does it look like when there is school-wide commitment to and engagement with collaboratively inquiring into data? Most often, schools look to existing improvement efforts and initiatives. For example, teams of teachers and administrators who are already focused on improving eighth-grade English language arts are already in perfect position to use data to guide their discussions and inform their improvement efforts. In other instances, teachers collaboratively engage with data analysis during their professional learning communities (see Book Three, Day 1, for more on professional learning communities), and some schools have established formal data teams composed of teachers within and/or across grade levels and content areas.

Regardless of the specific structure for engaging with data, Love et al. (2008) advocate for seven essential steps that district and school leaders can take to support collaborative inquiry into data.

1. *Make collaborative inquiry an integral part of your school operation and improvement efforts.* Engaging in the process of collaborative inquiry for every improvement effort strengthens the process of identifying areas in need of improvement, clarifying the problems to be solved, verifying the causes, generating solutions, and measuring the effectiveness of the improvement efforts.

2. *Build stakeholder support.* Generating interest in and support for collaborative inquiry involves communicating with a range of stakeholders, including district and school administrators, school faculty, department chairs, union representatives, instructional coaches, teacher leaders, school board members, school improvement teams, parents, and assessment/data coordinators.

3. *Assess and take steps to strengthen a collaborative culture.* Depending on the level of collaboration in your culture, you may need to spend time on the following: ensuring that people learn to work together, building a shared vision, and developing the knowledge and skills needed to work collaboratively.

4. *Select, prepare, and empower data coaches.* Although many different teams and groups of teachers engage in collaborative inquiry into data, it is essential to identify at least one person on each team who can lead, facilitate, and guide the work. Many schools identify this person as a "data coach" and provide the necessary professional development for them to facilitate their teams' immersion into collaborative inquiry. However, over time and as data teams gain experience, the role of facilitating can be shared among many members of the group.

5. *Organize data teams.* Whether you have existing teams already focused on improvement efforts or are creating new teams, it is important to make sure that these teams are clear about their roles and responsibilities, including their decision-making authority.

6. *Create time for collaboration.* Improvement efforts guided by teams of teachers are not something taken on after school, one week in the summer, or once a semester. Having a collaborative culture focused on improving teaching and learning requires that teams have time within their professional day to engage in this work. The exact amount of time will depend on your school's structures for ensuring teacher collaboration during the school day.

7. *Ensure timely access to robust data sources.* As discussed in Day 7 of this book, it is essential that teachers have access to a variety of student-learning data to guide their improvement efforts (pp. 28–44).

Reflection

Do you and your teams of teachers currently engage in collaborative inquiry? If so, in what ways and for what purposes?

Review the list of seven essential steps. Which ones have you actively taken steps toward implementing? Which ones might you still need to focus on? What specific next steps can you take to ensure that collaborative inquiry becomes a part of your school's culture?

DAY 12: DATA-DRIVEN DIALOGUE

Data-driven dialogue is a collective process designed to create shared understandings of issues and events using information from many different sources. It separates inquiry, analysis, and problem finding from the rush to decide and the rush to act.

Bruce Wellman and Laura Lipton

What's unique about dialogue? Isn't it the same as discussion?

As discussed in Book Four, Day 12, *dialogue* is reflective learning in which group members seek to understand each other's viewpoints and assumptions by talking together to deepen their collective understanding. With dialogue, there is inquiry to learn and a desire to discover and unfold shared meaning, to integrate multiple perspectives, and to uncover and examine underlying assumptions.

The purpose of *discussion,* on the other hand, is to decide something. Discussion eliminates some suggestions from a wider field, with the stronger ideas taking precedence. In discussion, there is normally an action outcome.

The definition of dialogue helps position it as the way of talking that enhances the process of collaborative inquiry into data. It is a structured process that facilitates the engagement with data in a way that focuses first on making meaning of the data before looking at solutions. Bruce Wellman and Laura Lipton (2003) developed a model of Data-Driven Dialogue that the authors of the *Data Coach's Guide* (2008) adapted to include four phases:

- *Phase 1: Predict.* This initial phase provides an opportunity for team members to "activate their prior knowledge and surface the assumptions that they bring to the data" and to acknowledge prior conceptions they may be bringing to the dialogue about the data and results (p. 74). For example, at this phase you ask, "What do we expect to see in this data? What are some questions we are asking?" Responses might include comments such as, "I anticipate that our fifth-grade students will increase their performance in mathematics" or "I wonder if we can tell from the data whether our new science program had an impact on students' learning of physical science?"

- *Phase 2: Go Visual.* This phase focuses on displaying the data on "large, visually vibrant, color-coded displays" or chart paper. Having the data displayed visually, rather than looking at a printout of a report or a list of percentages and numbers, contributes to group ownership of the data (p. 74).

- *Phase 3: Observe.* This phase engages team members in making only observational statements about the data, rather than those based on inferences or assumptions, and ensures that everyone clearly understands the data and what they mean. For example, at this phase you ask, "What do we notice? What are some patterns or trends that are emerging?" Responses might include comments such as, "I notice that 60 percent of our fifth-grade students were proficient in mathematics last year, and that has increased to 75 percent this year" or "There is an achievement gap of over 20 percent between our eighth-grade White students and African American students in science."

- *Phase 4: Infer/Question.* In this final phase, team members "generate multiple possible explanations or implications of what they are seeing in the data" and consider diverse perspectives before coming to a conclusion (p. 77). For example, at this phase you ask, "What inferences and explanations can we draw? What tentative conclusions might we make? What new questions are we asking about student learning?" Responses might include comments such as, "I think our pull-out programs may negatively influence all students' opportunities to learn mathematics" or "I'm thinking that our science program does not help students learn the practices of science, since we don't often engage students in exploring science concepts through investigations."

The four phases of Data-Driven Dialogue are foundational for teams engaged in collaborative inquiry, and facilitators or data coaches find that the process contributes to more effective understanding of the data and generation of solutions.

Reflection

How often do you engage in dialogue, rather than discussion? Is Data-Driven Dialogue a new concept for you? If so, which phase do you think might be easiest for you to facilitate? Which might be the most challenging?

Review the four phases and, at your next meeting involving an analysis of data, practice facilitating all four phases. Afterward, reflect on your facilitation and seek feedback on the effectiveness of the process from your colleagues.

DAY 13: ROOT CAUSE ANALYSIS

The benefits of RCA are that it uncovers relationships between causes and symptoms of problems, works to solve issues at the root itself, and provides tangible evidence of cause and effect and solutions.

Raymond Lewallen

Root cause analysis (RCA) is a methodology designed to identify and correct the basic cause(s) of a specific problem rather than just addressing the symptoms of the problem. There are various philosophies, tools, and processes for performing RCA, some of which are very sophisticated, requiring statistical analysis. Specific approaches lend themselves well to certain types of problems, such as health and safety, engineering, quality control in manufacturing, social problems, or education. Regardless of the approach, here are five basic principles of RCA:

1. The primary purpose of RCA is to identify factors that have contributed to a particular situation or event to remove these factors.

2. Often more than one underlying cause exists.

3. The way a problem is defined will affect the root causes identified. Accurate statements of the situation or event are critical.

4. Effective use of RCA requires developing a chain of events to distinguish between contributory factors and the root cause.

5. Used consistently over time, RCA can reduce the frequency of problems (Mind Tools, 2012).

One of the simplest approaches to RCA is called the Five Whys (Six Sigma, n.d.). It involves asking why as many times as necessary (usually five is sufficient) to get to the root cause. Table 5.2 illustrates a simple example.

In the example in Table 5.2, just three why questions were necessary to get to the two root causes. Obviously, one could have asked why the

Table 5.2 Example of the Five Whys

The Problem
A high school has determined that too many students are getting Ds or Fs in their required courses and that an effective way of addressing this problem is to require all such students to report for tutoring after school. However, the students are not coming. A group of teachers and support staff has been tasked with using RCA to identify why students are not attending the after-school tutoring.
Why?
Data from students reveal two reasons: There are an insufficient number of tutors; and the tutoring time conflicts with extracurricular activities, students' after-school employment, and other personal commitments that students may have.

Why are there an insufficient number of tutors?	*Why does the tutoring time negatively affect students?*
The person in charge of the tutoring program was authorized to hire only two tutors. That number turned out to be insufficient for the number of students.	Program planners assumed that being tutored was more important than any obligations that students may have.
Why could just two tutors be hired?	*Why did they make that assumption?*
The principal, who controls the budget, had budgeted for just two. **(root cause)**	They did not check with coaches, club sponsors, counselors, or students themselves to see if the requirement to attend tutoring would cause any conflict. **(root cause)**

Resolution
The answers to the why questions suggest two courses of action. The first is to work out a tutoring schedule that will not force students to choose between their after-school commitments and tutoring. Then, based on the schedule, determine how many more tutors are needed to meet the students' needs or schedule the tutors throughout the school day so they can work with more students.

principal had allotted just two tutors originally. One could also probe to determine if the program planners followed the district's policy and procedures for program design. However, in this case, three whys were sufficient to provide direction on what actions to take.

One final note: RCA works well for situations in which the problem can be well defined. It may not work for the more complex problems discussed in this book in Day 16. Those may require a different approach, as suggested in Day 28.

> **Reflection**
>
> Think of a problem your school or district is currently experiencing. Start asking why questions. Did you get to a root cause (or perhaps more than one root cause)? How can you use RCA in your leadership role within your school or district?

DAY 14: CAUSE AND EFFECT

> *Before the effect, one believes in different causes than one does after the effect.*
>
> Friedrich Nietzsche

You're writing a plan for improving the performance of middle school students in science. You have several options to choose from. Which of the following would you select?

- Adopting a new project-based science curriculum
- Providing professional development for teachers in inquiry-based science
- Starting an annual science fair at all middle schools in your district
- Starting an after-school science club
- None of the above
- All of the above

In all our years of consulting with schools, the most common failure we have seen is selecting interventions that can't possibly lead to the outcomes desired. For example, let's look at those just proposed. Adopting a new curriculum won't bring about the desired results unless there's a commitment to teaching the curriculum, teachers have professional development and on-going support, materials are readily available, and the curriculum is culturally relevant for the students.

Professional development alone will not work unless all teachers are committed to and are proficient in teaching the curriculum, have an in-depth understanding of the science content, and supporting materials are in place. A science fair or club may increase some students' interest in science, but these activities are usually not of sufficient duration or specifically targeted to increase students' conceptual understanding of science.

To begin to have the chance of impacting students' performance, an intervention must take into account the following four factors:

1. *Sufficient duration:* There must be enough teacher and student contact hours for the desired changes in attitudes and behavior to occur. Almost always more hours are necessary than are originally planned.

2. *Necessary supports:* New instructional or curricular interventions won't be successful without professional development that includes opportunities to deepen content and pedagogical content knowledge, to practice with the new instructional approaches, and to receive feedback over time until reaching proficiency. Supports also must include the required materials that are readily available to teachers. Professional development that does not include these components is a threat to achieving outcomes.

3. *Targeted instruction:* The activity must directly address the knowledge, skills, and attitudes that make up the desired outcomes. Teachers must engage in data analysis to identify student learning needs and select specific instructional strategies and activities to address the needs. Outcomes are at risk if teachers identify student learning problems that are based on hunches rather than on data or select an ineffective intervention.

4. *Commitment of administration and staff:* District and school administrators along with teachers and support personnel must be committed to the intervention. For example, administrators who adopt the curriculum but not the materials or teachers who continue to teach the former curriculum put the desired outcomes at risk.

Taking these factors into consideration when planning a school improvement effort can help in the setting of realistic outcomes that are more likely to be obtained.

Reflection

Think of an improvement effort that your school or district is currently involved in. Assess the desired outcomes in terms of duration, supports, instruction, and commitment. What is supporting you to achieve your outcomes? What is putting your outcomes at risk?

DAY 15: CAUSE AND EFFECT ANALYSIS: THE FISHBONE

Cause and effect are two sides of one fact.

Ralph Waldo Emerson

Day 13 in this book describes one approach to cause and effect analysis—the 5 Whys Strategy. The Fishbone process is another strategy for identifying potential causes to a specific problem. It is a strategy for analyzing multiple causes of a student-learning problem and is often used by teams who are engaged in collaborative inquiry into student learning data. The Fishbone creates a concept map that captures numerous causes that the team can then prioritize and generate solutions to address.

The Fishbone diagram (Figure 5.2) has been used as a Total Quality tool since the early 1960s, and the fields of engineering and machine production have their own labels for the categories (the spines on the skeleton of the fish). For data teams, these spines are labeled with categories that

Figure 5.2 Fishbone Graphic

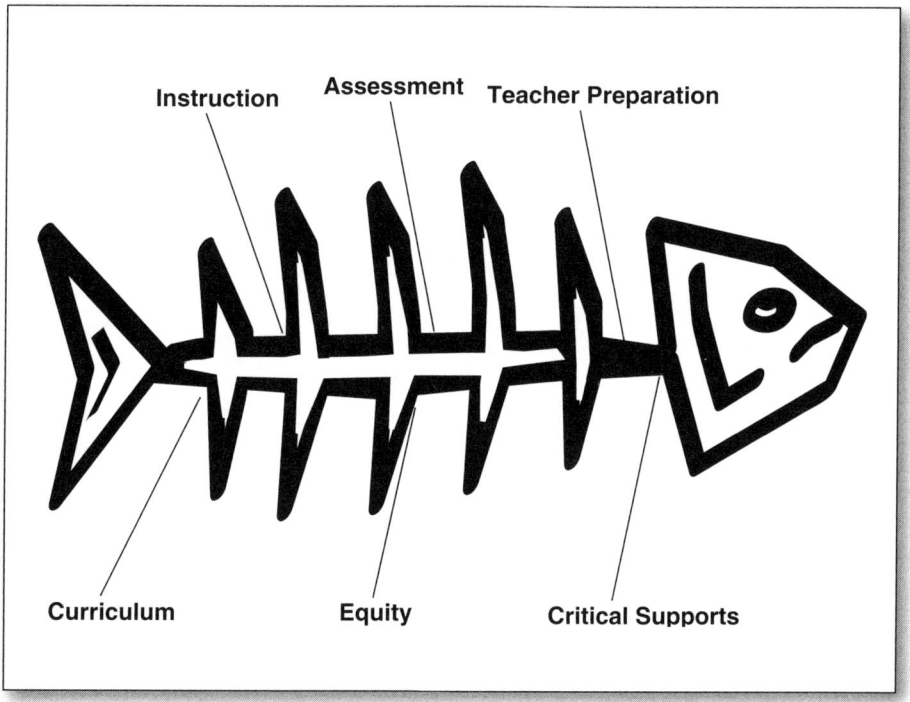

SOURCE: Love, N., Stiles, K. E., Mundry, S., & DiRanna, K. Copyright 2008. *The Data Coach's Guide to Improving Learning for All Students: Unleashing the Power of Collaborative Inquiry.* Thousand Oaks, CA: Corwin. Reprinted with permission.

align to areas of improvement over which teachers and administrators have control to change, which include curriculum, instruction, assessment, equity, and critical supports. The resulting fishbone is a visual depiction of the potential systemic causes of the student-learning problem.

What *is* on the fishbone is as important as what *is not* on it. The labels on the spines in Figure 5.2 should not have titles like "student related," "family/community related," or "school's population." Including categories such as these can lead to blaming and identification of causes that are *not* within the control of the team to change. For example, including a potential cause such as "increased enrollment of students of color" as the reason for decreasing student performance in English language arts places blame on the incoming students of color. An awareness of a changing demographic population is important, but the reason that it is important is to guide changes in the curriculum and instructional practices and student supports, not to place blame on those students for the decreasing test scores. Therefore, statements placed on the fishbone graphic should reflect only areas of the educational system that can be influenced by the school.

Once the potential causes have been proposed, teams can work through them to identify those that they believe are most urgent to resolve. For example, teams can ask themselves some of the following questions to help them come to agreement:

- Which causes are within our control to change?
- Which causes have the greatest impact on student learning?
- Which causes are we most eager to investigate through consulting the research to verify that there is a connection to student learning?
- Which causes do we have the time and resources to address? (Love et al., 2010, p. 263)

Reflection

What tools or strategies do you and your faculty use to identify potential causes for a student-learning problem? How often do you latch onto one cause and move forward with a plan of action before considering a variety of causes? How often do you find that blame is placed on students, their families, or the community? How have you facilitated discussions to refocus the conversation on factors that the school has control to change? What processes do you currently use to identify causes to resolve?

Identify an upcoming meeting where you plan to examine the potential causes of student learning problems, using the Fishbone graphic as a tool. Afterward, reflect on how the graphic contributed to the process of identifying potential causes, avoiding blame, and generating multiple causes to investigate.

DAY 16: IDENTIFYING PROBLEMS

The problem is not that there are problems. The problem is expecting otherwise and thinking that having problems is a problem.

Theodore Rubin

Achieving the results you desire depends on proactively identifying problems in your environment that are barriers to your success.

Every discipline (medicine, engineering, education) has its own methods for identifying problems (tests and indicators, logic, research, needs sensing). For education, one commonly used approach is discrepancy analysis, which identifies gaps between any two identified conditions. For example, a gap may exist between a district's current and desired graduation rates. The current rate is 63 percent; the desired rate is 100 percent. An intermediate goal is to meet the state average of 74 percent. Often federal, state, and local requirements, standards, or guidelines drive discrepancy analysis and the establishing of new goals.

It's important for leaders to identify problems so solutions can be proposed and implementation begun. In identifying a problem, ask yourself the following four questions:

1. *What exactly is the problem?* In the example above, the gap is not the problem but rather symptoms of a possible problem. Symptoms are usually the presenting problem; the actual problem and cause are usually buried below. See Day 13, Root Cause Analysis, for an approach to determining what's causing the problem.

2. *What is the reach of the problem?* How many students are affected by dropping out? Is it 15, 50, or 500? What is the drop-out rate by school? Is it higher in some schools than others? Who are the dropouts? What are their characteristics? Reach is important because it tells us how many and who are affected.

3. *What is the impact of the problem?* Are the drop-outs going into gangs that are terrorizing neighborhoods? Ending up in prison? Are employers unable to find recent graduates to fill positions? Are young women getting pregnant before or after leaving school? Impact lets us know how serious the problem is.

4. *How complex is the problem to solve?* Some problems are relatively easy to solve. In the example above, perhaps there was an error in the calculation; and the graduation rate is really 76 percent, actually higher than the state's. Perhaps the cause is the difficulty some students are having in meeting the district's new requirement of four years

of mathematics and science for graduation. That's not simple, but it is solvable. Perhaps there are multiple causes; in addition to the new requirements, there's a severe shortage of highly qualified mathematics and science teachers. Too many classes are staffed by long-term substitutes who lack the proper certification. The problem and its solution(s) can be extremely complex.

Unfortunately, there's no magic formula for determining which problems to address first. Is the number affected more important than the severity of the problem? Should one take on the more complex problems first or opt for a quick win with addressing a relatively simple one? These are value judgments that only the people involved can make. However, one guide is to ask yourself, "Which problem is the most urgent and one that has the potential to harm students if not resolved now?"

Duffy (2008), referencing Rittel and Webber (1973), uses the term *wicked problems*. A *wicked problem* is one in which each suggested solution redefines the problem. The horrendous school shootings across the country in the last few years are good examples of a wicked problem. Each proposed solution (banning automatic weapons and/or magazines, placing armed guards in schools, increasing services for individuals with mental illness, reducing the violence on television and in video games, etc.) suggests a different problem. So the actual solution remains unknown as does the problem, making resolution extremely difficult.

Furthermore, the ability to resolve a *wicked problem* may lie outside the control of the group most needing to solve it and involve multiple groups. (See Day 28, Seeking Collective Impact.)

Reflection

Reflect on one or two problems your school or district is facing. Which are relatively straightforward: you know the problem, the cause(s) of the problem, and the solution(s)? For each problem, what is the impact, severity, and level of complexity? Is either one a *wicked problem*? If so, who are the stakeholders involved in the *wicked problem*? What are their different causes and ideas for resolutions?

DAY 17: COMMUNICATING ABOUT PROBLEMS

> *I wonder how many children's lives might be saved if we educators disclosed what we know to each other.*
>
> Roland Barth

You're an elementary school assistant principal who supervises the two instructional coaches who work in your building. You suspect that one of the coaches may have developed a romantic relationship with a fifth grade male teacher whom she coaches. If so, this would definitely be a conflict of interest covered by board policy. A complicating factor is that the coach in question and her family have been friends with your school's principal for years. Do you: (1) switch coaches to remove the conflict of interest; (2) speak first with the coach to review the policy; (3) speak with the coach and the teacher together about your concern; (4) tell your principal what you think is going on; (5) ask personnel to deal with it; or (6) do nothing, hoping that this too will pass?

There's often a natural reluctance for educators to speak up about problems in schools. "The elephant in the room (school)" is just not spoken about publically although everyone knows that it is there. And the problems (elephants) may be legion—from low student achievement to lack of critical resources to violations of safety standards. People often question the personal impact of voicing the problem, asking, "What will happen to me if I speak up? Will I be ostracized or fired, or will my concern simply be ignored? Will I be blamed for starting trouble? Will my principal support me?" These are some of the questions that go through educators' minds as they ponder whether to speak or remain silent. The result is that problems are not identified or addressed, and desired results remain fleeting.

Unwillingness to voice concerns in an organizational setting is often related to a sense of safety. The thoughts expressed above that go through educators' minds reflect apprehension and fear. A sense of safety in a school or district needs not be left to the whims of events. Leaders can—and should—take steps to establish an environment in which all feel a level of security in going about their work. More specifically, leaders can take three steps to ensure a safe and non-threatening organization.

1. *Follow the Seven Norms of Collaboration* (see Book Four). Although the norms of collaboration refer to group behavior, remember that a group can be just two people. One can practice the norms in interactions with colleagues, parents, and students in any numerical arrangement. Posing Questions, Norm Number 3, includes asking questions with the intent of inquiring into others' thinking. The other norm particularly relevant to establishing safety is Number 7, Presuming Positive Intentions. As Garmston and Wellman (2009) point out, assuming that others have positive intentions "encourages honest conversations about important matters" (pp. 38–39). With positive intentions as a norm, listeners are less likely to perceive threats or personal attacks. Organizations that practice the Seven Norms of Collaboration will have a heightened sense of safety and feel more empowered to voice their concerns about specific problems and issues.

2. *Avoid blame.* Let's start by distinguishing between fault and blame. The content of a situation and the effectiveness of one's response is the fault. According to Blythe (2003), fault can be "described objectively, traced back, and assigned" (p. 1). On the other hand, blame is an emotional reaction to a situation. Blame is not objective; it can easily get out of hand. In fact, one study referenced by Main (n.d.) has shown that blame can be contagious. Blythe (2003) points out that the severity of a situation will worsen if blame has taken over.

Leaders can stop blame. First, they themselves accept responsibility for whatever unfortunate situation occurred and encourage any others at fault to do so. Colleagues will be much more forgiving and less likely to blame if those at fault are honest about their role. They can also encourage searching for root causes rather than blaming individuals. Often analysis will show causes, such as an ineffective policy or lack of adequate preparation of staff, which are institutional factors that affect a situation more than individuals do. Finally, leaders can offer support rather than punishment. Perhaps those perceived at fault did not have adequate resources and were doing the best they could with what they had.

Eliminating blame in an organization can be a major contributor to safety. It can create a willingness to take responsibility and ownership for situations and outcomes. Individuals become more willing to share successes and failures so that others can learn from what does and does not work. Working in this kind of environment also promotes risk taking as individuals are more likely to innovate when they know that they will not be blamed if they fail.

3. The third action that increases safety in an organization is *being trustworthy and building trust*, which are discussed in Days 24 and 25.

> **Reflection**
>
> Go back and reread the opening paragraph of this contemplation. If you were the assistant principal, how would you handle this situation? Obviously, there is no one right way. What you do depends on the outcome that you want to achieve and the environment in which you are functioning, including your own personal sense of safety. How safe do you and your colleagues feel in your organization? What can you do to heighten a sense of safety?

DAY 18: CRITERIA FOR SELECTING OUTCOMES

> *However beautiful the strategy, you should occasionally look at the results.*
>
> Winston Churchill

Students are not performing well in mathematics, and we believe that our curriculum is ineffective. If we adopt a new curriculum, student learning will improve, right?

What's "wrong" with the logic in this statement? What's "right" about it? Although adopting a new curriculum may very well be one solution to improving students' opportunity to learn mathematics, there are several missing links in the statement. For example, without professional development to help teachers learn the new pedagogical approaches and to deepen their own mathematics content understanding, simply putting the new curriculum into the classrooms is likely to fail.

Thinking through the intended outcomes of an intervention effort requires careful attention to the realistic results that might be expected. For example, in the scenario here, identifying, purchasing, and having a high-quality mathematics curriculum available to teachers is a realistic outcome. Whether or not it influences teaching and learning is dependent on specific related interventions, such as opportunities for professional development and practice using the curriculum.

A well-thought out intervention plan includes several components, including:

- A verified cause that is directly aligned with an identified student learning problem
- An appropriate number of intervention strategies that address the cause
- Explicit outcomes for each of the intervention strategies
- A plan for monitoring and evaluating the effectiveness of the intervention strategies in achieving the outcomes.

The authors of the *Data Coach's Guide* (Love et al., 2008) suggest that data teams use a logic model approach to planning how they will address the cause that is contributing to the student-learning problem. For each intervention strategy, they propose that team members ask which of four intended outcomes might result from each:

1. *Program or policy outcomes.* What do we expect to see as a result of changes in our content-area program or educational policies?

2. *Teacher-learning outcomes.* What do we expect teachers to know, understand, be able to do, and/or believe?

3. *Teacher-practice outcomes.* What do we expect to see happening in classrooms in terms of teacher practice?

4. *Student-learning outcomes.* What do we expect students to know, understand, be able to do, and/or believe? (p. 281)

No single intervention strategy can be expected to achieve all four goals, which is why most plans include several interconnected strategies. We know from research that achieving teacher-learning and teacher-practice outcomes is the only way to effectively achieve student-learning outcomes. (See Book Three, Day 21, for a discussion of the connection between teacher learning, teacher practice, and student learning.)

> **Reflection**
>
> How do you and your staff usually identify the outcomes from your intervention strategies? How often do you consider the "missing links" in outcome statements? Which of the four types of outcomes do you most often identify as results of your improvement strategies? Which ones are missing? How might you facilitate discussions with teachers to help them understand the four types of outcomes and their interrelationships? For information on how to develop a logic model, see Book 3, Day 27.

DAY 19: SELECTING THE RIGHT INTERVENTION

> *Taking action in a solution only works if the problem—not just the symptoms—has been correctly and completely stated, and the solution clearly fits.*
>
> Jim Sayers

The contemplations in Day 13 and 15 suggest processes for identifying root causes of problems that you have some control over and can change. Once you identify these, you can look for and select interventions or practices that will improve your results.

The U.S. Department of Education (n.d.) defines an intervention as "a specific program, product, practice, or policy aimed at improving student outcomes." The first step in selecting the right intervention is to find out what works. This involves reviewing existing evidence and research and looking internally to identify what approaches you have tried that work and considering whether they could be spread to other initiatives. For example, the Department of Education sponsors research and research summaries and publishes practice guides to help educators select and use interventions with evidence of effectiveness. The What Works Clearinghouse (http://ies.ed.gov/ncee/wwc/) is a Web site where leaders can find specific recommendations in areas such as how to help struggling readers, improve mathematics learning, address behavioral problems, and enhance writing skills.

However, only some of the existing research base provides evidence of the effectiveness of specific programs and curricula. Such evidence is hard to come by because of the costs and challenges of doing experimental research in educational settings. More often educators need to apply their professional judgment to determine if a program, curriculum, or instructional material is right for them and their students. Effective leaders make sure that their staff use thoughtful and systematic procedures for reviewing any intervention prior to its selection.

One example of a systemic process for selecting instructional materials is Analyzing Instructional Materials or AIM. Developed by our colleagues at WestEd with collaborators at BSCS, AIM is used widely to guide the systematic selection of instructional materials. Through this process, teams:

- *Identify criteria for the selection.* Criteria include: (1) content, for example, alignment to standards, accuracy, concept development; (2) work students do, for example, extent to which the program engages prior knowledge and supports metacognition; (3) assessments, for example, their quality, use, and accessibility; and (4) work teachers do, for example, the instructional model, the effectiveness of the instructional strategies, and the level of support and guidance for the users found in the materials.

- *Gather evidence.* Teams review the intervention or program using their criteria; they identify specific examples of how the program meets or does not meet criteria.

- *Analyze evidence and apply a rubric.* Teams work together to identify the strengths and limitations of the program.

- *Score components and summarize results.* Teams score the program on the basis of their criteria and select or reject the intervention for a pilot implementation. They continue to gather evidence throughout the pilot before making plans to scale up the intervention.

We suggest that all organizations have clear procedures such as this for the critical review and selection of any new intervention.

Reflection

What is your process for ensuring that you are selecting the right interventions to get desired results? In what ways do you use rigorous research and knowledge about best practices to inform your selections?

> How are the staff engaged in setting and applying criteria and in selecting interventions? Do you try out new programs and gather evidence of their impact before implementing on a wider scale? What changes would you like to make in how new interventions or programs are selected?

DAY 20: RAPID PROTOTYPING

The most common cause of failure in leadership is produced by treating adaptive challenges as if they were technical problems.

Ronald Heifetz, Alexander Grashow, and Marty Linsky

Getting results is at the core of effective leadership. The preceding contemplation discusses what leaders should consider in selecting evidence-based interventions for use in their organizations when such proven practices are available. However, there is not always a ready-made solution to your problem. Book Two, Day 19 introduces the idea that some of the problems we face are *adaptive challenges* where the solutions are unclear and the work of the leadership is to transform, reinvent, and discover (Heifetz, Grashow, & Linksy, 2009). The authors distinguish adaptive challenges from *technical problems* where the problem is clear and the possible solutions are known. The approach to solving technical problems is to choose the evidence-based solution or find the right expert and implement the solution. With adaptive challenges the approach must be one of learning and engaging stakeholders who are directly engaged in the work in discovering and trying out solutions.

Rapid prototyping is a model for addressing challenges that have no known solution. It has been used in the fields of manufacturing, instructional software design, and medicine. In translating it to education, Mehta, Gomez, and Bryk (2011) state that "the emphasis is on frontline practitioners systematically learning in practice to improve and developing structures through which localized knowledge is continuously tested and refined, accumulated over time, and spread across the field" (p. 2).

Teachers engage informally in rapid prototyping all the time when they notice something is not working in their classrooms and they test out a new approach. For example, they might create visual representations of complex text to increase students' comprehension. If their solution works, they may do more of it, refine their approach, and ultimately transform their practice to using visual representations all the time. Unfortunately, the individual teacher working in her own classroom creating workable solutions only benefits her students. If we want greater results for everyone, such inventions need to be shared publically.

Rapid prototyping involves teams designing new solutions so that everyone can learn from one another and contribute to producing new ideas. In one of the author's work with districts transforming their schools to become student-centered, teams from the district are using a form of rapid prototyping to identify and try out new practices. The teams use a rapid prototyping process with the following key steps:

- Teams identify a key focus area they wished to address that represents a *real-world problem* they face (e.g., What technology applications would enhance personalization?).
- Teams engage in *brainstorming* to identify ways to address the real world problem.
- Teams *prioritize* their brainstormed ideas and chose one practice to *test* in their sites.
- Teams decide what *evidence* they will gather on the effectiveness of the practice.
- Teams *implement* the chosen practice over a short period of time.
- Teams *gather and report data* regarding the chosen practice's effectiveness and *decide* whether to continue, revise, or expand their use of the practice based on results.

Through this ongoing process, teams can make continuous adjustments and improvements in practice based on real data in real time.

In the field of education, Morris and Hiebert (2011, p. 5) propose a rapid prototyping process for creating shared instructional products that guide classroom teaching. Their process has three key features: (1) "all members of the system share the same problems for which the products offer solutions; (2) improvements to existing products are usually small and are assessed with just enough data; and (3) the products are jointly constructed and continuously improved by contributions from everyone in the system." They note the importance of involving participants with different kinds of knowledge and expertise, as it results in more useful and higher quality products than those created by individuals.

Reflection

Is your organization facing adaptive challenges? What structures do you have in place to engage staff in generating and testing out new ideas for addressing them? In what ways do you encourage staff to invent and share new approaches to vexing problems?

> Identify groups of staff that face a shared problem. For example, you may have students in the high school who are over age and under credit—without creative solutions they are in danger of dropping out. Who on your staff cares about this problem and may have solutions? How can you engage them in generating plausible solutions, trying them out quickly, and learning from them in time to get results for these youth?
>
> What rewards and incentives are built into your culture to recognize and celebrate innovation? How could you make rapid prototyping and the sharing of new approaches an integral part of how you improve practice?

DAY 21: ASSESSING EVALUATION

One of the great mistakes is to judge policies and programs by their intentions rather than their results.

Milton Friedman

One of the ways you know you're getting the results you want is by evaluating your project or program. Program evaluation in education has evolved significantly in the last 20 years. What was considered "state of the art" then has been replaced with much more sophisticated approaches and beliefs. Table 5.3 captures many of the changes that have taken place.

Table 5.3 Evolution of Evaluation

Evaluation Then	Evaluation Now
Funders, prospective grantees, and program directors rarely required programs to be evaluated or collected data on results.	Evaluation is now required by most funders at the federal, state, and local levels. It is part of the emphasis on greater accountability and desire to learn what works.
Rarely were funds set aside for evaluation.	The amount of money recommended for evaluation is at least 10 percent, but often more, of a project's or program's total budget for each year.
The typical evaluation was a satisfaction survey.	Most evaluations use a mixed-method approach with multiple measures, such as test results, observations, surveys, and interviews, and sometimes include a comparison or control group.
Evaluations were often carried out by internal staff. An external evaluator was not considered necessary.	Evaluations are considered more credible if they are conducted by persons external to the organizations or by an internal/external team.

Evaluation Then	Evaluation Now
Projects or programs established goals.	Projects and programs have specific goals, objectives, and desired outcomes, often documented in a program's logic model or theory of action.
Project or program goals were not measurable.	Goals, objectives, and outcomes are measurable.
Evaluation data were largely descriptive in nature and focused on simple levels of impact such as the project's reach (e.g., number of teachers and students participating).	Evaluation data are gathered at different levels of impact from numbers reached to whether the program has its intended outcomes. (See Book Three, Day 29 for a description of levels of impact.)
Data linking student achievement to their teacher's performance were either not available or considered confidential. There was no consideration of using student achievement data as part of teacher evaluation.	Data linking student achievement to teacher performance are readily available in many districts and are now being used for teacher evaluation. There is greater emphasis on the links between a program/project, teacher learning/practice, and student learning.

Reflection

Reread the list above. Put a check mark in the cell that most closely describes your school's or district's approach to ongoing evaluation of your programs. Are your practices still primarily reflective of the list under "Evaluation Then"? What can you do to make your evaluation efforts more credible? For example, if your programs/projects do not have specific goals, objectives, and outcomes, engage colleagues in the development of a logic model or theory of action to help you clarify the aspects you want to evaluate. (See Book Three, Day 27.) If you only gather evidence or data on one or two levels of impact, consider what you can do to extend your evaluation data collection efforts to learn more about the impact of your program or project. If you do not have expertise within the district to conduct the evaluation, consider whether you might partner with a local college or university to conduct external evaluation.

DAY 22: REFLECTING ON RESULTS

What our schools quickly appreciated is that structured and facilitated conversations guided by protocols yield far greater results for impacting teacher practice and improving school culture than weekly faculty meetings that have an unclear focus and loose agenda.

Learning Forward

Throughout the school day and week there are thousands and thousands of interactions between teachers and students and their families and among staff. Each of these interactions provides an opportunity to reflect on and raise awareness of the results you are seeking and how you are progressing. However, reflecting on results in a substantial way requires subtle shifts in the focus and purpose of our interactions with each other.

In a quick conversation with a parent who asks how her child is doing in the new school, a teacher can choose to assure the parent that the child is doing well and working well with classmates. Or the teacher could choose to use the interaction to communicate what the student's learning goals are, how the child is doing in reaching them, and offer an observation such as, "Yesterday your child helped three other children solve a math problem in a creative way. That is so important because we are working on promoting collaborative learning in this school."

In many grade-level team meetings, teachers often examine lesson plans and discuss the activities they are planning to use. They help each other think through what they will do and how. The focus of these discussions is solely on the execution of the lesson. In follow-up meetings the teachers might discuss how the lesson worked and what they might do differently next time. What is different when a group of teachers is focused on results? They start their conversation by examining the impact of their past lessons and ask what results they are getting. They acknowledge successes and plan to build on them, and they recognize failings and devise new strategies to address them.

Likewise, meetings among faculty and conversations between teachers and supervisors create an opportunity to reflect on results, but the conversation needs to be well designed for this purpose. "What results are we getting?" and "How do we know?" are two key questions that guide such conversations. For example, if a school's goal is increasing student engagement, a conversation that is designed to reflect on results would be guided by questions such as: "What are you noticing in your classroom that suggests students are more engaged in their learning? What types of activities are students doing when they are more engaged or less engaged? What do these results suggest for what is needed next?" For a school with the goal of reducing disciplinary referrals, a conversation about results might start by identifying cases in the school where referrals have declined and asking these teachers to reflect on and share what is working, why, and what evidence they have to support their conclusions.

Developing a culture for ongoing reflection on results doesn't happen overnight, but it can begin by consciously changing the questions asked and the focus of everyday conversations. The National School Reform Faculty suggests a protocol for use in examining success that can begin to build the habits of mind to reflect on results, called the Success Analysis Protocol (www.nsrfharmony.org). The protocol guides groups of teachers to collaboratively examine successes through the following process: sharing of one case of success; asking clarifying questions that can be answered by facts; analyzing and discussing insights and how the successful case varies from usual practices; and reflecting on the reasons the group believes the case was successful. Other cases of success are then shared through the same process followed by the group compiling and discussing a list of factors that contributed to the successful cases.

> **Reflection**
>
> What is the focus and nature of conversations and the topics of meetings in your setting? To what extent do your conversations focus on learning from your results?
>
> How often do staff members engage in collaborative discussions about successes and the reasons for them? Do staff members have the meeting structures and protocols to help them reflect on results? What more might you do to change the focus of conversations in your setting?
>
> What questions will you ask in your next meeting or conversation to promote more reflection on results?

DAY 23: PLANNING FOR SUCCESS

Every choice you make has an end result.

Zig Ziglar

Improvement efforts undertaken by schools and districts in the past 30 years have not brought about the changes desired, according to *The Futures of School Reform* (Mehta, Schwartz, & Hess, 2012). Most of the changes going on today are found in pockets across the country rather than being more evenly diffused. Although many educators and stakeholders posit a variety of solutions, there is growing agreement that a different approach is needed.

Thornton and Perreault (2008) believe that schools have not been successful at improving because they have adopted quick fix solutions and not looked at the major changes needed to improve complex organizations like schools. These two authors emphasize the interdependence of the different components that make up schooling. Little success is possible unless solutions to problems are designed with this interdependence at their core. Table 5.4 lists the reasons why so many school improvement efforts fail

Table 5.4 Barriers and Facilitators Affecting Success

Less Likely to Be Successful The initiative:	More Likely to Be Successful The initiative:
Is linear (proceeds according to plan in a lockstep manner).	Incorporates feedback, complex relationships, and interdependent relationships.
Does not incorporate the interactions necessary with other components of the organization.	Recognizes the involvement of other parts of the system.
Does not evaluate as it progresses.	Evaluates at each step of the way.
Fails to align identified needs and planned improvements.	Aligns the identified needs and the proposed intervention.
Fails to address the root causes of problems.	Directly addresses the root causes of the identified problem(s).

and identifies the characteristics of improvement efforts that are more likely to be successful (Thornton and Perrault, 2008, pp. 40–43).

So here's an example. School A adopts a new mathematics curriculum in response to students' low proficiency scores on the state assessment. It is not clear, however, that the current curriculum is the cause of the low scores. All elementary grades begin using the new curriculum at the same time. The curriculum developer sponsors a one-day orientation for teachers. The only measure of success will be if the test scores improve in a year. Furthermore, there's no formal interaction among the teachers for them to reflect on their experiences with the curriculum.

School B adopts a new science curriculum based on recent information that the state standards-based test is more inquiry oriented while the current curriculum, now 15 years old, is more traditional. The curriculum will be phased in over a three-year period, starting with the primary grades. Curriculum developer–sponsored professional development is set for four days over the year, accompanied by an online network of users. The district provides intensive week-long summer institutes to engage teachers in learning science content and the pedagogical strategies embedded within the new curriculum. Throughout the year, teachers meet monthly by grade level to discuss their progress and examine student work. Formative assessment is built into the curriculum so comparable data exist for teachers to assess students' progress. During April and May the intermediate-level teachers will join the monthly meetings to transition the curriculum to the next grades. In addition to student performance data, the school district has engaged an external evaluator to assess the first year's experience, resulting in data that can help refine the implementation plan in subsequent years. Finally, the teachers conduct two meetings during the year to introduce the curriculum to parents along with sending out a monthly newsletter.

> **Reflection**
>
> If your school has an improvement effort underway, does it resemble School A or School B? How successful do you think it will be? Will you get the results you desire? If so, what aspects of the plan are strong? If not, what aspects of the plan need adjusting? What can you do to help make any adjustments that will increase the likelihood of achieving results?

DAY 24: COMPONENTS OF TRUST

Trust is the lubrication that makes it possible for organizations to work.

Warren Bennis

Do you trust your colleague who does quality work but does not meet her deadlines? Another colleague who has excellent ideas but erupts into anger when something goes wrong?

Why is it that you can trust some people in some ways and not in others? Because trust is not a single quality but a composite of several. In fact, a review of the literature shows that there are between three and fifteen components with the differences being largely the level of specificity. So what behaviors exemplify trust? Covey (2006) lists the following 13:

1. Talking straight
2. Demonstrating respect for others
3. Creating transparency
4. Righting wrongs when they occur
5. Showing loyalty
6. Delivering results
7. Getting better or improving constantly and deliberately
8. Confronting reality

9. Clarifying expectations

10. Practicing accountability

11. Listening first

12. Keeping commitments

13. Extending trust to others (pp. 136–229)

Trust in organizations is essential and a crucial factor in leadership and in getting results (Covey, 2006; Heathfield, 2013b; Stroh, 2010). In Book One, Day 17 we describe the negative impact on entire school and community cultures when a lack of trust exists. Thus, a major responsibility falls on leaders to establish and maintain a sense of trust throughout an organization. You can't espouse talking straight and then lie to staff, keeping commitments when you regularly cancel meetings on short notice, or confronting reality when you ignore a festering problem. As a leader, you greatly contribute to the standard of trust.

Reflection

In a study of reform in Chicago Public Schools Anthony Byrk and colleagues (2010) found that relational trust in a school community is critical to sustaining comprehensive school change. They write that effective leadership must attend to "continuing effort to build trusting relationships across the school community" (p. 204). In what ways does your work support this? Where do you see evidence of the 13 characteristics of trust in your actions?

DAY 25: KEEPING THE TRUST

I contend that the ability to establish, grow, extend, and (where needed) restore trust among stakeholders is the critical competency of leadership needed today.

Stephen Covey

Since it is essential to have trusting relationships to achieve desired goals and results, leaders need to conscientiously maintain trust. So just what does a leader need to do? You may not be able to control the level of trust experienced in your larger organization, but you certainly can influence it within your area of responsibility. This is essential if you want your school improvements to be successful, as trust can make the difference between achieving and failing.

The best way to ensure trust is to avoid actions that destroy trust. According to Heathfield (2013b), there are four major ways of destroying trust in an organization's culture. They are as follows:

1. *Telling lies (either of commission or omission):* Usually an attempt at confusion or deception is behind either telling an outright lie or telling only part of the truth. The more powerful the perpetrator is in the organization, the greater the negative impact that will occur.

2. *Failing to walk the talk:* Behaving in a contrary way from one's words engenders distrust. Do I believe what you say or what you do? The nonverbal behavior (Book Four, Day 10) is usually indicative of a person's real intent or character.

3. *Failing to do what one has promised to do:* If you promise that no one will be transferred next year and two people are relocated, you have just violated trust. Failing to keep one's promises includes major discrepancies such as the one just mentioned, to more minor behaviors such as being consistently late for meetings or not returning telephone or e-mail messages.

4. *Making random and capricious changes for no apparent reason:* Abrupt changes of course and institutional surprises without a credible rationale also destroy trust. Those affected are likely to be confused and often angry, especially if they are directly affected by the change.

So none of us is perfect. Mistakes do occur. If you or your colleagues commit one of these violations of trust, what can be done to restore a sense of safety that trust provides (Heathfield, 2013a). Here are some suggestions:

1. *Apologize for lying or leaving out important details:* Sooner or later, the deceit is likely to become public. Your only believable recourse is to apologize, as hard as that may be. And remember that there are four parts to an effective apology: saying that you are truly sorry, what it is that you're sorry for (to clarify that you're not sorry for getting caught), what you are going to do to make up for your transgression, and how you plan to avoid making that same mistake again. (Note that not all situations call for a four-part apology, e.g., accidentally bumping into or interrupting someone.)

2. *Note your failures to walk your talk:* Committing this error is inevitable; it is likely to happen to all of us at some points in our careers. Again, the best recourse for a discrepancy in your words and actions is an apology to those affected. Encourage your co-workers to bring to your attention any discrepancies in the future and to discuss more appropriate ways in which you can walk your talk.

3. *Make up for a failure to do what you had promised:* Here prevention is your best bet. Avoid over-promising or over-predicting. If you do err, the four-part apology is appropriate with emphasis on how to prevent this mistake from recurring in the future. Again, this applies to both major and more minor actions such as missing an appointment.

4. *Acting thoughtfully with transparency, keeping in mind the impact of a decision:* If changes are made thoughtfully with transparency, employees are less likely to lose trust. They have had input into the decision and have been informed as the planning process evolved. There are no surprises. If, however, a violation has occurred, putting a process in place so that it is less likely to occur in the future will help lessen the negative impact.

Especially challenging are instances in which a decision that you have made and communicated is negated by circumstances out of your control. Perhaps two people do have to be transferred. If that's the case, be transparent in your communication, letting others know immediately. If possible, have those responsible for making the change explain why it became necessary. And finally, explain what you plan to do to minimize the impact on the two leaving and those who stay.

> **Reflection**
>
> Covey (n.d.) says that "the first job of any leader is to inspire trust" (p. 1). Small actions over time build trust. The best way to build trust is with more trust. Write down five actions you can take to promote or restore trust in your area of influence. Act on those ideas and determine what happens over a three-month period.

DAY 26: TIME REQUIRED FOR RESULTS

> *Reading proficiency in the district averages just 48 percent. Math proficiency is even worse, at 36 percent. Those numbers actually reflect a small improvement, but at that rate it'll take 156 years for students in Santa Fe schools to become proficient in reading and math, and that's unacceptable.*
>
> Superintendent Joel Boyd

How long does it take to narrow the achievement gap? For all students to achieve proficiency? To significantly increase the graduation rate? We used to think in terms of years, but evidence is growing that significant improvement can be achieved in a much shorter period of time, a year, for example (Bambrick-Santoyo, 2010; Chenoweth, 2008; Mehta et al., 2012; Schmoker, 2011). Here are some key factors that can speed up the rate of change for improvement efforts.

Focusing efforts on what will actually make a difference in student achievement. Schmoker (2011) illustrates how focusing on instruction is more likely to bring about change than structural or procedural innovations, such as student academies or schedule changes. Schools need to focus on what makes a difference to the largest numbers of students: "a coherent, content-rich curriculum; massive increases in reading, writing, and discussion across the curriculum; and a focus on the most ordinary, well-known elements of effective lessons" (p. 70).

Making instructional changes that are driven by data. Bambrick-Santoyo (2010), along with his many examples, makes a strong case for data-driven instruction. The focus of data-driven instruction is not what teachers teach but whether students learn. Teachers must have frequent and accurate data to determine what adjustments they need to make in their teaching so that every child succeeds.

Having buy-in by all involved. Total buy-in is critical for an improvement effort, but it doesn't have to happen at the beginning. Unlike those who demand commitment from the onset, Bambrick-Santoyo (2010) prefers to let buy-in develop. His experience is that the results received from data-driven instruction win over most teachers as soon as they see students learning.

Having a leader that exerts a strong influence. A recent report from The Wallace Foundation (2013) leads off by stating that considered separately, most school variables have, at most, small effects on learning. It's the cumulative effects, the existence of a critical mass that produces the desired effect. And it's the principal who is responsible for setting the vision and managing the people, data, resources, and processes to bring about improvement. The most well-planned improvement effort in the world will not work without strong leadership.

"So how long will it take," you ask? The time your school improvement effort will take to achieve the intended outcomes depends in large part on the presence of critical factors such as those above. The more critical factors in place, the better your chances are for success in a reasonable amount of time.

> **Reflection**
>
> Think of an improvement effort you have been involved in where changes were made in a timely manner. What were the critical factors that contributed to its going well? Think of one that dragged on and on and perhaps was eventually abandoned? What critical factors were absent or not well represented? How can you use this information to strengthen your improvement efforts?

DAY 27: GETTING BETTER RESULTS

None of us is as smart as all of us.

Ken Blanchard

You have a very important decision to make. You need to devise a schedule that will allow teachers in your school to have common planning periods. They want to establish professional learning communities by grade levels. Which of the following approaches is likely to help you make the best decision?

a. Call three other schools that have common planning periods. Select one that most closely matches your situation.
b. Review the literature. Go with what you find cited most often.
c. Input the data into your scheduling software; follow whatever the program suggests.
d. Convene a group of interested staff. Hold a session (or sessions) to see what schedules you and the group can come up with.

Although *a, b,* and *c* are all likely to provide you with helpful information, it's *d* that's likely to provide the best solution. You ask, "How can that be?" It's synergy, according to systems advocates (Senge et al., 2000). "And what's synergy?" It's the "interaction of elements that when combined produce a total effect that is greater than the sum of the individual elements, contributions, etc" (The Free Dictionary, 2012). In other words, through interaction your group is likely to come up with a better decision than you working alone.

Synergy is not calling up your three closest colleagues to ask their opinion nor is it having a brainstorming session (although both can be effective strategies for garnering input); it's much more than that. For synergy to emerge, the following factors need to be present:

- The person convening the group has a legitimate problem and values a group approach. (Participants see the task as authentic.)
- Each person's contribution is respected. (An outrageous suggestion can trigger one that's highly workable.)
- Individuals in the group are knowledgeable about the topic. (For instance, they use data such as that gathered in *a, b,* and *c* above in their deliberations.)
- Sufficient interest in the problem in essential to generate energy that can lead to synergy. (Energy precedes synergy.)
- Heterogeneity among group members ensures different perspec-

tives. (This diversity of ideas can be managed through setting of group norms and following the Seven Norms of Collaboration, discussed in Book Four.)
- Group members learn to think together. (They suspend their assumptions and judgments.)

Not only is the product likely to be better, there's likely to be greater ownership as the product has come from the group. Also, the process builds efficacy in decision making among group members (Senge et al., 2000).

Reflection

Think of a time when you made a decision totally by yourself. What was the outcome? Was it what you wanted? What might you have done to get a better result?

Now think of a current situation you're involved in. How could a synergistic group possibly help you work through this situation? What are some other ways in which you could use groups to effect better decision making?

DAY 28: SEEKING COLLECTIVE IMPACT

Schools need outside partners to assist in eliminating the barriers to effective education.

Jeffrey Henig, Helen Janc Malone, and Paul Reville

There is a growing recognition of the systemic links between education and many other sectors, which is leading some organizations to engage in a process called *collective impact.*

According to Kania and Kramer (2011), collective impact is the "commitment of a group of important actors from different sectors to a common agenda for solving a specific social problem" (p. 2). Collective impact is not your typical partnership of two or three organizations. In collective impact, local groups put aside their individual agendas to focus on one shared agenda. Many agencies, including schools, coming together to focus on increasing the high school graduation rate, reducing gang violence, cleaning up a polluted river, or reducing and preventing childhood obesity are examples of a shared agenda with collective impact.

The opposite of collective impact is *isolated impact*. Isolated impact is oriented toward discovering a solution to a problem within a single organization with the hope of scaling up that discovery. Historically, schools have used this "try to find a cure" approach as their improvement strategy. However, there's no evidence that this approach works very well. As Kania and Kramer (2011) state, "No single organization is responsible for any major social problem, nor can any single organization cure it" (p. 4). Collective impact works best with wicked problems (discussed in Day 16); those where the problem is unknown as are the solutions. For example, reducing gang violence is an excellent example of a problem whose causes may be unknown as are the solutions, and this is a problem that lends itself to problem-identification and the generation of solutions through the efforts of a variety of committed organizations.

Kania and Kramer (2011) have identified five components of successful collective impact efforts:

1. *A common agenda:* All participants in collective impact must have a common goal. Differences have to be surfaced, discussed, and resolved. This doesn't mean that every single person has to agree on all of the details, but they do need to agree on the major goals.

2. *Shared measurement system:* Agreement on a common agenda is not possible without agreement on what the measures of success will be. Ongoing evaluation helps keep all efforts aligned and allows participants to hold each other accountable.

3. *Mutually reinforcing activities:* Every group of stakeholders works out of their strength, and their contribution fits into an overarching plan.

4. *Continuous communication:* Developing trust is a huge challenge. Participants need a substantial amount of contact time with each other for trust to develop and to see that they are being treated fairly.

5. *Backbone support organizations:* Managing a collective impact effort requires a separate organization and staff with specific skills. Usually single organizations are not in a position to undertake such an effort. Having a backbone organization manage the effort enables the participating agencies and organizations to focus exclusively on their agenda and implementation of their activities.

And, of course, the effort needs an appropriate level of funding in order to operate. That can come from the participating organizations as well as external grants.

> **Reflection**
>
> Knowing what you now know about *wicked problems* (see Day 16) and *collective impact*, are there any problems in your school or district that might be appropriate for a collective approach? If so, what are they? Who inside or outside of your organization might initiate such an effort? What about key community organizations who might be interested in the problem? Could you visit an interested organization and start the dialogue on the value of a collective approach? Could you look at some cases of collective impact and determine the extent to which they might apply to your community? How could you help get the work underway?

DAY 29: SUSTAINING A FOCUS ON CONTINUOUS IMPROVEMENT

> *Clear and deeply felt values, a passionate sense of purpose, and meaningful connections with others generate energy to sustain the momentum of continuous improvement.*
>
> Dennis Sparks

The title of this contemplation intentionally focuses on sustaining continuous improvement rather than results. All too often, organizations set goals, implement actions to achieve the goals, perhaps meet the goals, and then move on to the next set of goals. Throughout Book Five we have emphasized the importance of focusing on results but simply achieving results does not lead to continuous improvement. Rather, continuous improvement is a mind-set that requires a shift from achieving a specific set of outcomes or results, to one in which the focus is on ongoing efforts to improve within a culture where everyone is learning and growing. In other words, a culture in which everyone is focused on continuously improving.

For decades, organizations have used the PDCA Cycle—Plan-Do-Check-Act—to guide continuous improvement. (See Book Two, Day 6.) Originally conceptualized in the 1950s by Deming, the cycle has evolved and been used throughout the field of education (Senge et al., 1999). The PDCA Cycle is one that can greatly contribute to the process of continuous improvement, and includes:

- *Plan*—Identify an opportunity or area in need of improvement and plan for change.
- *Do*—Implement the plan on a small scale.

- *Check*—Use data to analyze the results and determine whether the improvement effort made a difference.
- *Act*—If the improvement effort was successful, implement it on a wider scale, continuing to gather data to assess the results. If the effort was not successful, begin the cycle again.

When organizations are committed to using continuous improvement cycles like PDCA, how do leaders sustain the focus on these efforts without being derailed by competing demands? Leaders can engage in specific actions, such as:

- *Communicating expectations*, by ensuring that everyone is committed to the vision as well as the ways in which to achieve the vision; generating both short-term and long-term goals and outcomes, with interim benchmarks to inform progress; and providing ongoing opportunities for dialogue and reflection.
- *Providing professional development based on needs*, by assessing current learning needs and anticipating emerging needs that develop over time; designing learning opportunities for teachers and others who enter into the organization at different points in time; providing coaches and mentors to support a sustained focus on the practices that are being implemented; and providing leadership development for emerging teacher leaders.
- *Creating a culture that values the improvement process*, by celebrating successes; promoting innovative and creative thinking and actions, such as rapid prototyping; and fostering and allowing room for experimentation and mistakes.
- *Using data to monitor impact and results*, by making a variety of sources of data accessible to everyone; providing time and resources that are needed to analyze and engage with the data; and being on the lookout for unanticipated indicators of success.
- *Reflecting on effectiveness*, by knowing what success does and does not look like based on previously established goals and outcomes; examining potential causes for both success and failure; and considering reasons for variations in the results, such as changes in the context or changes in implementation of the practices.

Reflection

Does your organization focus mostly on achieving results or engage in a process of continuous improvement? If the former, what more might you do to foster a culture that values continuous improvement? For example, are people empowered with the knowledge and skills to engage in processes like the PDCA Cycle? How might you ensure they have the resources needed?

Review the list of suggested actions and identify any that you might need to focus on more frequently. Make your own list of actions that are already embedded within your repertoire of leadership actions and those that need to be enhanced. What specific steps will you take to enhance those practices?

DAY 30: RESULTS OVER TIME

Change with the seasons of life. Don't try to stretch a season into a lifetime.

Unknown

"Well, that's that for a good while," you say after working for the past three years to get a preschool program in place. You're finally getting the results you want. Now you can go on to something else and not concern yourself with the program anymore. Right? No, sorry, while the kind of attention the program needs will change, it will still require attention to thrive.

It's the nature of things to change unless they are attended to on a regular basis. You clean your desk off on Monday morning, and by Monday evening it's a mess again. You need to nurture your relationships if you want them to continue. You have to keep after those weeds, or they will push out the flowers that you planted last summer. The same thing happens with policies, programs, and projects. Once established, they do not remain static. Events occur, and they begin to change. Deming (1986) captured this phenomenon when he warned, "it is possible and in fact fairly easy for an organization to go downhill even though everyone in the organization performs with devotion" (p. 26). For education, here are some examples that can start a policy, program, or project on a downhill slide unless attended to.

The students change. Redistricting doubles the number of children in your preschool program who are English language learners.

Personnel change: One of your teachers is moving out of state, and one is on maternity leave. Staff turnover along with shortages of preschool teachers is one factor that can negatively affect your program.

Lack of resources: An operating levy that failed has led to a 15 percent cut in the money available for resources this year. That means that your program won't be able to replenish the activity kits that your teachers use with the preschoolers. The lack of resources calls for changes in the curriculum.

Declining support: You initially had great support from parents for your preschool program. However, as their children completed the program and moved on to kindergarten and first grade, that support began to wane. Plus, you've heard rumors that the primary teachers in the school aren't pleased with the curriculum.

Changing priorities: Your superintendent retired, and her successor has reordered district priorities. Preschool programs are no longer on the list. Be it a new superintendent, principal, board of education, a group of parents, or the community at large, your program is vulnerable to officials' power and interest.

These aren't the only threats to your program; a whole range is always out there. By anticipating and tending to them, you make adjustments in your program that enable it to continue to function successfully.

What will eventually happen to your preschool program way down the road? It may be abandoned because it's not needed or people won't support it; over time it may mutate into a highly successful but very different program from the one you began. In the meantime, however, by tending to the program you can regularly renew and regenerate its vitality and effectiveness. The most important thing to track is your impact. What gains are students making? In what areas? What is the strength of their gains? Are there any students not making gains? If so, why? Are the gains holding as preschoolers move into kindergarten and first grade? If not, why not? What adjustments do you need to make in the program?

> **Reflection**
>
> Think of a program that you are responsible for, and ask yourself the following questions:
>
> - Does your program have any current threats? If so, what are they? What about long-term threats? How can you mitigate against these threats?
> - Is your program producing the outcomes that you desire? If not, why not? What do you need to do to achieve these outcomes?
> - What do you need to do to continue to tend to the growth and development of the program and support its staff and managers?

DAY 31: CONTINUING TO LEARN

The mind that opens to a new idea never returns to its original size.

Albert Einstein

We are the proverbial creatures of habit. We go to work each day, perform our job, interact with colleagues, participate in meetings, and go home. We may think from time to time about being more efficient, or we may engage in professional learning to increase our knowledge and skills. However, how often do we ask ourselves if we're doing the right work? What are the underlying assumptions about our work? How accurate are those assumptions? Is what we're doing actually meeting the needs of those we serve? Are their lives better because of our work? What could be done that might be more effective? These are the questions that remain buried as we go through our daily routines.

Pfeffer and Sutton (2000) describe this phenomenon as follows: "People and the organizations in which they work are often trapped by implicit theories of behavior that guide their decisions and actions. Because the theories are not surfaced or conscious, they can't be refuted with data or logic. In fact, people may not even be conscious of how the theories are directing their behavior . . . " (p. 91).

Breaking the typical pattern is not easy, but it can be done with persistence. Introduction of new information into one's experience is key. Here are four suggestions:

1. *Write down your set of assumptions underlying the work you do and analyze them.* Ask yourself questions such as the following: "Do you actually believe these assumptions, or have you inherited them from another place or time? Do the assumptions support the outcomes you desire? Do other people need to share your assumptions if you're going to be successful? If so, how do you know that they have a similar belief system? How might you find out? What assumptions might you want to change?"

2. *Solicit feedback regularly.* Even in organizations that value feedback, people may not readily give it unless you ask, "How are the communities of practice working?" "What can be done to help those that are having some difficulties?" "How well is this new group of teacher interns matched with their mentor teachers? Do we need to make any changes?" "I've been out a lot lately. Are people complaining that I'm hard to reach?" Asking questions like these can give you new information that you might otherwise not be aware of. As a result, you can make course

corrections early before serious problems develop or have some data that support that all is well.

3. *Vary your daily routines.* Changing what you normally do each day can give you a different perspective. Driving to work a different way shows you an intersection where children cross that is not well marked. Having lunch with someone you don't know well broadens your rapport with and understanding of staff. One of the authors worked in a district where every administrator had to teach one day each year. She still has vivid memories of how she had to depend on the kindergartners to get through the day. She and the other administrators always came away with a new view on what being a teacher in this district was like.

4. *Stay abreast of new research and developments and share that information with staff.* Information about education is exploding these days. Research and evaluation reports abound. Professional journals provide the latest on developments in the disciplines along with successful projects and best practices. *Education Week* gives an overview of what is happening in education at the national, state, and local levels. Being knowledgeable of key developments strengthens your credibility and trustworthiness. What message would you send if you provided copies of the key publications and Web sites to your staff? What impact might that have?

What these four actions have in common is that they can give you a different perspective that can challenge old beliefs, provide you with critical information that you need to know, or give you new ideas to consider. Actively seeking the new keeps you from being trapped by your own beliefs and behaviors.

Reflection

Would you like to have a fresh perspective? Choose one of the actions discussed above, such as asking for feedback or varying your routine, and try it for a week. What did you learn? What did you notice that you had not seen before? How are your colleagues interacting with you? How did your changes in behavior help you gain a new perspective?

Review the Table of Contents for *Leading Every Day* and check the contemplations you would like to refer back to as you continue to learn as a leader. Seek out new ideas and challenges and commit to always seeking results.

REFERENCES

Bambrick-Santoyo, P. (2010). *Driven by data: A practical guide to improve instruction.* San Francisco: Jossey-Bass.

Bevis, J., & Chudgar, V. (2007). *Writing effective policies part 1: Dissecting an email use policy.* Retrieved February 1, 2012, from http://www.mcafee.com/us/resources/white-papers/foundstone/wp-writing-effective-policies.pdf

Blythe, B. (2003, March/April). *How to avoid blame in the aftermath of a crisis* [News and Articles]. Crisis Management International. Retrieved January 1, 2013, from http://www.cmiatl.com/news_article51.html

Boudett, K. P., & Mundy, L. (2006). Organizing for collaborative work. In K. P. Boudett, E. A. City, & R. J. Murname (Eds.), *Data wise: A step-by-step guide to using assessment results to improve teaching and learning* (pp. 11–28). Cambridge, MA: Harvard Education Press.

Bryk, A. S., Sebring, P. B., Allensworth, E., Luppescu, S., & Easton, J. Q. (2010). *Organizing schools for improvement: Lessons from Chicago.* Chicago: The University of Chicago Press.

Chenoweth, K. (2008). *"It's being done": Academic success in unexpected schools.* Cambridge, MA: Harvard Education Press.

Collins, J. (2001). *Good to great: Why some companies make the leap . . . and others don't.* New York: HarperCollins.

Connors, R., Smith, T., & Hickman, C. 2010. *The Oz principle: Getting results through individual and organizational accountability.* New York: Penguin Group.

Covey, S. (n.d.). *How the best leaders build trust.* Retrieved January 1, 2012, from www.leadershipnow.com/CoveyOnTrust.html

Covey, S. (2006). *The speed of trust: The one thing that changes everything.* New York: Free Press.

Deming, W. E. (1986). *Out of the crisis.* Cambridge, MA: MIT Press.

Desimone, L., Smith, T., & Phillips, K. (2007). Does policy influence mathematics and science teachers' participation in professional development? *Teachers College Record, 109*(5), 1086–1122.

Duffy, F. (2008). Open systems theory and system dynamics: The twin pillars of transformational change in school districts. In B. Després (Ed.), *Systems Thinkers in Action* (pp. 1–23). Lanham, MD: Rowman & Littlefield Education.

Fullan, M. (2011, May). *Choosing the wrong drivers for whole systemic reform.* (Centre for Strategic Education Seminar Series Paper No. 204). Melbourne, VIC: Centre for Strategic Education.

Garmston, R., & Wellman, B. (2009). *The adaptive school: A sourcebook for developing collaborative groups.* San Francisco: Jossey-Bass.

Gilbert-Jamison, T. (2012). *Leadership through accountability—The 5 essentials.* Retrieved December 14, 2012, from http://ezinearticles.com/?Leadership-Through-Accountability—The-5-Essentials&id=2195094

Heathfield, S. (2013a). *How to rebuild trust at work.* Retrieved January 1, 2013, from http://humanresources.about.com

Heathfield, S. (2013b). *Top 5 ways to destroy trust*. Retrieved January 1, 2013, from http://humanresources.about.com

Heifetz, R. A., Grashow, A., & Linsky, M. (2009). *The practice of adaptive leadership*. Boston: Harvard Business School Press.

Hyatt, M. (2012, March). *How real leaders demonstrate accountability*. Retrieved December 14, 2012, from http://michaelhyatt.com/leadership-and-accountability.html

Interaction Associates. *Dimensions of success*. Retrieved January 2, 2013, from http://www.interactionassociates.com/ideas/facilitative-leadership-balancing-dimensions-success

Kania, J., & Kramer, J. (2011, Winter). *Collective impact*. Stanford Social Innovation Review. Retrieved January 1, 2013, from http://www.ssireview.org/articles/entry/collective_impact

Leonard, M. (2013). *Effective policy—17 characteristics of good policy*. Retrieved February 1, 2012 from http://ezinearticles.com

Love, N., Stiles, K. E., Mundry, S., & DiRanna, K. (2008). *The data coach's guide to improving learning for all students: Unleashing the power of collaborative inquiry*. Thousand Oaks, CA: Corwin.

Main, E. (n.d.). *How to stop the blame game from wrecking your workplace*. Rodale News. Retrieved January 1, 2013, from www.rodale.com/blame-game

Mehta, J. D., Gomez, L. M., & Bryk, A. S. (2011, March). Schooling as a knowledge profession. *Education Week, 30*(26), 36.

Mehta, J., Schwartz, R., & Hess, F. (2012). *The futures of school reform*. Cambridge, MA: Harvard Education Press.

Mind Tools. (2012). *Root cause analysis*. Retrieved January 1, 2013, from www.mindtools.com

Morris, A. K., & Hiebert, J. (2011, January-February). Creating shared instructional products: An alternative approach to improving teaching. *Educational Researcher, 40*, 5–14.

National School Boards Association. (2012). *Accountability*. Retrieved December 14, 2012, from http://www.nsba.org/sbot/toolkit/Accountability.html

Pfeffer, J., & Sutton, R. (2000). *The knowing-doing gap: How smart companies turn knowledge into action*. Boston: Harvard Business School Publishing Corporation.

Reeves, D. (2012, April). Research shows. *American School Board Journal, 199*(4), 36–37.

Rittel, H., & Webber, M. (1973). Dilemmas in a general theory of planning. *Policy Sciences, 4*, 155–159.

Schmoker, M. (2011). Turnaround: A tale of two schools. *Kappan, 93*(2), 70–71.

Shoemaker, P., Krupp, S., & Howland, S. (2013). Strategic leadership: The essential skills. *Harvard Business Review, 91*(1-2), 131–134.

Senge, P., Cambron-McCabe, N., Lucas, T., Smith, B., Dutton, J., & Kleiner, A. (2000). *Schools that learn*. New York: Doubleday.

Senge, P. M., Kleiner, A., Roberts, C., Ross, R. B., Roth, G., & Smith, B. J. (1999). *The dance of change*. New York: Doubleday.

Six Sigma. (n.d.). *Determine the root cause: 5 Whys.* iSix Sigma. Retrieved January 1, 2013, from www.isixsigma.com

Sparks, D. (2007). *Leading for results* (2nd Ed.). Thousand Oaks, CA: Corwin.

Stroh, L. (2010). *Trust rules: How to tell the good guys from the bad guys in work and life.* Mission Viejo, CA: Nortia Press.

The Free Dictionary. Retrieved November 12, 2012, from www.thefreedictionary.com/synergy

The Wallace Foundation. (2013). *The school principal as leader: Guiding schools to better teaching and learning.* New York: Author. Retrieved February 22, 2013, from http://www.wallacefoundation.org/knowledge-center/school-leadership/effective-principal-leadership/Pages/The-School-Principal-as-Leader-Guiding-Schools-to-Better-Teaching-and-Learning.aspx

Thornton, B., & Perreault, G. (2008). Using systems thinking to improve twenty-first century schools. In B. Després (Ed.), *Systems Thinkers in Action* (pp. 39–54). Lanham, MD: Rowman & Littlefield Education.

U.S. Department of Education. (n.d.). *What Works Clearinghouse Glossary.* Washington, DC: Author. Retrieved February 28, 2013, from http://ies.ed.gov/ncee/wwc/glossary.aspx

Wellman, B., & Lipton, L. (2003). *Data-driven dialogue: A facilitator's guide to collaborative inquiry.* Sherman, CT: MiraVia.

Index

Abundance mentality, 39
Accountability, 203
Accountable leader, being an, 202–204
Actions and beliefs, aligning, 22–23
Adams, Abigail, 99
Adams, John Quincy, 3
Adaptive challenges, 230
Additive learning, 101
Affective conflict, 185
Affirmation, 13, 15
Alignment, of beliefs and behaviors, 107–108
Ambiguity, strategies for coping with, 29–30
Analyzing Instructional Materials (AIM), 229
Angelou, Maya, 18, 42
Anthony, Scott, 20
Argyris, Chris, 159
Assessment, 13, 232–233
Assessment-centered environments, 100
Assumptions, recognizing, 59–60
Attending, 77

Barrett, Richard, 61–62
Barron, Jon, 201
Barth, Roland, 40, 145, 181, 224
Behaviors, 107–108
Beliefs, 107–108, 114
Bennis, Warren G., 32, 146, 237
Berkum, Scott, 34
Bernhardt, Victoria, 208
Berra, Yogi, 134
Bershad, Carol, 73
Bias, and conditions to avoid, 168–169
Blanchard, Kenneth, 8, 179, 242
Block, Peter, 187
Boyd, Joel, 240
Brainstorming, 166

Buck, Pearl S., 35
Byrk, Anthony, 238

CampbellJones, Franklin, 167
Carnegie, Dale, 62
Carroll, Lewis, 190
Cause and effect, 219–222
Change, 46–91
  agent, leader as, 13
  as continuous improvement, 53–54
  balancing with constants, 57–58
  building ownership for, 82–83
  complexity and pace of, 55
  coping with, 29–30
  downside of, 81–82
  efforts, managing multiple, 76–78
  history, examining, 80–81
  impact of, 49–50
  individuals as agents of, 83–84
  initiating, implementing, and institutionalizing, 88–89
  missing piece in, 56–57
  origins of, 65–66
  people first and, 48
  planning for, 63–65
  process, 47–48
  resilience, 69–70
  resistance to, decreasing, 72
  self-assessment, 85–86
  speed of, 54–56, 69
  stages of, 50–53
  theory of, 135
"Charles Darwin School" (of learning), 24
Chenowith, Karin, 35
"Chicago Cubs Fan School" (of learning), 24
Choices, 5–6
Churchill, Winston, 226
Clemmer, Jim, 65
Client-centered focus, 17–18

Coach, group leader as, 147
Cobb, Jeff, 55
Coercive power, 9
Cognitive conflict, 185
Cognitive dissonance, 101
Cohen, Dan, 56
Collaboration, group norms of, 147–149
Collaborative inquiry, 211–215
Collaborative leadership, 26–27
Collective impact
    components of successful, 244
    seeking, 243–245
Communication, 13
    nonverbal, 159–160
    open, 153–154
    verbal, 157–159
Communities of learning. *See* Learning communities, leading
Community-centered environments, 100
Compromise, 184
Concerns-Based Adoption Model (CBAM), 51–52, 130
Conflict, 184–188
Confusion, strategies for coping with, 29–30
Conner, Daryl, 29, 49, 55, 69
Connors, Roger, 202
Consensus, 178–179
Constants, balancing with change, 57–58
Constituents, knowing your, 75–76
Consultant, group leader as, 147
Content equity, questions to explore, 120
Context, 115–117
Contingent rewards, 13
Continuous improvement
    building a culture of, 205–206
    change as, 53–54
    learning as, 249–251
    sustaining a focus on, 245–247
Conversations, group, 146
Covey, Stephen, 9, 38, 75, 238
Crisis, leading through a, 30–32
Crum, Thomas, 183
Cultural blindness, 97
Cultural competence, 97
Cultural destructiveness, 97
Cultural incapacity, 97
Cultural precompetence, 97
Cultural proficiency, 96–98, 167–170
Culture, 13, 23–24
Curriculum, 13
Cyclical energizing, 86

Data
    engaging with, 213–215
    equitable access to, 206–208
    evaluation, 137–138
    power of, 209–210
    providing (group norm #5), 157
    purposeful use of, 208–209
    sources, for questions, 208–209 (table)
Data Coach's Guide to Improving Learning for All Students (Love, Stiles, Mundry, and DiRanna), 216, 227
Data-driven dialogue, 215–217
Davenport, Thomas H., 102
Decisional capital, 16
Decision making, group, 177–178
De Gues, Arie, 93
Dialogue, 163, 215
    as reflective learning process, 164–165
    data-driven, 215–217
    discussion versus, 162–164
Dimensions of Success model, 198
DiRanna, Kathryn, 211
Disappointment, dealing with, 68–69
Discipline, 13
Disciplines, nature of (science and mathematics), 114–115
Discussion, 162–164, 216
Disruptive people, dealing with, 188–190
Diversity, promoting, 11–12
Dixon, Nancy M., 132
DuFour, Richard, 24, 94
Duhigg, Charles, 14, 31

Educational programs, evaluating the effectiveness of, 137
Effective groups, leading, 144–195
    conversations, 146
    decision making, 177–178
    development, domains of, 192–194
    leaders, four roles of, 146–147
    norms of collaboration, 147–162
Einstein, Albert, 28, 37, 100, 114, 249
Eller, John, 147
Ellis, Dave, 6
Emerson, Ralph Waldo, 221
Emotional intelligence (EQ), 27
Epiphany, 98
Equity, ensuring, 119–120
Ethical leadership, 41–42
Evaluation
    assessing, 232–233

data, gathering, 137–138
evolution of, 232–233 (table)
Evans, Robert, 23, 71
Expertise, defining, 103–105
Experts, characteristics of, 104

Facilitator, group leader as, 147
Failing forward, 71
Feedback
　giving, 179–181
　receiving, 181–182
Fifth Discipline, The (Senge), 78
Firestone, Harvey S., 174
Fishbone, 221–222, 221 (figure)
Five Whys, 218–219
Flexibility, 13
Focus, 13
Follett, Mary Parker, 103
Forrester, Jay, 78
Friedman, Bonnie, 128
Friedman, Milton, 137, 232
Fullan, Michael, 53, 70, 86, 93, 133
Futures of School Reform, The (Mehta, Schwartz, and Hess), 235

Gaines, Ernest J., 139
Gandhi, Indira, 153
Gang, Jeanne, 155
Garmston, Robert, 157, 177
George, Bill, 30–31
Goals, of an organization, 61–62
Grashow, Alexander, 230
Greenleaf, Robert, 157
Grief process, stages of, 67
Groups. *See* Effective groups, leading
Guskey, Thomas, 189

Habits, 14–15
Hague, Frank, 83
Hall, Gene, 47
Harris, Sydney J., 85
Haynes, Marion E., 165, 175, 185
Heart of Change, The (Kotter and Cohen), 56
Heath, Chip, 56
Heath, Dan, 56
Heifetz, Ronald, 230
Henig, Jeffrey, 243
"Henry Higgins School" (of learning), 24
High-leverage changes, 79
Hord, Shirley, 47
Horner, Martin, 205
Houle, David, 20

Houle, Ed, 55
Human capital, 16
Huxley, Aldous, 95

Ibsen, Henrik, 2
Ideals/beliefs, 13
Ideas, putting on the table
　(group norm #4), 155–156
Impact, 135
Inclusiveness, conditions to promote,
　168–169
Individuals, as agents of change, 83–84
Innovation, eight pillars of, 21–22
Innovative thinking, embracing, 20–22
Input, 13
Inquiry, collaborative, 211–215
Instruction, 13
Integrity, 39
Intellectual stimulation, 13
Intervention, 228
　plan, components of, 227
　selecting the right, 228–230
　student performance and, 220
Isna-la-wica (Lone Man), 19
Isolated impact, 243

Jackson, Jesse, 182
Johnson, Ruth S., 119, 213
Johnson, Samuel, 164

Kaser, Joyce, 58, 74, 136, 137
Killion, Joellen, 112
King, Martin Luther, 41, 96, 178
Knowledge, 114
　acquisition, 95–96
　bases, 114
　transfer, 102–103
　generating and sharing, 15–17
　sharing, 132–134
Knowledge-centered environments, 100
Kotter, John P., 54, 56, 72, 76
Kouzes, James M., 22, 60, 82
Kübler-Ross, Elisabeth, 67

Ladder of inference, 159
Lambert, Linda, 26
Leaders, 2–3
　accountable, being, 202–204
　approaches used by, 13–14
　effective, five practices of, 199
　group, four roles of, 146–147
　responsibilities of, 2–3
　role of, to achieve results, 199–201

support for, 35–37
  See also Leadership
Leadership, 1–45
  actions and traits, 34–35
  balancing with management, 32–33
  basic assumptions about, 22–23
  collaborative, 26–27
  effective practices of, 3–5
  ethical, 41–42
  individual, sustaining, 86–87
  modeling, 40–41
  practices, 3–5
  results-based, 12–14; 196–253
  See also Leaders
Leading. *See* Change; Effective groups, leading; Leaders; Leadership; Learning communities, leading; Results
Learning. *See* Continuous improvement; Learning communities; Professional learning; Schools
Learning communities, leading, 92–143
  additive learning, 101
  by example, 138–139
  critical issues to consider, 117–119
  environments, types of, 100
  experiences, powerful, 98–99
  how people learn, 99–100
  in organizations, 95–96
  modeling commitment to, 138–139
  professional learning, practice-based, 106
  taking responsibility for learning, 139–141
Lessons learned, capturing, 132–134
Lewallen, Raymond, 217
Lieberman, Ann, 115
Lindsey, Randall, 167
Linsky, Marty, 230
Linton, Curtis, 7
Lipton, Laura, 215–216
Loehr, Jim, 86
Logic model, 134
Logistical supports, providing, 174–175
Lone Man (Isna-la-wica), 19
Loss, accepting, 66–68
Loucks-Horsley, Susan, 50, 108, 117, 126
Love, Nancy, 111, 211

MacKenzie, Alec R., 172
Malone, Helen Janc, 243
Management, balancing with leadership, 32–33. *See also* Leadership

Mathematics and science, knowledge and beliefs in, 114–115
Maturity, 39
Mayer, Marissa, 209
Meeting room, setting up, 175–177
Meetings
  beginnings and endings of, 190–192
  structuring effective, 172–174
Mental models, 59
Metaphors, in verbal communication, 158
Miller, Lynne, 115
Misalignment, of beliefs and behaviors, 108 (table)
Mission, of an organization, 61–62
Mistral, Gabriela, 129
Mobilization, 82
Monitoring/evaluating, by leaders, 13
Moral imperative, 7–8
Motivation, dimensions of, 62–63
Mundry, Susan, 73, 126, 211

Networking, 19–20
New, trying something, 28–29
Newman, Paul, 151
Newton, Isaac, 12
Nietzsche, Friedrich, 219
Nonverbal communication, paying attention to self and others (group norm #6), 159–160
Norms, 148
Norms of collaboration, 148

Open communication, features in, 153–154
Optimizer, leader as, 13
Order, establishing, 13
Organizations
  goals and missions of, 61–62
  leading learning in, 95–96
  safe and non-threatening, 225–226
Outcomes, 134
  achieving realistic, 135–137
  selecting, criteria for, 226–228
Outputs, 134
Outreach, 13
Ownership, building for change, 82–83

Paradox, living with, 33–34
Paraphrasing (group norm #2), 151–153
Parker, Palmer, 33
Parks, Rosa, 79
Parsons, Beverly Anderson, 135
Participation, eliciting, 165–167

Pausing (group norm #1), 149–151
Payne, Charles M., 23, 25
Peale, Norman Vincent, 160
Perkins, David, 175
Peters, Tom, 88
Pfeffer, Jeffrey, 81
Philosophical approach, 126
Philosophy, balancing with pragmatism, 126–128
Plan-Do-Check-Act (P-D-C-A) cycle, 54, 245–246
Plan/planning, 64, 235–237
Policy, role of, 204–205
"Pontius Pilate School" (of learning), 24
Positive intentions, presuming (group norm #7), 160–162
Posner, Barry Z., 22, 60, 82
Power
  coercive, 9
  legitimate, 9
  of data, 209–210
  using appropriately, 8–9
Power of Habit, The (Duhigg), 31
Practice-based professional learning, 106
Pragmatic approach, 126
Pragmatism, balancing with philosophy, 126–128
Predictable surprises, 81
Presenter, group leader as, 147
Principals, effective, 200
Prioritization, 82
Problems
  communicating about, 224–226
  facing, 70–71
  handling, 182–183
  identifying, 223–224
  wicked, 224, 245
Process, 47–48, 198
Professional development
  critical issues in, 117–119
  design, 108–113
  in context, 115–117
  programs, 124
  strategies, selecting and combining, 123–125
  student impact, 125–126
Professional learning
  communities, 94
  effective, 105–107
  practice-based, 106
  strategies for, 120–123
Program logic models, 134–135
Prototyping, rapid, 230–232

Questions
  data sources for, 208–209 (table)
  good (for leaders to ask), 37–38
  posing (group norm #3), 153–155

Race, meaning of, 8
Racial achievement gap, 7
Racial dialogue, 7–8
Racial perspectives, 8
Rapid prototyping, 230–232
Reagan, Ronald, 204
Recognition, 82
Reeves, Douglas, 201
Reflexive learning process, 164–165
Reflexive practice, 128–129
Relationships, 14, 27–28, 198
Research review, 201–202
Resiliency, 69–70
Resistance to change, 71–75
Resources, 14
Results
  better, getting, 242–243
  leading for, 12–14, 197–199
  over time, 247–248
  reflecting on, 233–235
  role of leaders in achieving, 199–201
  role of policy in achieving, 204–205
  time required for, 240–241
Reville, Paul, 243
Rewards, contingent, 13
Right thing, doing the, 42–43
Rigorous evidence, using, 201–202
Roberts, Laraine, 167
Roles
  establishing clear, 170–172
  of group leaders, 146–147
  of leaders in achieving results, 199–201
  of policy in achieving results, 204–205
Roosevelt, Eleanor, 5, 69
Root cause analysis (RCA), 217–219
Rubin, Hank, 26
Rubin, Theodore, 223

Santayana, George, 80
Sayers, Jim, 228
Scaling up, 129–130
Schlechty, Phillip C., 197
Scholtes, Peter, 37
Schools
  ethical, 42
  improvement in, 25
  inconsistencies in, 107
  of learning, 24

Schumacher, Michael, 192
Schwartz, Tony, 86
Science and mathematics, knowledge and beliefs in, 114–115
Self-assessment, 85–86
Senge, Peter, 10, 59, 78, 131
Shakespeare, William, 66
Shared vision, 3, 10–11, 60–61
Shift Age, 55
Sills, Beverly, 68
Singleton, Glenn, 7
Situational awareness, 14
Situational learning, 102–103
Smith, Margaret Schwan, 120
Smith, Tom, 202
Social capital, 16
Sparks, Dennis, 105, 123, 205, 245
Stanton, Elizabeth Cady, 170
Stereotyping, 168–169
Stiegelbauer, Suzanne, 50
Stiles, Katherine, 211
Success
 planning for, 235–237
 promoting, for every student, 41
 recognizing and celebrating, 18–19
Sufficient consensus, 178
Support, for leaders, 35–37
Surprises, predictable, 81
Surround, defining the, 175
Switch (Heath and Heath), 56
Synergy, 242–243
Systems thinking, 78–79

Talking, ways of, 162 (figure)
Taylor, Jim, 17
Team building, 131

Team learning, 131–132
Technical problems, 230
Theokas, Christina, 35
Thoreau, Henry David, 48
Transformation decade, 20
Transformative learning, 100–102
Trust, 24–26, 237–240

Using Data Process, 211–213
Utility power, 9

Vaill, Peter B., 138
Value conflicts, resolving, 187–188
Verbal communication, paying attention to self and others (group norm #6), 157–159
Visibility, 14
Vision and standards, committing to, 110–111

Wallace Foundation, 2, 199
Warhol, Andy, 52
Wellman, Bruce, 157, 177, 215–216
Wenger, Etienne, 15
Wheatley, Margaret, 27, 146, 159
Whitehead, Alfred North, 57, 63
Whiteness, 8
Whittemore, Flora, 186
Wicked problems, 224, 245
Win/win solutions, 38–40
Wise, Bob, 110
Wojciki, Susan, 21
Wright, Frank Lloyd, 107

Ziglar, Zig, 235

The Corwin logo—a raven striding across an open book—represents the union of courage and learning. Corwin is committed to improving education for all learners by publishing books and other professional development resources for those serving the field of PreK–12 education. By providing practical, hands-on materials, Corwin continues to carry out the promise of its motto: **"Helping Educators Do Their Work Better."**